THE FLY TYING
ARTIST

Creative Patterns for Common Hatches

Rick Takahashi

STACKPOLE
BOOKS

Guilford, Connecticut

To all fly fishers and fly tiers who have and enjoy all that our sport has to offer; and to those who want to pick up a fly rod and step into the water, or to sit at the vise and create art.

Kevin Browning enjoying the fall below Pueblo Reservoir.
JIM BROWNING PHOTO

Published by Stackpole Books
An imprint of The Rowman & Littlefield Publishing Group, Inc.
4501 Forbes Blvd., Ste. 200
Lanham, MD 20706
www.rowman.com

Distributed by NATIONAL BOOK NETWORK
800-462-6420

British Library Cataloguing in Publication Information available

Library of Congress Cataloging-in-Publication Data

Names: Takahashi, Rick, author.
Title: The fly tying artist : creative patterns for common hatches / Rick Takahashi.
Description: Guilford, Connecticut : Stackpole Books, [2019] | Includes index.
Identifiers: LCCN 2018021174 (print) | LCCN 2018032255 (ebook) | ISBN
  9780811768078 (e-book) | ISBN 9780811717694 | ISBN
  9780811717694 (hardback : alk. paper) | ISBN 9780811768078 (e-book)
Subjects: LCSH: Fly tying.
Classification: LCC SH451 (ebook) | LCC SH451 .T26 2019 (print) | DDC 688.7/9124—dc23
LC record available at https://lccn.loc.gov/2018021174

The paper used in this publication meets the minimum requirements of American National Standard for Information Sciences—Permanence of Paper for Printed Library Materials, ANSI/NISO Z39.48-1992.

Printed in the United States of America

CONTENTS

Greenback cutthroat trout from high up in Rocky Mountain National Park.

ACKNOWLEDGMENTS

I could not pursue writing books about my love of fly fishing and fly tying if it were not for my wife, Susan, who provides me with the opportunity to spend hours on end in my studio doing what I do; she supports me and without her I couldn't do this. My son, Josh, and daughter, Haley, are my constant support crew allowing me to pursue these projects of mine. To my parents, Clara and Henry Takahashi, whose constant encouragements and bringing up my sisters and me with the belief of treating others with kindness and respect; to never give up when the odds are stacked against you, are constant reminders of how to live our lives every day. To my sisters Dee Dee, Becky, and Caprice, who always believed in their brother.

Without Ross Purnell, I would have never had the opportunity to do any of the things I've done in the fly-fishing industry. Ross gave me my first opportunity to get involved in publishing for the Virtual Fly Shop; later, as he moved to *Fly Fisherman* magazine, he helped me to become involved with the magazine with several assignments dealing with illustrating, fly tying, and writing. Ross is someone I have counted on for years; he has encouraged me and supported my efforts.

I owe a great deal of appreciation to Jay Nichols for asking me to write my first and second book and to guide me through all the intricacies of publishing. In my eyes, Jay Nichols is the best publisher in the business, as evidenced by the number of books published under his leadership. Thank you for taking a chance on me to write a book.

I am grateful to Van Rollo, who is one of the hardest working and most knowledgeable fly-fishing representatives in the industry, for helping to get my patterns as part of Umpqua's lineup and for all the years of friendship. To Brian Schmidt, the late Bruce Olson, and Dave Student of Umpqua Feather Merchants for taking a chance on me and including my fly patterns in their catalog. To Bill Chase of Angler's Sport Group for supporting my fly tying with Daiichi hooks.

I would like to thank the following companies and individuals for allowing me to be part of their Pro Staff: Dr. Tom Whiting of Whiting Farms, Martin Bawden of Flymen Fishing Co., Gary Barnes of Semperfli, Kent Govett of Canadian Llama, Jay Burge of Finest Fly Tying Benches, Bill Chase of Angler Sports Group, Keven Evans of Force Fly Fishing, Dave Student of Umpqua, and Bruce Corwin of Solarez. I love tying with their products and appreciate the support they have given me in my fly-tying efforts.

I would like to thank John Rohmer of Arizona Dubbing, John Le Coq of Fishpond, and Bill Black for their support of my fly-fishing addiction. I would also like to thank Mr. Yonenoi of C and F Design for supporting me in my fly-tying efforts; thanks to James Shaughnessy of Beulah Fly Rods for the critical and aesthetic designs of your fly rods: making the art of casting a joy. Beulah designs fly rods for any water or fishing condition you might encounter; I love fishing these fly rods.

Photographs are an essential part of the process of writing a book and I appreciate the help of my friends who are far better photographers than I; I am indebted to my close friends Brian Yamauchi, Israel Patterson, Jim Browning, Tom Flanagan, and Mark Tracy who contributed the bulk of the photos for this book. These photographers share the joy of fly fishing through the lens of the camera and have what I consider "the best eyes for composition and a knack for subject matter that excites." In addition to their photography, they are also highly skilled anglers.

There are many individuals who have influenced me throughout my fly-fishing and fly-tying life. Dr. Donn Johnson opened up the whole world of fly fishing by teaching me how to fly fish, how to tie flies, and influenced me in the appreciation of the aesthetics of the angling world. Tim England was a huge influence to me lending advice on fly tying and illustration. Fly tiers like Vince Wilcox, Vincent Su, Curtis Fry, Cheech Pierce, Greg Garcia, Hans Weilenmann, Tim England, Scott Stisser, Brian Yamauchi, Eric Ishiwata, Juan Ramirez, Dave Mosnik, Al Troth, Bubba Smith, Shane Stalcup, Ron Yoshimura, Jin Choi, Takashi Nakajima, Jim Auman, Brian Chan, Jude Duran, Phil Iwane, Phil Rowley, Pat Dorsey, Jim Cannon, Gary Okizaki, Charlie Craven, John Barr, Tim Mack, Deward Yocum, Joey Solano, Tim Drummond,Craig Mathews, Gary Lafontaine, Steve Thrapp, John Harder, Jeff Elhert, David Sanchez, Jim Ferguson, Jeff Goff, Dennis Martin, Steve Solano, Marty Stabb, Dr. James Rose, Ron Yoshimura, Judson Knolls, Chris Kreuger, Bob Dye, Mike Kruise, Dick Shinton, Scott Kemp, Shea Gunkel, Robert Younghanz, Eric Pettine, Doc Sheets, Mark Boname, Jason Haddix, Greg Sheets, Kevan Evans, Rich Pilatzke, Ray Johnston, Joe Comacho, Chris Taylor, James Ushiyama, John Larson, Tim Jacobs, Merne Judson, Dan McGann, Lauren Lehigh, Joe Johnson, Jake Ruthvin, and Mike Valla—all of these tiers have shared with me their expertise, their love of fly fishing and tying, and above all their friendship. Tiers like Ed Shenk, Gary

The rainbow trout has been a guiding factor to why I've spent a lifetime fly fishing and tying flies. This rainbow shows its springtime colors on the South Platte River. JIM BROWNING PHOTO

Lafontaine, Shane Stalcup, and Craig Mathews have been a big influence to my learning how to tie flies. A great deal of appreciation goes to Jerry Hubka for coauthoring *Modern Midges* and *Modern Terrestrials*.

I'd like to thank Steve Solano, owner of Rocky Mountain Fly Shop; Brian Chavet, previous owner of Elkhorn Fly Rod and Reels; Gordon Waldmeier, owner of Angler's Roost; and Jim and Dan McGann, current owners of Elkhorn Fly Shop for allowing me to be a shop rat and fly-tying instructor.

I'd like to thank Ben Furimsky of the Fly Fishing Show for allowing me to tie at the Denver Fly Fishing Show and to present my demonstrations. Thanks to Fred Portillo of the West Denver TU fly-tying clinic for allowing me to demonstrate and to share the knowledge of fly tying with others. I'd also like to thank Roger Maves of Ask About Fly Fishing and Peter Stitcher of Fly Fishing Rendezvous for allowing me to participate in their events.

I am very thankful the Umpqua Feather Merchants carry several of my patterns in their catalog. Currently Umpqua is carrying my Crystal Chironomid, Go2 Prince, Go2 Caddis, Go2 Pheasant Tail, Mini Minnow Olive/White, Rainbow Mini Minnow, Bopper Hopper, and Lil Froggy.

INTRODUCTION

I am convinced to the bottom of my soul that I was born to be a fisherman and, more specifically, an angler and fly tier. My earliest memories of childhood are filled with images of fishing paraphernalia: hooks, sinkers, multicolored Wright and McGill leaders spooled on a multicolored plastic spool, Pflueger Ideal split shot in the blue and black or white tin boxes. These are not the common images most associated with childhood—images of pets, favorite toys, friends, and so on. I do have those memories but in my mind they are secondary; my most vivid recollections of childhood have to do with fishing.

Even though I had never been fishing, I knew I wanted to fish. I don't recall my folks fishing when I was a young child; they were too busy working and raising a family. But I believe in my soul that I was destined to be a fisherman; it was my karma and led me in the direction of a lifelong pursuit to become a fisherman.

I remember my uncle Paul visiting my family when he was on leave from the army; he brought gifts for our family that consisted of small items called *omiyage*. His gift to me was an ocean fishing survival kit consisting of a squid jig and line packaged in a small olive-colored canvas bag with US Army printed on it. I took that lure out every day and looked at it without having any idea of how it was used. As time went on, I collected various pieces of fishing equipment, which I kept in a tin Band-Aid box that I taped to a belt. I would take those items out to inspect them on a daily basis much the way I still do in my adult life.

It is still clear in my mind the day I caught my first trout. This singular event has shaped my fishing to this day. I was perhaps four or five years of age and was invited by a neighbor's dad to go and participate in a Huck Finn Fishing Derby at Washington Park, located in the middle of Denver, Colorado. The sponsors of the event had blocked off a small channel on two ends and stocked it with rainbow trout. I remember being given a small gold salmon egg hook from Eagle Claw that was packed in a cardboard and plastic sleeve.

A red salmon egg was placed on my hook, and I was escorted to the edge of the channel where I dropped my line into the flow. In short order I had hooked a rainbow trout that was probably 8 to 10 inches long. I hoisted that fish up and didn't allow it to be taken off the hook; I didn't care if I caught another. I looked at that fish and remember thinking it was the most beautiful creature I'd ever seen. From that day, the one fish that has captured my imagination, wonder,

This photo was taken very near the spot where I saw my first angler and learned what a fly represented, on the South Platte River below the town of Deckers, Colorado. PHIL IWANE PHOTO

and respect has been the trout. No other fish has motivated me to pursue every aspect of fly fishing, and no other fish species has captured my interest as much as the trout. To this day, even the smallest trout continue to thrill me.

When I was six years old, I bought my very first fly with the money I earned keeping my room clean and not beating up on my sisters. I took the twenty-five cents my dad had given me and went shopping at a local hardware store which sold fishing equipment. I spent hours looking around

Learning to watercolor trout was a natural outcome of my artistic appreciation of the fish.

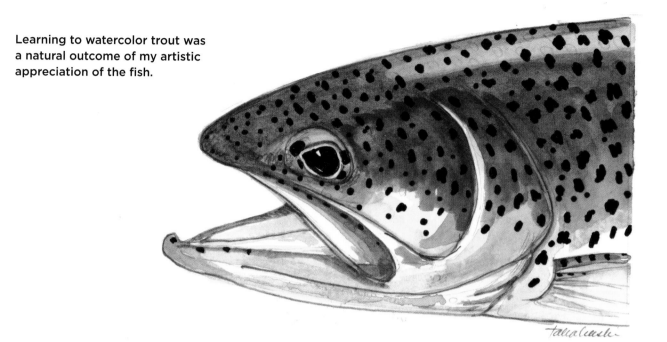

at the various pieces of fishing equipment, taking each item out for a closer inspection. When I came across a Royal Coachman dry fly, I didn't know what it was but knew it had something to do with fishing because of the hook. I purchased the fly and took it home. I took that fly out every day for a long period of time just to look at it; I thought it was beautiful, just like the first trout I caught. I noticed the fly was held together with tying thread at the eye of the hook. I also noticed the spikey brown stuff (hackle) was coming out all around the hook; I had to figure out what the brown stuff was, so I took a razor, cut the thread, and unwrapped it. All of a sudden the hackle came unwound. All I remember was that I had to learn how to tie flies, and thus began my learning to tie flies and a lifelong passion.

I had started to tie flies from a fly-tying kit my uncle Ted Takahashi bought me when I was seven years old. He came to visit our family during his leave from the US Army and told me he would buy me whatever I wanted—a fly-tying kit, of course. After tying up a few flies, I took them to Jim Poor of Anglers All and showed him the flies for his critique. He told me that they were the worst flies he'd seen and that I needed to go home and practice tying. It was the best advice I could have ever gotten. I did what he told me to do and practiced tying almost every day. In fact, I still practice tying at least six flies a day and have done so for nearly sixty-five years.

My second love in life is art; in fact, I was so enamored with art that I was held back in first grade because I would rather look at the pictures in the books and draw than learn to read. My uncle Paul, the person who gave me the squid jig, was also a trained artist who studied art at the Chicago Institute of Art. During one of his visits he taught me how to draw an F-86 Saber Jet, a tank, and a hot rod. My parents were also artistically talented, and I was given

every opportunity to pursue art. In fact, the entire clan on the Takahashi side of the family are very artistic. I later earned a bachelor's degree in art and a master's in special education. I taught art to special needs students as well as becoming an art educator for my entire teaching career.

Many of the patterns described in this book are flies that I have developed on my own. Having said that, I can't help but believe that I have also been influenced by many talented fly tiers whose images of their patterns are subconsciously embedded in my mind and have influenced my tying. My honest attempt is to bring to you flies I believe I developed out of my desire to create an impressionistic replica of what I had seen when collecting bugs, but I also realize that there may exist similarities to other patterns developed by other fly tiers.

Most of the patterns I tie and fish are simple in design and concept. I tie and design my flies around a Japanese design aesthetic philosophy called *shibui*. A simplified explanation of *shibui* in Japanese describes a design aesthetic that values simple, unadorned minimalism and elegant beauty. The seven key components of *shibui* design are simplicity, modesty, naturalness, implicitness, silence, everydayness, and imperfection. I have always been fascinated by the concept of minimalism and have incorporated that sense in my artwork and in my fly tying. I also incorporate the Bauhaus design concept of form following function. I do, however, like to tie patterns with substantially more steps and use of materials when required.

I try to tie each pattern to the best of my abilities. I believe strongly that good craftsmanship can save a poor design and poor craftsmanship can ruin a good design. Therefore, I try to tie the next pattern better than the last, but having said that, I try to remember that sometimes imperfections are a part of the *shibui* experience.

Ushi's Pink Panties Midge Pupa fooled this rainbow trout on the San Juan River.
DAVE SANCHEZ PHOTO

Umpqua signature fly designer Rick Takahashi demonstrates his fly-tying techniques
at the Denver Fly Fishing Show. PHIL IWANE PHOTO

Chilly Spinney Mountain Reservoir, South Park, Colorado. JIM BROWNING PHOTO

I am a strong believer in the fact that fly tiers unknown to each other and separated by varying degrees of distance can create almost identical patterns. Fly tiers who pay attention to what fish are feeding on and examine those specimens closely can come up with the same result. I have often come across fly tiers who think they are the first to come up with a new pattern when in fact that pattern has already been tied.

Case in point: I had developed a pattern I call the Crystal Chironomid, which I developed after close examination of midge pupae that I collected on East Delaney Butte Lake while out in my belly boat. I observed that the pupae ascending to the surface were very silvery in appearance, segmentation was wider than other insects I had collected, the abdomen was two-thirds the length of the total insect, the thorax contained the wing buds, and the head of the pupa sported a feathery gill. I tried to incorporate all these features into the pattern and came up with the Crystal Chironomid. I used the proportions of a pattern I'd seen and tied from Gary Borger's book—the Bow Tie Buzzer.

I fished this pattern for a year or so and as usual shared the pattern with others. My friend Steve Solano, who owned Rocky Mountain Fly Shop and was very knowledgeable about fly patterns, told me I should look at a fly tier from

Scotland named David McPhail. I got on the internet and looked him up and found that he had tied many different types of chironomid patterns, and some of my patterns looked similar to his; his tying techniques are superior and he is now one of my favorite tiers. I soon learned that the United Kingdom is the master of chironomid fishing in stillwater.

I wanted to include in this book a few of the patterns I tie and some of the techniques I employ. It is my wish to inspire you to tie—not necessarily my patterns specifically, but tying the patterns with your own twist. The patterns described have all caught fish, and I want to share these patterns with you in hopes you'll also have success. Many of the patterns are similar in appearance; this is due to my "tinkering" with each pattern. I love to see how I can use various types of materials in the patterns I design.

My patterns are based on observations I've made while fishing and being an artist with a vivid imagination. I love to sit down at the vise to tie. Those days when I am unable to fish are spent at the vise tying flies. I almost love to tie flies more than I love to fish, and some days it's vice versa. In any case, I'm blessed to have fishing as part of my life and am honored to share the water with many fishermen I've come to count on as my friends.

-1-

BAETIS SERIES

Paintbrush BWO Dun

The Baetis family of mayflies were the first mayflies that I learned to fish as a youngster on the South Platte River near Deckers, Colorado. My first encounters occurred during midmornings when I noticed a large number of trout rising to the surface to intercept some sort of insect; I'd see noses coming out of the water with mouths open or bulges just under the surface of the water as the trout took advantage of emerging mayflies.

Upon close inspection of the water's surface, I noticed hundreds of little sailboat-like insects riding on the top of the water, and as I tracked the path of the insect I saw trout lined up facing upstream, intersecting these miniature sailboats. I then became aware of hordes of the flying insects in the air; rising from the surface a good number never even took flight as they were sucked in by the feeding trout. For those that took flight I could make out their long, hanging tail fibers as they made their way to the streamside vegetation.

I went to the library to check out books on fly fishing, and through some rudimentary research I discovered that these insects, reminiscent of mini sailboats, were in fact mayflies. I decided that it might be prudent of me to collect some of these mayflies on my next outing on the water. On my next fishing trip, I took a glass jar and filled it with stream water and then proceeded to try and collect some mayflies.

I constructed an insect collection screen made of fabric mesh used on window screens by wrapping the mesh around broom handles that I cut off an old broom and nailing the mesh to the wooden handle; I didn't do a good job of nailing and mostly pounded the nail into the wood, then bent the nail over with a hammer to secure the mesh to the wooden handle. Thus equipped, I proceeded to try to catch some of these mayflies as they drifted downstream. I caught quite a few mayflies and put them in the jar for

later inspection. After consulting a number of fly-fishing books that discussed insect identification, I determined that the mayflies I had collected were known as Blue-Winged Olives.

I was just beginning to tie flies but had no clue as to the construction of these mayflies; that was to come years later. As I got older, I was able to tie a crude-looking mayfly, but I didn't know how to fly-fish at the time and was using a spinning rod with a bubble to try to catch trout.

Eventually I learned how to fly-fish, and as my tying skills improved with hours of practice I started to concentrate on learning as much as I could about the Blue-Winged Olive mayfly. I learned the life cycle of the mayfly, how to collect immature mayfly nymphs, and how to preserve what I had collected. I took my little jars of insects to our local fly shop, and they helped me identify the insects I had collected, sharing the common names of these insects in their various stages of the life cycle.

One aspect of my fly tying that remains a constant is the need to push the design limits of whatever I'm tying, trying to create as many permutations of a given insect as I can possibly envision and to incorporate a variety of tying materials and approaches until I exhaust my creativity. As an artist and educator, I've always believed there are several solutions to a problem and that several techniques may be used to reach the same conclusion. New materials are constantly being introduced into the arsenals of fly tying and beg the fly tier to experiment on how these materials might be applied no matter how alien or inappropriate they may appear. With this thought in mind, I often will tie several patterns using similar techniques but with different materials.

Collecting the nymphs of the Baetis mayflies was beneficial to me in that I had to learn to identify, at least in

1

Dry-fly fishing at its finest: A freely feeding cutthroat trout leisurely takes insects off the surface. ISRAEL PATTERSON PHOTO

Israel Patterson with a brownie from the North Fork of the Poudre River. ISRAEL PATTERSON PHOTO

general terms, what a Baetis nymph looked like. Upon casual inspection I noted that the nymph's abdomen was very slender in shape, the thorax was slightly larger in width, the abdomen and thorax were almost even in proportions, and it had six legs and two tails. I took the nymphs I had collected to my local fly shop, Angler's All, located in Englewood, Colorado. Jim Poor taught me the name of the insect, the Blue-Winged Olive, and showed me some patterns to imitate the nymph. As a kid, that was way too much information for me to digest, but it provided the starting point of a lifelong investigation and fascination with this bug.

My first attempts at tying the nymph were crude and clunky in appearance and looked nothing like what I had collected. It then occurred to me that I really didn't have the proper materials to begin to tie this pattern, and more important, I didn't possess the skill level to even attempt tying these flies. It would take years of tying practice before I would become proficient enough to attempt this pattern successfully. However, Jim Poor did introduce me to tying a Gold-Ribbed Hare's Ear in his style of tying—omitting a wing case and tying in the round. The Gold-Ribbed Hare's Ear—with and without a wing case—was the only nymph I tied for years.

Years later, as I became a more seasoned fly tier who was able to purchase the variety of materials to tie flies of any shape, size, or color, I attempted to tie my own versions of the nymph. Remembering what I had observed as a youngster, I began to seek out materials that would facilitate what I had in mind for tying the nymph.

Key Materials for Baetis Nymphs

The Baetis nymph is rather slender in appearance, has three tails, and ranges in color from olive to olive-brown to rust. Some nymphs have darker-colored wing cases before emergence and are adept at swimming.

ABDOMEN

A wide range of materials replicates the slender nature of the Baetis nymph's abdomen, including feather fibers from various species of birds and waterfowl, and finer-textured fur dubbing materials such as beaver, rabbit, muskrat, or nutria.

One of my favorite dubbing materials for dry flies and some nymphs is Superfine Dubbing. This dubbing has long fibers, which allow me to make a very slender abdomen, and with the addition of more dubbing can produce a body larger in shape. I use it both for nymphs and adult insects; tying a tighter, sparser body helps the fly float and thus makes it an ideal dubbing material for dry flies. I use coarser types of dubbing designed to hold water when tying nymph-type patterns.

I use biot quills for making abdomens when I want to show segmentation, especially in the style of Shane Stalcup. By understanding how to tie in the biot quill, you can produce an abdomen with a ridged rib or a smooth body. Notice that when you peel off a biot from the stem, there is a notch at the base of the biot. The notch that is facing up, away from the hook, will produce a body with a fuzzy or raised rib; tying the notch so that it faces toward the rear will produce a smooth body. When tying in the biot, always wrap the first wrap with your fingers, then line up the biot and hackle pliers prior to tying in.

Tying thread also makes excellent abdomens. I sometimes will lay an underbody using the color of the thread as a base, then color the tying thread with a dark waterproof marker to use as a rib. I always coat the thread abdomen with either a thinned-out head cement or use a thin UV resin to provide a protective coating so that the thread will hold up longer to the teeth of the fish. I use thinned-out head cement because some of the head cements make too thick of a covering, which can crack when hemostats apply pressure when removing the hook; thin out your head cement or look for a cement that will not leave a heavy coating.

I've been using Veevus 16/0 threads lately for tying many of my favorite smaller flies, because of the smaller diameter and strength of the thread. I can create flies that are slimmer in profile and can avoid thread buildup. I also like to tie with UNI 6/0 and 8/0 threads for flies larger than size 22. I use Danville's threads and UTC's 70 denier for many of the patterns I tie. Each of the thread types has found its way into my tying, and I can interchange many of them.

Nature's Spirit and Spirit River produce some of the finest peacock herls, which I use in tying many of my quill-bodied flies. I like to strip the fuzz off the individual herls with an eraser or my thumbnail and then tie them in by the tips to create a beautiful striped color segmentation of the mayfly's abdomen; these dyed peacock herls come in a wide range of colors to match your tying needs.

I've also discovered that the use of a polyester paintbrush fiber wrapped around the hook shank creates a very acceptable quill-like appearance lending segmentation to the body. Spacing of the paintbrush fiber in evenly wrapped turns with a darker olive makes a sexy-looking abdomen. I wrote an article in *Fly Fisherman* magazine titled "A Painters Touch," in which I extoll the virtues of this material.

WING CASE

Many mayfly nymphs have a darker wing case before emergence. Materials like Larva Lace's precut foam in dark gray to black is an excellent choice for creating wing cases that are darker, and will produce a shiny wing case. Shane Stalcup's Medallion Sheeting with a darker mottled effect mimics nicely the dark coloration of the wing case. Pheasant tail fibers as used in Sawyer's Pheasant Tail Nymph are an excellent choice for a wing case on that style of nymph. Goose biots also make a fine wing case; I often use two biots to form an impression of a splitting wing case with the addition of pearl-colored tinsel up the center of the biots to mimic the gaseous bubble underneath the forming wing. Yarns of various types such as Antron, Z-Lon, and Fluoro Fiber are a good choice when suggesting a wing case and then tied back to form legs. Pearl-type tinsels are also effective for creating a flashback type of look, again mimicking that gaseous bubble that reflects the sunlight, thus attracting attention to the nymphs.

THORAX

I favor using some sort of dubbing for the thorax of the Baetis nymph—dubbings like blended muskrat, Superfine Dubbing, Spirit River's Fine Dubbing, Trout Hunter's dubbing materials, SLF dubbing materials, and Hareline's natural fur dubbing. For more visual, add colorful dubbings such as Ice Dub in peacock colors, Arizona Simi-Seal, and, one of my favorite new dubbings, Jan Siman Synthetic Peacock Dubbing from Kevin Compton's Performance Flies, which comes in a wide array of colors.

LEGS

For legs, I sometimes use a dubbing brush made out of fur from the face of a hare's mask to create a soft-hackle effect, with the fibers streaming toward the rear of the fly to provide a sense of movement. If tying a thorax using fur dubbing, I like to pick the fibers for the illusion of legs. Partridge body feathers tied in a soft-hackle style reminiscent of Shane Stalcup are also an excellent choice.

HOOKS

Daiichi 1760 and 1260 hooks are my favorite hook styles to tie all manners of nymph fly patterns. I like the slight curve of the hook, which I use to tie mayfly nymphs, chironomids, and terrestrials; it's a versatile hook style for my tying needs. Tiemco 200R and Dai-Riki 270 are also a good hook to use when tying nymphs.

THREADS

In recent years I've come to favor Veevus threads in various colors starting with 16/0 and going to 10/0 in size; the threads are very strong at small diameters. I also like to tie with UNI, Danville, and UTC thread in various colors in the 8/0 to 210-denier size.

Key Materials for Baetis Dun Patterns

TAILING

A variety of materials, both natural and synthetic, will produce the visual effect of the tail; however, I favor tying with natural materials for the nymphs I'm trying to imitate. Natural materials such as wood duck flank feathers, partridge, dyed mallard flank feathers, hackle fibers, Whiting Farms Coq de Leon, and moose body hair are generally my first choice for tails. Synthetic materials such as Z-Lon, Antron, polyester paintbrush fibers, and Microfibetts are also used in tandem or coupled with the natural materials.

I like to use John Betts Microfibetts but have found as I've grown older and my eyes are not what they used to be that I needed to find an alternative tailing material. I have recently been tying my mayfly tails using tapered polyester paintbrush fibers that I have found in various hardware stores. Not all polyester paintbrush fibers are tapered; some are cut with a blunt end and are not useful as a tailing material. Many of the tapered paintbrush fibers I use come in a variety of colors such as amber, olive, white, and clear; I use them all. I found that the tapered paintbrush fibers are a little thicker in diameter than the Microfibetts. In the beginning I was concerned that the paintbrush fibers might be too thick and push the fly away from the trout's mouth, but so far that hasn't been the case.

I also use Nature's Spirit moose body hair for sparse tails on some of the mayfly patterns I tie, along with other natural hairs such as the hock portion of deer and elk. Other natural hairs that I use are tailing materials from Hareline such as Tinted Mayfly Tails. Whiting Farms Coq de Leon spade feathers as well as the spade feather of their capes are also used for tailing materials; in the past I've used guard hairs from select mink tails, too.

ABDOMEN

As with tying a nymph, I've designed many patterns using tying thread to make abdomens. I create an underbody using the color of the thread as a base, then color the tying thread with a darker waterproof marker and apply it as I would any ribbing material. I always coat the thread abdomen with either a thinned-out head cement or use a thin UV resin to provide a protective coating so that the thread will hold up longer to the teeth of the fish. I usually protect the thread body of the fly by using thinned-out head cement; do not apply a heavy coating of cement, as it will fracture if you apply pressure from hemostats when removing the fly from the trout's mouth.

Stripped quills from a peacock herl is one of my favorite abdomen materials. I strip the fibers of the herl using either an eraser or my thumbnail pressed against my index finger to rub in the opposite direction of the natural direction of the fibers. Nature's Spirit and Hareline produce a wide color range of peacock herls for tying quill-bodied flies.

I like to use fine-textured dubbings like Superfine, Antron, or any fine-textured dubbing applied sparsely to the thread to create a thin body profile; using sparse application techniques will often result in the color of the thread showing through the dubbing, just like the dubbing techniques of the old masters.

I like to use a polyester paintbrush fiber as a rib on many of the patterns I tie. Evenly spaced wraps of the paintbrush fibers create a good-looking abdomen. I buy my polyester paintbrush fibers at my local hardware store and look for natural colors.

THREADS

I've been using Veevus 16/0 threads lately for tying many of my favorite smaller flies, because of the smaller diameter and strength of the thread. I have found that I can create flies that are slimmer in profile and can avoid thread buildup. I also like to tie with UNI 6/0 and 8/0 threads for flies larger than size 22. I like Danville's threads and UTC's 70 denier for many of the Baetis patterns that I tie.

WING MATERIALS

I generally use one of several materials for wings on a mayfly. I like to use polyester yarns for a fuller visual effect or Antron yarns for a more slender wing profile. I like to tie my wings using this type of yarn as a single wing rather than as a split wing in the majority of cases; I've found that the yarn wing materials usually come back together when wet.

When tying a split-wing style, I prefer to use duck breast or flank feathers with a "V" cut out of the tip and the fuzz at the base removed so the feather has even tip lengths. I tie these in with the feather facing forward, then pulled back into an upright posture. I wrap a small dam of thread in front of the wing materials, forcing the wing to stand straight up, perpendicular to the hook shank; I use this dam technique with all the wings I tie for mayflies.

My favorite style of wings for mayflies is deer hair applied in the Compara-dun style. I believe that you can mimic almost any mayfly pattern by having a selection of colored deer hair in various textures, a 12-selection dubbing box of Superfine, various tailing materials like Microfibetts, tapered paintbrush fibers, Antron yarn, and various dry-fly hook styles.

There are several materials that I look to for creating wing cases for my nymphs. One is dark-colored Swiss Straw that I have unfolded and then cut into strips the width of the wing case I want to tie. I have in the past unfolded the Swiss Straw, sprayed it with a light coat of spray glue like Scotch 77, then re-folded it in two layers of

Kevin Browning enjoying the fight in the South Platte River's Cheesman Canyon. JIM BROWNING PHOTO

materials—this forms a slightly thicker wing case material. The black and dark gray strips of foam from Larva Lace are another material I'll use for nymph wing cases. I generally cut the foam into thinner strips prior to tying in; I like the shiny surface look it gives when stretched while being tied in.

I also have used colored Antron yarn fibers in brown, stonefly brown, dark gray, and black when tying in a wing case. The yarn has an added advantage of being pulled alongside the body to simulate legs. Many yarns can be effectively used for wing cases and legs.

I also will use a dubbing loop with various types of dubbing to create a soft-hackle effect. When you insert a sparse amount of dubbing into the loop, a gentle brush-out of the material after it is tied in creates the illusion of legs and adds movement.

HACKLE

I've found that Whiting Farms is the best producer of hackle for tying dry flies. Using their capes and saddle hackles for hackling dry flies is beyond comparison; however, I also tie with Metz and Keough hackles for larger dry flies. I never dreamed that I would be able to tie a small dry fly with a saddle hackle but have found Whiting Farms midge saddle my go-to hackle for tying small dry flies from size 16 to 24.

HOOKS

I have several hook styles that I like to tie dun patterns with. The Daiichi 1220 and 1222 hook is one of my favorite hook styles to tie mayfly adults. This hook style has a slight bend at the waist and gives a slightly swept-back look to the dries. I also like tying with Tiemco's 100 style hook when tying mayfly adults.

COPPER MICRO BAETIS

- **Hook:** #18-22 Daiichi 1180
- **Thread:** Olive 16/0 Veevus
- **Bead:** Copper brass sized to fit hook
- **Tail:** Olive tapered polyester paintbrush fibers
- **Underbody:** Tying thread
- **Rib:** Olive paintbrush fiber
- **Wing Case:** Brown or black holographic tinsel
- **Legs:** Hare's ear dubbing in a dubbing loop

TYING THE COPPER MICRO BAETIS

I developed this pattern after fishing a small RS2 designed by the great Rim Chung in sizes 18-22. I had found through my experiments that a copper bead might be more effective in attracting the trout's attention than traditional gold and silver brass beads. I wanted to use the polyester tapered paintbrush fibers for the tail and the same material for the rib of the body over an underbody of tying thread. I wanted to create a sense of a soft hackle by using a dubbing loop made of rabbit, which took care of the thorax portion, then using black or brown holographic tinsel as a wing case. I often apply a layer of Solarez Bone Dry UV resin over the wing case and back half of the bead.

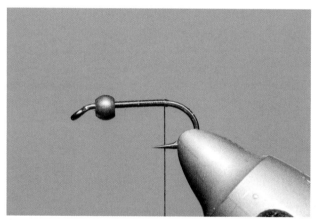

1. Slide the bead on the hook so that it rests behind the hook eye. Attach tying thread behind the bead and wrap the thread in touching wraps back to the hook bend opposite the bead; trim excess thread.

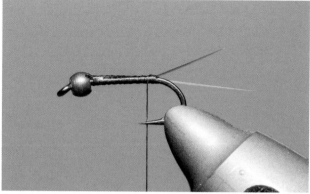

2. Position two tapered paintbrush fibers at the hook bend, making the extended tail about half the length of the body. Wrap thread over the tailing material to behind the hook, then wrap the thread back to the base of the hook opposite the barb; trim excess tail material. Tease the tail fibers apart and make figure eight wraps between the fibers, forcing them to split. Wrap the thread back over the hook shank to form a tapered body shape.

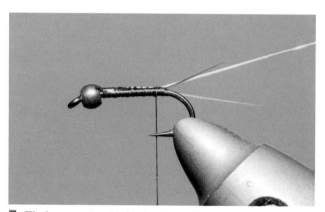

3. Tie in one strand of paintbrush fiber at the midpoint of the hook with the fiber facing to the rear of the hook; wrap thread over the fiber to the hook bend in touching wraps.

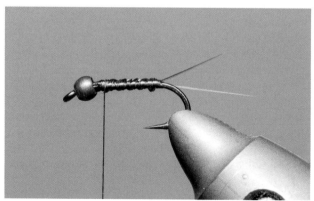

4. Wrap tying thread forward to behind the bead, then wrap the polyester paintbrush fiber forward in evenly spaced wraps to the bead. Tie off and trim excess paintbrush fiber.

5. Wrap thread about one bead width back from the bead and tie in the brown holographic tinsel.

8. Pull holographic tinsel over the collar of hair to form a wing case. Tie off, trim tying thread, and whip-finish.

6. Form a dubbing loop and insert a small bunch of hare's ear dubbing; twist the dubbing loop trapping the hare's ear. Take a dubbing brush (Dennis Collier's Dubbing Brush used here) and tease out the trapped hair.

9. Tease the dubbing with your brush to release the trapped fibers and create the impression of legs.

7. Wrap the hare's ear dubbing forward to the eye; tie off and trim excess. This is what the dubbing brush collar should look like

10. When tying the Copper Micro Baetis, you can use various colors for the underbody, and if you can find different colored paintbrush fibers, you can tie up variations such as shades of olive, rust, and cream, or use any type of body material you like. Try using various shades of hare's ear dubbing or dubbings with similar qualities of texture.

PAINTBRUSH BAETIS EMERGER

- **Hook:** #18-22 Daiichi 1220 or 1222, Tiemco 200R, or Dai-Riki 270
- **Thread:** Dun 16/0 Veevus or olive dun 8/0 UNI
- **Tail:** Brown and amber Antron yarn fibers
- **Underbody:** Tying thread
- **Rib:** Olive polyester paintbrush fiber
- **Thorax:** BWO Superfine Dubbing
- **Wing:** Dun polyester yarn or Antron yarn
- **Legs:** Natural CDC and dun polyester fibers from the wing
- **Head:** Tying thread

TYING THE PAINTBRUSH BAETIS EMERGER

I developed this pattern for when Baetis were hatching and the trout were not keying to the adult but rather to the emerging phase. I incorporated a trailing shuck and used a polyester paintbrush fiber to create a ribbed effect on the abdomen. The poly yarn in the loop wing also creates the impression of legs and helps buoy the fly in the surface film. The CDC feather is not for flotation but rather to help trap air bubbles on the fly's body to simulate the gaseous bubble used to facilitate the nymph's ascent to the surface. I treat the fly with Shimizaki Dry Shake to create the bubble. I also fish this pattern subsurface from the bottom to the top of the water column. I'm describing this pattern to show the development of my bead-head version of a Baetis that has emerged but is pulled subsurface before the wings have fully dried.

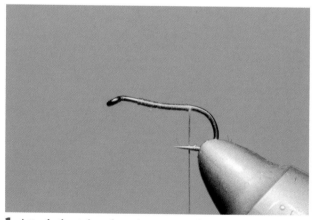

1. Attach the tying thread two eye widths back from the hook eye. Trim tag end of thread, make several touching wraps to secure the thread to the hook, and wrap thread back to the hook bend opposite the barb.

2. Wrap the thread in touching wraps back to the original tie-in point. Tie in a sparse amount of polyester or Antron yarn that will be used as the shuck of the emerging mayfly; take four to six fibers of the brown and amber yarns and mix together to form the shuck. Trim the excess fibers from the front edge of the yarns. Wrap the tying thread over the yarns in touching wraps to create a smooth foundation for the abdomen, making sure that the Antron fibers are positioned on the top of the hook shank. Trim the Antron fibers equal to the length of the abdomen; if desired, trim the fibers by slanting your cuts to form a point at the end of the fibers (a tying technique taught to me by Charlie Craven).

3. Wrap thread to the midpoint of the hook shank, tie in the polyester paintbrush fiber by its tip, then wrap tying thread in touching wraps over the paintbrush fiber back to the hook bend opposite the barb. Form a slight taper to the thread underbody and position the tying thread at the midpoint of the hook.

4. Wrap the polyester paintbrush fiber forward, allowing a small space between each wrap if desired. Tie off and trim excess paintbrush fiber just past the midpoint of the hook.

5. Cut 1½ inches of dun polyester or Antron yarn and divide in half lengthwise. Tie in the tip of yarn in front of the thorax, or at the one-third portion of the hook shank as shown, with the yarn facing toward the rear of the hook.

6. Select a large CDC fiber and trim the fluff from the base, then trim a V shape out of the tip as shown.

7. Place the "V" between the yarn wing with tips facing toward the rear of the hook. Tie in and pull the stem of CDC forward until you reach the desired length of the legs; trim excess. Wrap thread to one eye width back from the hook eye.

8. Fold the yarn forming a loop, then tie it off the loop one eye width back from the hook eye.

9. Divide the yarn evenly into two halves; tie each half, forcing the yarn to face toward the rear of the hook on one side of the hook, forming the outriggers. Perform the same procedure on the opposite side of the hook. Wrap tying thread over the yarn, forcing the yarn to face toward the rear of the hook. Trim each side the same as the thorax in length to form the outriggers. Color the outriggers with an olive permanent marker.

10. Whip-finish the head—it may appear to be slightly larger than what you usually expect from the head, but mayflies do have larger heads in real life. Color the head of the fly with a dark brown permanent marker.

11. The Baetis Emerger gives the appearance of a mayfly starting to emerge from its nymphal shuck with the wings partially unfolding. This pattern can be fished from the surface to the bottom of the stream.

TAK'S BAETIS ADULT PARACHUTE

- ■ **Hook:** #18-22 Daiichi 1220 or 1222 or Tiemco 100
- ■ **Thread:** Olive dun 8/0 UNI
- ■ **Tail:** Dun tapered paintbrush fibers
- ■ **Abdomen:** Light olive Nature's Spirit stripped peacock herl
- ■ **Wing:** Dun polyester yarn
- ■ **Hackle:** Dun Whiting Farms midge saddle

TYING TAK'S BAETIS ADULT PARACHUTE

I designed the Baetis Adult Parachute to create a low-riding adult mayfly that gives a better imprint on the surface of the water. I tied off the thread at the base of the wing and hackle rather than folding the wing and hackle out of the way in order to make finishing wraps prior to whip finishing. This technique was used with Vincent Sue's 720 vise.

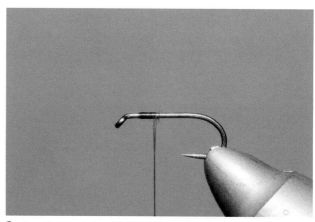

1. Attach tying thread two eye widths back from the hook eye, trim tag end of thread, and make several touching wraps to secure the thread to the hook. Position thread one-third the distance from the hook eye and the bend of the hook; this is the position on the hook shank I like to tie all my wings the same no matter what type of material I'm using.

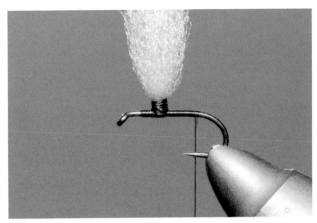

2. Cut the strand of polyester yarn into a 2-inch length; divide the strand of yarn into two separate strands. Tie in one strand of the polyester yarn in the middle of yarn with several wraps to secure to the hook. Hold both ends perpendicular to the hook shank, forming a tight V shape straight up with a slight amount of tension.

4. Wrap thread backwards with touching wraps to the hook bend opposite the barb. This is the position I tie the majority of my tails in; going farther down the bend will cause the tail to point at an angle, whereas tying in the tail material at the barb of the hook should ensure the tail extends back in line with the hook shank.

3. Make several wraps directly in front of the yarn, forming a small ball of thread that will cause the yarn wing to stand perpendicular to the hook shank. Wrap thread directly in back of the yarn, using several wraps to secure the yarn. Wrap the thread around the base of the wing to start the bundling process (posting of wing). Continue to wrap thread up the post to the desired height, then back down to the hook shank. Change the direction of the wrap and follow the same procedure to make a thicker base.

5. Select two polyester paintbrush fibers, evening up the tips. Measure how long you want the tails to be and place the polyester paintbrush fibers at the hook bend opposite the barb. Position the fibers to lie on top of the hook shank and then wrap the thread forward over the tail fibers in touching wraps to the base of the wing.

6. Trim off the excess tail fibers behind the base of the wing, then wrap thread back to the hook bend. Make one wrap behind the tail material, then make a figure eight wrap between the polyester paintbrush fibers to splay them out to the side at a 45-degree angle. Wrap thread back to behind the wing to form a smooth underbody.

9. Take a dun Whiting Farms midge saddle hackle and size it for proper length of fibers for the size of hook you are using. Remove the fibers from the base of the hackle to expose a bare stem. Determine which way you want the hackle to face. I prefer to tie in the hackle with the shiny side facing down or toward the eye of the hook; in this direction the hackle fibers will cup up when wrapping around the wing post. This allows the fly to sit lower in the surface film and, by having the hackle fibers cupping upward, lessens the number of fibers being trapped in the whip-finish. Some tiers prefer to have the hackle fibers facing down; it is determined by your preference.

Attach the bare stem directly in front of the wing post, then secure and trim excess butt of the stem. Wrap thread behind the wing and allow it to hang down. Grasp the hackle with hackle pliers if needed, then wrap the hackle up the wing post and then back down.

7. Wrap thread to the hook bend opposite the barb. Tie in the stripped Nature's Spirit peacock quill by its tip at the base of the wing and wrap the tying thread over the stripped quill back to the base of the tail, then wrap thread forward to just behind the rear of the wing. (Strip the peacock herl by placing it between your forefinger and thumbnail. Rub your thumb against your finger with pressure on the herl from the top section of the herl to the base until all the barbs are removed and you have a clean herl.) You can also substitute a fine-textured dubbing like Superfine to form a slender body.

8. Wrap the stripped quill forward in touching wraps to the rear base of the wing to form the abdomen; secure and trim excess quill. I like to wrap the thread to the hook eye and then back to the wing to form a thread thorax, or you can dub the thorax if desired.

10. Allow the hackle and hackle pliers to hang on the back side of the wing post; the weight of the hackle pliers will hold the hackle in place prior to tying in.

11. Wrap the tying thread around the base of the hackle stem, making sure to trap the hackle stem in the process; once secured keep taking wraps around the base of the post by dropping each wrap below the hook shank, making sure not to trap any hackle fibers. The hackle stem will be tied in because of the hackle hanging down. I like to position the thread in front of the wing post, then use a half-hitch tool to secure the wraps; I can then use a whip-finisher to finish off the head or continue to make several more half hitches. Trim thread and the hackle stem. You can also whip-finish the fly underneath the hackle if desired, then trim the thread.

13. Baetis Parachute; this style of adult dun sits lower in the water to give a better imprint on the surface when viewed from below. You can use different colored stripped peacock herl, biots, or other quill materials to form the body. I prefer to use Nature's Spirit dyed peacock herl because the color remains the same when the fuzz of the herl is removed. Protect the stripped quill with a light coating of head cement.

12. Trim the underside of the thorax of any loose hackle fibers; apply a small amount of head cement if desired.

Baetis (BWO)

NYMPHS

THREAD BAETIS NYMPH

- **Hook:** #18-22 Daiichi 1260 or TMC 200R
- **Thread:** Tan 8/0 UNI
- **Tail:** Dun or olive polyester tapered paintbrush fibers
- **Underbody:** Tying thread
- **Rib:** Tying thread colored with dark brown or black Sharpie
- **Wing Case:** Dark brown Antron fibers
- **Thorax:** Tying thread
- **Legs:** Dark brown Antron fibers
- **Note:** Coat body with thinned head cement.

STRIPPED QUILL BAETIS NYMPH

- **Hook:** #18-22 Daiichi 1260 or TMC 200R
- **Thread:** Tan 8/0 UNI
- **Tail:** Dun or olive polyester tapered paintbrush fibers
- **Underbody:** Tying thread
- **Rib:** BWO Nature's Spirit stripped peacock herl
- **Wing:** White polyester yarn
- **Thorax:** Olive Superfine Dubbing
- **Legs:** Whiting Farms CDL hen feather
- **Note:** Coat body with thinned head cement.

COPPER HEADED BAETIS NYMPH

- **Hook:** #18-22 Daiichi 1260 or TMC 200R
- **Thread:** Tan 8/0 UNI
- **Bead:** Copper glass bead
- **Tail:** Whiting Farms dark Coq de Leon hen fibers
- **Underbody:** Tying thread colored with light olive Chartpak marker
- **Rib:** Tying thread colored with black Sharpie
- **Wing Case:** Brown goose biot coated with Solarez Bone Dry UV resin
- **Thorax:** Blended muskrat dubbing
- **Legs:** Dark brown Antron fibers

GUNMETAL BAETIS NYMPH

- **Hook:** #18-22 Daiichi 1260 or TMC 200R
- **Thread:** Tan 8/0 UNI
- **Bead:** Gunmetal glass bead
- **Tail:** Whiting Farms dark Coq de Leon hen fibers
- **Underbody:** Tying thread colored with light olive Chartpak marker
- **Rib:** Tying thread
- **Wing Case:** Brown Swiss Straw
- **Thorax:** Tying thread
- **Legs:** Whiting Farms dark Coq de Leon hen fibers

A crisp 14-degree day on the South Platte River, ideal weather conditions for a Baetis hatch. JIM BROWNING PHOTO

BAETIS QUILL NYMPH

- **Hook:** #18-22 Daiichi 1260 or TMC 200R
- **Thread:** Olive dun 16/0 Veevus
- **Tail:** Dun or olive polyester tapered paintbrush fibers
- **Abdomen:** Olive Nature's Spirit stripped peacock herl
- **Wing Case:** Brown Medallion Sheeting
- **Thorax:** Olive Superfine Dubbing
- **Legs:** Organdy fibers dyed brown

BIOT BAETIS NYMPH

- **Hook:** #18-22 Daiichi 1260 or TMC 200R
- **Thread:** Olive dun 16/0 Veevus
- **Tail:** Dun or olive polyester tapered paintbrush fibers
- **Abdomen:** Blue-Winged Olive goose biot
- **Wing Case:** Black goose biot covered with Solarez Bone Dry UV resin
- **Thorax:** Hare's ear Nature's Spirit Emergence Dubbing
- **Legs:** Dark brown Antron fibers

ANTRON BAETIS NYMPH

- **Hook:** #18-22 Daiichi 1260 or TMC 200R
- **Thread:** Black Veevus 16/0
- **Tail:** Dun or olive polyester tapered paintbrush fibers
- **Abdomen:** BWO or light olive Nature's Spirit stripped peacock herl
- **Wing Case:** Dark brown goose biot covered with Solarez Bone Dry UV resin
- **Thorax:** Olive Shane Stalcup dubbing
- **Legs:** Organdy fibers dyed brown with permanent marker

WIRE RIBBED BAETIS NYMPH

- **Hook:** #18-22 Daiichi 1260 or TMC 200R
- **Thread:** Tan 8/0 UNI
- **Tail:** Dun or olive polyester tapered paintbrush fibers
- **Abdomen:** Tying thread colored with light olive Chartpak marker
- **Rib:** Brown Performance Flies wire (extra-small)
- **Wing Case:** Dark brown Antron
- **Thorax:** Blended muskrat dubbing
- **Legs:** Whiting Farms dark Coq de Leon fibers

PAINTBRUSH BAETIS NYMPH

- **Hook:** #18-22 Daiichi 1260 or TMC 200R
- **Thread:** Olive dun 16/0 Veevus
- **Tail:** Wood duck flank feather fibers
- **Underbody:** Tying thread
- **Rib:** Olive polyester paintbrush fiber
- **Wing Case:** Dark gray Larva Lace foam
- **Thorax:** Tying thread
- **Legs:** Brown hen hackle fibers

THREAD BAETIS NYMPH WITH SHUCK

- **Hook:** #18-22 Daiichi 1260 or TMC 200R
- **Thread:** Olive 16/0 Veevus
- **Tail:** Amber and dark brown Antron fibers
- **Underbody:** Tying thread
- **Rib:** Tying thread colored with dark brown or black Sharpie
- **Wing Case:** Brown goose biot
- **Thorax:** Tying thread
- **Legs:** Dark brown Antron fibers
- **Note:** Coat body with thinned head cement.

THREAD BODIED BIOT NYMPH

- **Hook:** #18-22 Daiichi 1260 or TMC 200R
- **Thread:** Olive 16/0 Veevus
- **Tail:** Dun or olive polyester tapered paintbrush fibers
- **Underbody:** Tying thread
- **Rib:** Tying thread colored with dark brown or black Sharpie
- **Wing Case:** Brown goose biot
- **Thorax:** Tying thread
- **Legs:** Dark brown Antron fibers
- **Note:** Coat body with thinned head cement.

COPPER HEADED BAETIS NYMPH

- **Hook:** #18-22 Daiichi 1260 or TMC 200R
- **Thread:** Olive 16/0 Veevus
- **Tail:** Light olive Antron fibers
- **Underbody:** Tying thread
- **Rib:** Tying thread colored with dark brown or black Sharpie
- **Wing Case:** Black goose biot covered with Solarez Bone Dry UV resin
- **Thorax:** Tying thread
- **Legs:** Dark brown Antron fibers
- **Note:** Coat body with thinned head cement.

SYNQUILL BAETIS NYMPH (OLIVE)

- **Hook:** #18-22 Daiichi 1260 or TMC 200R
- **Thread:** Olive 70-denier UTC
- **Tail:** Mallard dyed wood duck fibers
- **Body:** Hareline Synthetic Quill dyed with olive permanent marker
- **Wing Case:** Black goose biot covered with Solarez Bone Dry UV resin
- **Thorax:** Muskrat dubbing
- **Legs:** Olive partridge fibers

SYNQUILL BAETIS NYMPH

- **Hook:** #18-22 Daiichi 1260 or TMC 200R
- **Thread:** Olive brown 70-denier UTC
- **Tail:** Olive tapered paintbrush fibers
- **Body:** Synquill olive material
- **Underbody:** Tying thread
- **Wing Case:** Dark brown Antron yarn
- **Thorax:** Tying thread
- **Legs:** Olive hare's ear dubbing

MAGIC BAETIS NYMPH

- **Hook:** #18-22 Daiichi 1260 or TMC 200R
- **Thread:** Olive 70-denier UTC
- **Tail:** Whiting Farms dark Coq de Leon fibers
- **Underbody:** Tying thread
- **Rib:** Chartreuse Stretch Magic (.5 mm)
- **Wing Case:** Brown Swiss Straw
- **Thorax:** Tying thread
- **Legs:** Organdy fibers dyed brown with permanent marker

FLASHBACK PAINTBRUSH BAETIS NYMPH

- **Hook:** #18-22 Daiichi 1260 or TMC 200R
- **Thread:** Olive dun 8/0 UNI
- **Tail:** Brown and olive Antron fibers
- **Underbody:** Tying thread
- **Rib:** Olive polyester paintbrush fiber
- **Wing Case:** Pearl Flashabou
- **Thorax:** Medium to dark olive dubbing
- **Legs:** Brown Whiting Farms hen hackle fibers

PAINTBRUSH DROWNED BAETIS NYMPH

- **Hook:** #18-22 Daiichi 1260 or TMC 200R
- **Thread:** Olive Veevus 16/0
- **Bead:** Gold metal
- **Tail:** Olive tapered paintbrush fibers
- **Underbody:** Tying thread
- **Rib:** Olive polyester paintbrush fiber
- **Thorax:** Olive Superfine Dubbing
- **Wing/legs:** White polyester yarn
- **Underwing:** Natural CDC
- **Collar:** Peacock Ice Dub
- **Note:** Polyester legs colored with pale olive permanent marker.

TAK'S SPLIT WING BAETIS NYMPH

- **Hook:** #18-22 Daiichi 1260 or TMC 200R
- **Thread:** Dark dun 16/0 Veevus
- **Tail:** Dun tapered paintbrush fibers
- **Body:** Olive brown or green Nature's Spirit stripped peacock herl
- **Wing Case:** Brown goose biots
- **Flash:** Pearl Krystal Flash
- **Thorax:** Muskrat dubbing
- **Legs:** Olive partridge fibers

RUSTY BAETIS NYMPH

- **Hook:** #18-22 Daiichi 1260 or TMC 200R
- **Thread:** Rust 8/0 UNI
- **Tail:** Brown pheasant tail fibers
- **Underbody:** Tying thread
- **Rib:** Tying thread
- **Thorax:** Tying thread
- **Wing Case:** Brown biot covered with Solarez Bone Dry UV resin
- **Legs:** Hareline Predator Tinsel

COPPER MICRO BAETIS NYMPH

- **Hook:** #18-22 Daiichi 1180
- **Thread:** Olive 16/0 Veevus
- **Bead:** Copper brass
- **Tail:** Olive tapered polyester paintbrush fibers
- **Underbody:** Tying thread
- **Rib:** Olive paintbrush fiber
- **Wing Case:** Brown holographic tinsel
- **Legs:** Olive hare's ear dubbing loop

BLACK MICRO BAETIS NYMPH

- **Hook:** #18-22 Daiichi 1180
- **Thread:** Olive 16/0 Veevus
- **Bead:** Black tungsten
- **Tail:** Olive tapered polyester paintbrush fibers
- **Underbody:** Tying thread
- **Rib:** Olive paintbrush fiber
- **Wing Case:** Brown holographic tinsel
- **Legs:** Olive hare's ear dubbing loop

COPPER D-RIB MICRO BAETIS NYMPH

- **Hook:** #18-22 Daiichi 1180
- **Thread:** Olive 16/0 Veevus
- **Bead:** Copper brass
- **Tail:** Olive tapered polyester paintbrush fibers
- **Abdomen:** Light olive D-Rib
- **Wing Case:** Black goose biot covered with Solarez Bone Dry UV resin
- **Legs:** Organdy fibers dyed brown

RUSTY MICRO BAETIS NYMPH

- **Hook:** #18-22 Daiichi 1180
- **Thread:** Rust brown 70-denier UTC
- **Bead:** Copper brass
- **Tail:** Olive tapered polyester paintbrush fibers
- **Abdomen:** Tying thread
- **Rib:** Copper wire
- **Wing Case:** Brown Medallion Sheeting
- **Legs:** Dark hare's ear dubbing

THREAD BODIED BAETIS NYMPH

- **Hook:** #18-22 Daiichi 1180
- **Thread:** Olive 70-denier UTC
- **Tail:** Olive tapered polyester paintbrush fibers
- **Abdomen:** Tying thread
- **Rib:** Tying thread colored with black Sharpie
- **Wing Case:** Black biot
- **Legs:** Organdy fibers dyed brown
- **Note:** Coat body with thinned head cement.

FLASHBACK MICRO BAETIS NYMPH

- **Hook:** #18-22 Daiichi 1180
- **Thread:** Olive 70-denier UTC
- **Bead:** Copper brass
- **Tail:** Olive partridge fibers
- **Abdomen:** Olive D-Rib
- **Wing Case:** Pearl Krystal Flash
- **Legs:** Organdy fibers dyed brown

OLIVE BAETIS NYMPH

- **Hook:** #18-22 Daiichi 1180
- **Thread:** Olive 70-denier UTC
- **Tail:** Olive tapered polyester paintbrush fibers
- **Abdomen:** Tying thread
- **Rib:** Tying thread colored with black Sharpie
- **Wing Case:** Black biot
- **Legs:** Organdy fibers dyed brown
- **Note:** Coat body with thinned head cement.

ORGANDY BAETIS NYMPH

- **Hook:** #18-22 Daiichi 1180
- **Thread:** Olive 70-denier UTC
- **Tail:** Amber and brown Antron yarn fibers
- **Underbody:** Tying thread
- **Rib:** Olive polyester paintbrush fiber
- **Thorax:** Olive Superfine Dubbing
- **Wing Case:** Organdy fibers
- **Legs:** Organdy fibers

EMERGERS

PAINTBRUSH BAETIS EMERGER (STYLE 1)

- **Hook:** #18-22 Daiichi 1260 or TMC 200R
- **Thread:** Olive dun 16/0 Veevus
- **Tail:** Mixture of brown and amber Antron fibers
- **Abdomen:** Olive polyester paintbrush fiber
- **Thorax:** Olive Superfine Dubbing
- **Wing:** Dun polyester yarn
- **Legs:** Olive CDC fibers

PAINTBRUSH BAETIS EMERGER (STYLE 2)

- **Hook:** #18-22 Daiichi 1260, 1220, or 1222 or TMC 200R
- **Thread:** Olive dun 8/0 UNI
- **Tail:** Brown and amber Antron fibers
- **Underbody:** Tying thread
- **Rib:** Olive polyester paintbrush fiber
- **Wing Case:** White or light dun polyester yarn
- **Thorax:** BWO Superfine Dubbing
- **Legs 1:** Natural CDC fibers
- **Legs 2:** Polyester yarn colored with light olive Chartpak marker

DUNS

THREAD BODY HAIR BWO

- **Hook:** #18-22 Daiichi 1220 or 1222 or TMC 100
- **Thread:** Olive dun 8/0 UNI
- **Tail:** Olive polyester paintbrush fibers
- **Underbody:** Tying thread
- **Rib:** Tying thread colored brown with permanent marker
- **Wing:** Bleached deer hair
- **Hackle:** Dun Whiting Farms midge saddle

LOOP WINGED PAINTBRUSH BWO DUN

- **Hook:** #18-22 Daiichi 1220 or 1222 or TMC 100
- **Thread:** Olive dun 8/0 UNI
- **Tail:** Dun tapered paintbrush fibers
- **Underbody:** Tying thread
- **Rib:** Dark gray polyester paintbrush fiber
- **Wing:** Dun polyester yarn
- **Hackle:** Dun Whiting Farms saddle

STRIPPED QUILL BAETIS PARACHUTE

- **Hook:** 18-22 Daiichi 1220 or 1222 or TMC 100
- **Thread:** Olive dun 8/0 UNI
- **Tail:** Dun tapered paintbrush fibers
- **Abdomen:** Olive brown Nature's Spirit stripped peacock herl
- **Wing:** Dun polyester yarn
- **Hackle:** Dun Whiting Farms saddle

PAINTBRUSH BWO PARACHUTE

- **Hook:** #18-22 Daiichi 1220 or 1222 or TMC 100
- **Thread:** Olive dun 8/0 UNI
- **Tail:** Dun tapered paintbrush fibers
- **Underbody:** Tying thread
- **Rib:** Dark gray paintbrush fiber
- **Wing:** Medium dun polyester yarn
- **Hackle:** Medium dun Whiting Farms saddle

HAIR BAETIS PARACHUTE

- **Hook:** #18-22 Daiichi 1220 or 1222 or TMC 100
- **Thread:** Olive dun 8/0 UNI
- **Tail:** Dun tapered paintbrush fibers
- **Underbody:** Tying thread
- **Rib:** Olive brown Nature's Spirit stripped peacock herl
- **Wing:** Cow elk
- **Hackle:** Medium dun Whiting Farms saddle

BAETIS IRON DUN

- **Hook:** #18-22 Daiichi 1220 or 1222 or TMC 100
- **Thread:** Iron dun 8/0 UNI
- **Tail:** Dun tapered paintbrush fibers
- **Body:** Tying thread
- **Wing:** Dark dun deer hair
- **Hackle:** Medium dun Whiting Farms saddle
- **Note:** Coat body with thinned head cement.

SAN JUAN DARK DUN

- **Hook:** #18-24 Daiichi 1220 or 1222 or TMC 100
- **Thread:** Olive dun 8/0 UNI
- **Tail:** Dun tapered paintbrush fibers
- **Abdomen:** Olive brown Nature's Spirit stripped peacock herl
- **Wing:** Dun Comparadun deer hair
- **Hackle:** Dark dun Whiting Farms saddle

SAN JUAN BAETIS COMPARADUN

- **Hook:** #18-24 Daiichi 1220 or 1222 or TMC 100
- **Thread:** Olive dun 8/0 UNI
- **Tail:** Dun tapered paintbrush fibers
- **Underbody:** Tying thread
- **Abdomen:** Olive brown Nature's Spirit stripped peacock herl
- **Wing:** Dark dun or black MFC Widow's Web
- **Thorax:** Tying thread

LOOP WING BAETIS DUN

- **Hook:** #18-22 Daiichi 1220 or 1222 or TMC 100
- **Thread:** Olive dun 8/0 UNI
- **Tail:** Dun tapered paintbrush fibers
- **Abdomen:** Olive brown Nature's Spirit stripped peacock herl
- **Wing:** Dun polyester yarn
- **Hackle:** Dark dun Whiting Farms saddle

LOOP WING THREAD BODIED BAETIS DUN

- **Hook:** #18-22 Daiichi 1220 or 1222 or TMC 100
- **Thread:** Olive dun 8/0 UNI
- **Tail:** Dun tapered paintbrush fibers
- **Abdomen:** Tying thread
- **Wing:** Dun polyester yarn
- **Hackle:** Dark dun Whiting Farms saddle
- **Note:** Coat body with thinned head cement.

STRIPPED QUILL BWO

- **Hook:** #18-22 Daiichi 1220 or 1222 or TMC 100
- **Thread:** Olive dun 8/0 UNI
- **Tail:** Dun tapered paintbrush fibers
- **Underbody:** Tying thread
- **Rib:** Olive brown Nature's Spirit stripped peacock herl
- **Wing:** Dun Whiting Farms midge saddle
- **Note:** Coat body with thinned head cement.

BWO PAINTBRUSH DUN

- **Hook:** #18-22 Daiichi 1220 or 1222 or TMC 100
- **Thread:** Olive dun 8/0 UNI
- **Tail:** Dun tapered paintbrush fibers
- **Abdomen:** Olive brown Nature's Spirit stripped peacock herl
- **Wing:** Two dun CDC feathers
- **Hackle:** Dun Whiting Farms midge saddle
- **Note:** Coat body with thinned head cement.

BLACK WINGED BAETIS DUN PARACHUTE

- **Hook:** #18-24 TMC 2488 BL
- **Thread:** Olive dun 8/0 UNI
- **Abdomen:** Tying thread
- **Wing:** Black MFC Widow's Web
- **Hackle:** Grizzly Whiting Farms saddle
- **Note:** Coat body with thinned head cement.

BLACK WIDOW BWO

- **Hook:** #18-24 TMC 2488 BL
- **Thread:** Olive dun 8/0 UNI
- **Underbody:** Tying thread
- **Rib:** Olive brown Nature's Spirit stripped peacock herl
- **Wing:** Black MFC Widow's Web
- **Hackle:** Oversized grizzly Whiting Farms saddle clipped on bottom
- **Note:** Coat body with thinned head cement.

POLY WING PAINTBRUSH DUN

- **Hook:** #18-22 Daiichi 1222
- **Thread:** Olive dun 8/0 UNI
- **Tail:** Dun or gray tapered paintbrush fibers
- **Underbody:** Tying thread
- **Rib:** Olive paintbrush fiber
- **Wing:** Light dun polyester yarn
- **Thorax:** Tying thread

BLACK WINGED DUN

- **Hook:** #18-22 Daiichi 1222
- **Thread:** Olive dun 8/0 UNI
- **Tail:** Tapered paintbrush fibers
- **Abdomen:** Tying thread
- **Rib:** Tying thread colored brown with permanent marker
- **Wing:** Black MFC Widow's Web
- **Hackle:** Oversized grizzly Whiting Farms saddle clipped on bottom
- **Note:** Coat body with thinned head cement.

-2-

BASS SERIES

I've had the opportunity to watch and talk with some true artists who fashioned their bass flies using deer hair. I personally know some very talented deer hair fly tiers such as Dennis Martin, Jason Goodale, Jason Haddix, and Tim Jacobs, and I have admired the work of Billy Munn, Dave Whitlock, and Bob Messinger. Tim England, though, is one of the best deer hair fly tiers I have ever known. He showed me the basics of tying with deer hair and shared as much as I was able to understand and to translate to the tying vise. I was fortunate to have watched Tim England as he went through the process of developing many of his expertly crafted bass patterns tied with stacked deer hair into tight, compact bodies. It appeared to me that Tim always designed his patterns to have form following function; he had the ability to select materials that would give his bass flies the perfect shape with movement. I witnessed him catching many, many bass with his flies.

Baby Frog

I quickly found out that tying with deer hair involves a host of skill acquisition before one can tie a successful pattern. It became clear that practice and more practice are required to acquire the rudimentary skills to tie a deer hair bass fly not only successfully but with craftsmanship. I decided I wanted to design bass patterns that were more in line with my skill level and could be produced with less time at the vise. I started experimenting with foam materials to produce what I had in my mind's eye—flies that were easy to tie, showed movement, and required less time to tie the pattern.

As I set forth to conjure up ideas as to what I wanted to produce, I started to think about the qualities I wanted to incorporate in the pattern, the shape of the pattern, the color of the flies . . . more like what I had learned from Gary Borger's philosophy of size, shape, and color. I love

to fish for bluegills, sunfish, bass, and crappies, and I remembered how floating flies such as poppers, gurglers, deer hair poppers, and large dry flies always seemed to attract the fish because of their movement, which usually enticed the fish to take these flies. I wanted to infuse my flies with one or more of the qualities I'd come to recognize were the triggers causing the fish to accept the flies out of hunger or anger.

Key Materials for Bass Patterns

FOAM

I decided that I would use foam as the major construction component on all my surface warmwater flies, and would supplement with feathers and synthetic leg materials to create the movement I had in mind. One of my favorite tiers is Juan Ramirez, the creator of the Hopper Juan. His use of foam for this pattern intrigued me; the folding back of foam strips over themselves to create a rounded head was something I wanted to play around with. I looked at patterns like Bubba Smith's Cartoon Hopper, too, and liked the layered effect of stacking the foam to make a thicker-bodied fly as well as multiple-colored foam bodies and then gluing eyes onto the head. All these ideas helped me to come up with my own pattern.

ROUND RUBBER LEGS

I wanted to have my flies exhibit movement, which I learned can attract warmwater species of fish to the flies and then attack perhaps out of anger or hunger. I observed from the patterns of Tim England and others that the addition of some sort of appendages made their patterns more effective. I liked the way round rubber legs can create the

Top left: A handful of Mr. Bucket Mouth, who fell prey to Tak's Baby Frog.

Top right: Dinner plate–size bluegill caught on a Tak's Baby Frog.

Bottom left: Plump warmwater fish such as this bluegill often fall prey to a variety of fly patterns tied to use movement, which elicits strikes from opportunistic fish. DAVID SANCHEZ PHOTO

movement I wanted and that they come in a variety of solid and barred colors. I also like to incorporate Sili Leg–type materials in my patterns wherever I feel they are appropriate. Some of the patterns I've designed can be crossover types of patterns, such as my Ghost Minnow, Mini Minnow, and a few of my crawfish patterns, where I use them for both trout and warmwater fish.

HOOKS

I have been intrigued by some of the hooks that have been designed for deer hair bass fly tiers; why not try them for some of my patterns? I remember originally tying with Mustad stinger hooks. When I became more involved with tying the foam patterns, I continued to use the large-gaped stinger hooks popular for bass poppers; the large gape is ideal for the hooking qualities of these style hooks. I use the stinger hooks from Daiichi, Tiemco, and Saber, and with many of the smaller patterns I go with small, saltwater-style hooks.

UV RESINS

Brian Carson of Clear Cure Goo, which is unfortunately no longer in business, sent me some of his 3-D molded eyes in various sizes and color combinations to use for some of the patterns I was designing, and I found I could easily incorporate them into several of the patterns I was tying.

They added a somewhat realistic appearance and looked cool. A gel superglue worked well for adhering the eyes to the foam, and I covered the eyes with Solarez Bone Dry UV resin to prevent them from becoming unattached when put under heavy fishing pressure. There are several other manufacturers of UV resins—such as Loon, Deer Creek, Bug Bond, and Semperfli—that have also proven to be highly effective.

Designing the Baby Frog

I had the opportunity to fish a farm pond that was filled with bigger than average bass, bluegills, sunfish, crappies, and catfish. While fishing on these ponds, I noticed the music of frogs croaking along the shorelines filled with lily pads, reeds, and cattails. While sitting in my float tube, I noticed a baby frog swimming around near some reeds. As I watched, a huge bass attacked that baby frog. I knew then that I needed to come up with a frog pattern. I knew that frogs are a favorite food for bass and that a bass will readily take a frog swimming on the surface. I started to have visions of frogs being eaten by largemouth bass. I decided that I wanted to create my own foam frog that I could cast easily with a 5- or 6-weight fly rod. I felt the frog would have to be smaller than the traditional-size patterns being fished, so I set out to create a baby frog pattern that could be eaten by the size of fish I usually encounter in my local ponds. Thus the Baby Frog was born.

Following my tying philosophy of designing flies that are simple in construction and impressionistic of the organism I'm try to imitate, I created a tapered body with a wide head that tapered to a point at the rear of the fly. I chose a green strip of foam for the top of the frog and white foam for its belly. River Road Creations produces green, tan, and yellow 2 mm foam sheets with black elongated spots to mimic the frog's spots.

I wanted to add large eyes to continue the illusion of a live frog, and round rubber legs to mimic the legs of the frog while creating movement. I remember taking two lengths of round rubber legs and tying an overhand knot at one end. I then cut the two pieces of round rubber leg to look like kickers of a grasshopper. (I believe I saw Charlie Craven do the same procedure for his highly effective Charlie Boy Hopper.) What I remember most, however, is that when the overhand knot was tied, the two pieces of round rubber legs splayed out, perfect for creating the look of a frog's webbed feet. Taking enough of the round rubber legs to give the illusion of frog hind legs and leaving a shorter tag end resulted in giving the pattern its front legs.

I added a red dot under the chin mainly because I'd seen something similar on the face of poppers and on wooden bass lures and thought it looked cool. I added black dots on the back of the frog for looks only; unless the frog turned over, the fish can't see the dots on the top of the frog's body. I thought it looked more convincing.

I have tested this pattern in several colors over the past three years and found it to be very effective as a warmwater pattern, catching bass, bluegill, and sunfish. I use a bass stinger hook to tie this pattern, which usually ranges from size 10 up to 2/0; these larger stinger hooks help keep the smaller fish from grabbing the fly, but not always—I caught some small bass that were no larger than the frog pattern. Umpqua Feather Merchants has selected my Baby Frog pattern for their catalog.

TAK'S BABY FROG

- **Hook:** #6-10 Daiichi 2720, Tiemco 8089, Saber 7060, or Mustad 37187
- **Thread:** White 140-denier UTC
- **Body Top:** Green foam (2 mm)
- **Body Bottom:** White foam (2 mm)
- **Eyes:** 3-D molded eyes attached with gel superglue
- **Eye Coating:** Solarez Bone Dry or Thin UV resin
- **Legs:** Green/black barred round rubber legs
- **Color (optional):** I sometimes put a dot under the chin of the pattern with a red Sharpie and use a black Sharpie for spots on the back. River Road Creations has colored foam in tan, yellow, and olive with black spots on the foam to resemble the spotting of the frog's back.

TYING TAK'S BABY FROG

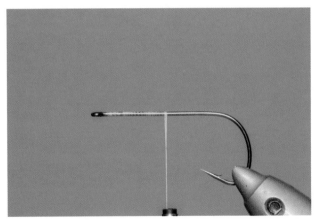

1. Attach tying thread at the hook eye and wrap thread back to the midpoint of the hook shank with touching wraps, then wrap the thread in spiral wraps forward to one eye width back from the hook eye.

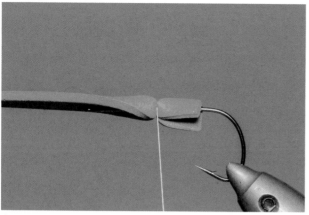

2. Cut two long strips of 2 mm foam, one green (or chartreuse, yellow, light green, or tan) and one white, ⅜ inch wide by 4 inches long; set aside. Place the colored strip on top of the hook with the long strip facing forward toward the hook eye. Tie in the foam on top of the hook shank, leaving a ½-inch piece of foam extending toward the hook bend. Take several tight wraps to secure the foam to the hook shank.

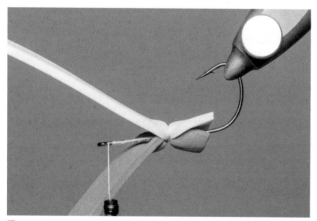

3. Rotate the hook over in the vise and attach the white piece of foam at the same tie-in point with a ½-inch piece extending back over the hook; tie in securely. Lift each piece of foam back slightly and allow the thread to slip in between the foam. Wrap the thread forward in evenly spaced wraps to one eye width back from the hook eye and take several wraps.

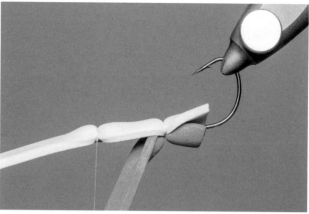

4. Fold the white piece of foam over the hook shank and tie in at the eye with several tight wraps of tying thread.

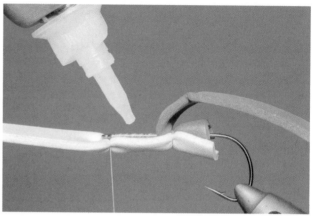

5. Rotate the vise so that the green piece of foam is facing up. Apply a small amount of gel superglue along the inside of the foam.

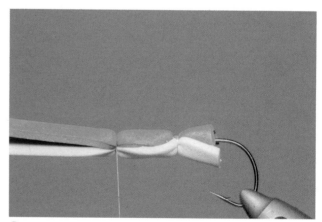

6. Fold the colored piece of foam over and tie in at the hook eye with six tight wraps of thread. Gently squeeze the foam together to bond the two pieces. When the gel superglue dries, the glue will keep the body from rotating on the hook.

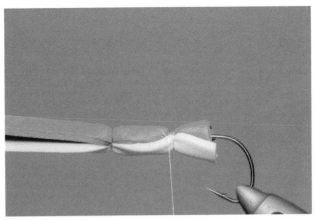

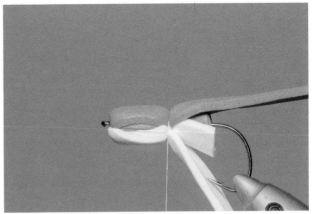

7. Place the tying thread across the top of the foam in a diagonal fashion and secure at the crease formed at the rear of the body. Rotate the vise.

9. Rotate the fly in the vise and make several more wraps of thread to secure the foam to the rear of the hook, thus completing the shape of the frog's body.

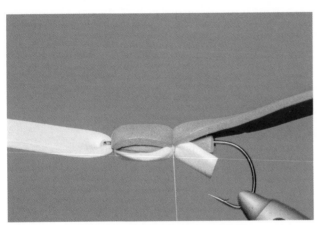

8. Apply superglue to the foam, then fold the top piece over toward the hook bend and secure in the same position as the foam already on the hook. Adding the superglue will reinforce the body of the fly. Make several wraps to secure the foam at the rear of the body. Rotate the vise and apply superglue, then pull the bottom foam over and secure at the rear of the body with several wraps of thread. Again, the addition of the superglue will strengthen the bond of the foam.

10. Trim the excess foam by cutting at a 45-degree angle on both sides of the foam body, creating a shallow point at the tail of the fly. Repeat process for the remaining layers of foam.

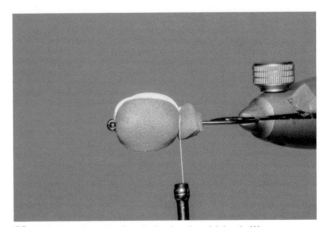

11. This is what the frog's body should look like.

Float tubing allows the warmwater angler access to waters that are hard to reach from shore due to vegetation overgrowth. DAVID SANCHEZ PHOTO

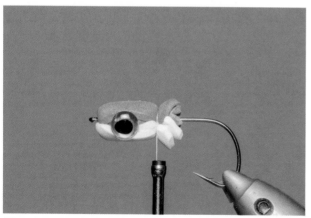

12. Add a small dot of gel superglue on the side of the foam body at the midpoint of the head and attach a 3-D eye; repeat on the opposite side of the head. Apply a coat of Solarez Bone Dry UV resin to the eye, overlapping the resin onto the foam; this should completely cover the eye. Set resin with UV light, and repeat process on the opposite side of the head. The Solarez Bone Dry UV resin has the thinnest consistency of the Solarez lineup of resins and applies a thin coat to protect the eyes without undue buildup of resin.

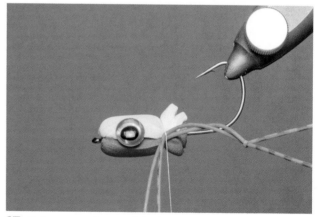

13. Select two pieces of the barred round rubber legs equal in length and tie an overhand knot approximately 1 inch from the end of the material. The knotted end of the round rubber will simulate a webbed frog's foot. Repeat the process. Attach the round rubber legs to the body, allowing the legs to extend back 1 inch or less, depending on your preference, from the body; secure with several wraps of tying thread. Repeat the process for the opposite side of the body.

14. The remaining rubber legs will then form the front legs of the frog and should splay out on the sides behind the eyes. Trim both sides of the front round rubber legs a little shorter but even.

Optional: Draw a dot under the chin of the frog using a red Sharpie, if desired. You can add black or olive dots on the top side of the frog's head, but this is for the fly tier not the fish. The fly will be viewed from the bottom, so the fish will not be able to see the dots on the back unless the fly lands upside down on the water's surface.

15. The Baby Frog gives an impressionistic representation of a baby frog. Additional colors (top color) can include chartreuse, olive, yellow, brown, and tan.

BASS TURD

- **Hook:** #4-8 Daiichi 2720 or Tiemco 600SP or 811S
- **Thread:** White 140-denier UTC
- **Body:** Tan, chartreuse, dark olive, light green, green, red, purple, blue, white, or yellow (or combinations of colors) foam (2 mm)
- **Eyes:** 3-D Molded Eyes attached with gel superglue
- **Eye Coating:** Solarez Bone Dry UV resin
- **Legs:** Colored MFC Centipede Legs or barred rubber legs, matching color to enhance the color scheme of the pattern.
- **Color (optional):** I sometimes put a dot under the chin of the pattern with a red Sharpie and use a black Sharpie for spots on the back.

TYING THE BASS TURD

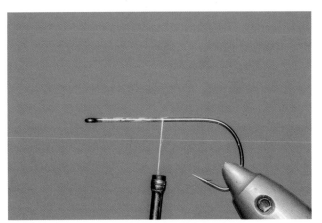

1. Attach tying thread at the hook eye and wrap thread back to the two-thirds point of the hook or even with the point of the hook, then wrap the thread to one eye width back from the hook eye.

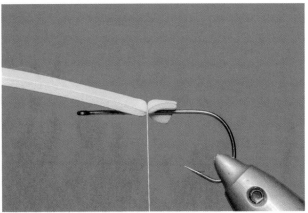

2. Cut a long strip of 2 mm foam approximately ¼ to ⅛ inch wide and tie in the tag end of the foam with the foam facing toward the hook eye; take several wraps to secure foam to the hook.

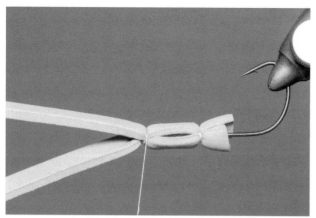

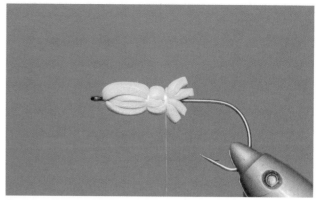

3. Invert the hook and tie in an identical piece of 2 mm foam opposite the first strip as shown. (You can cut two strips of foam out of the same color or one strip of one color and the other strip with another color of your choice to create a two-toned body.) Lift the foam away from the hook and wrap the tying thread to the hook eye. Apply a small amount of gel superglue to the inside surface of the foam. Fold the second strip of foam forward as indicated and tie off at the same position as the first strip at the hook eye. Gently squeeze the two halves together to form a tight bond; this will help decrease the rotation of the foam.

5. Trim the butt end of the foam as indicated and whip-finish but do not trim thread.

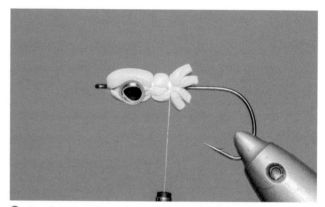

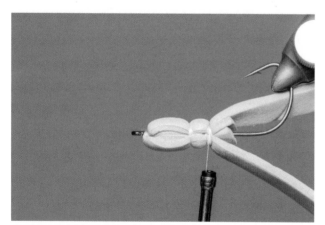

6. Apply a small amount of gel superglue to the side of the head at the halfway point of the first segment of the head and position a 3-D eye over the glue; gently press into position. Repeat the process on the opposite side of the head. Cover the eye, go slightly over the edge of the eye with Solarez Bone Dry UV resin, and set with UV light.

4. Invert the fly and position the tying thread so that it lies across the foam and toward the rear of the hook in the position that the first piece of foam was tied in. Fold the top piece of foam over facing the direction of the bend of the hook. Take several wraps of thread at the two-thirds position to form the first segment of the body of the fly. Fold the remaining piece of foam over to complete the first segment of the body to the rear of the hook, then tie in the foam as shown at the two-thirds position. Repeat the same process to create the second segment as shown; this will create two distinctive rounded body segments.

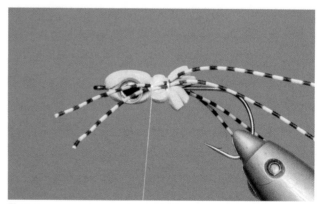

7. Select two pieces of the MFC Centipede Legs or any barred round rubber leg material, approximately 1½ to 2 times the length of the body. Tie in the legs as shown to the rear segment on each side of the body. After you have secured the rear segment, pull the thread along the midsection of the foam to the first segment and tie in the legs as shown. Whip-finish and trim thread. You can add head cement to the thread for more security.

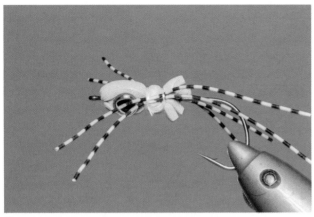

8. The Bass Turd is an attractor type of fly with extended legs to give motion to the fly when twitched on the surface of the water. Smaller versions of this pattern make a fly for bluegills.

Bass Bugs

BABY FROG (OLIVE/WHITE)

- ▪ **Hook:** #6-10 Daiichi 2720, TMC 8089, or Saber 7060
- ▪ **Thread:** White 140-denier UTC
- ▪ **Underbody:** White 5-inch-long piece of 2 mm foam ⅛ inch wide wrapped around hook
- ▪ **Body Top:** Olive foam (2 mm)
- ▪ **Body Bottom:** White foam (2 mm)
- ▪ **Eyes:** 3-D molded eyes covered with Solarez Bone Dry UV resin
- ▪ **Legs:** Chartreuse/green Wapsi Barred Round Rubber Legs
- ▪ **Color (optional):** I sometimes put a dot under the chin of the pattern with a red Sharpie, black Sharpie for spots on the back.

BABY FROG (LIGHT GREEN/WHITE)

- ▪ **Hook:** #6-10 Daiichi 2720, TMC 8089, or Saber 7060
- ▪ **Thread:** White 140-denier UTC
- ▪ **Underbody:** White 5-inch-long piece of 2 mm foam ⅛ inch wide wrapped around hook
- ▪ **Body Top:** Light green foam (2 mm)
- ▪ **Body Bottom:** White foam (2 mm)
- ▪ **Eyes:** 3-D molded eyes covered with Solarez Bone Dry UV resin
- ▪ **Legs:** Green/black Wapsi Barred Round Rubber Legs
- ▪ **Color (optional):** I sometimes put a dot under the chin of the pattern with a red Sharpie, black Sharpie for spots on the back.

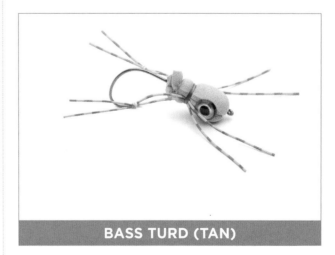

BASS TURD (TAN)

- ▪ **Hook:** #6-10 Daiichi 2720 or TMC 600SP or 811S
- ▪ **Thread:** White 140-denier UTC
- ▪ **Body:** Tan foam (2 mm)
- ▪ **Eyes:** 3-D molded eyes covered with Solarez Bone Dry UV resin
- ▪ **Legs:** Tan/brown MFC Centipede Legs

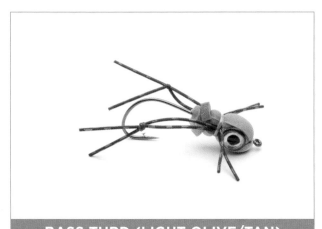

BASS TURD (LIGHT OLIVE/TAN)

- **Hook:** #4-8 Daiichi 2720 or TMC 600SP or 811S
- **Thread:** White 140-denier UTC
- **Body Top:** Light olive foam (2 mm)
- **Body Bottom:** Tan foam (2 mm)
- **Eyes:** 3-D molded eyes covered with Solarez Bone Dry UV resin
- **Legs:** Olive/silver Wapsi Centipede Legs

BASS RIBBIT (BLACK/TAN)

- **Hook:** #4-10 Daiichi 2720, TMC 8089, or Saber 7060
- **Thread:** Yellow 140-denier UTC or color to match color scheme
- **Body:** Black and tan foam (2 mm)
- **Eyes:** 3-D molded eyes covered with Solarez Bone Dry UV resin
- **Legs:** Tan/black MFC Centipede Legs

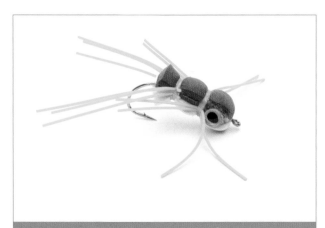

BASS RIBBIT (GREEN/WHITE)

- **Hook:** #4-10 Daiichi 2720, TMC 8089 or Saber 7060
- **Thread:** Yellow 140-denier UTC
- **Body:** Green and white foam (2 mm)
- **Eyes:** 3-D molded eyes covered with Solarez Bone Dry UV resin
- **Legs:** Yellow MFC Centipede Legs

BASSCOTTI (OLIVE/LIGHT GREEN)

- **Hook:** #4-8 Daiichi 2720, TMC 8089, or Saber 7060
- **Thread:** White 140-denier UTC
- **Body:** Light green foam (2 mm)
- **Top:** Olive foam (2 mm)
- **Legs:** Chartreuse/black MFC round rubber legs
- **Indicator:** Red foam (2 mm)

BASSCOTTI (TAN/ORANGE)

- **Hook:** #4-8 Daiichi 2720, TMC 8089, or Saber 7060
- **Thread:** White 140-denier UTC
- **Body:** Tan foam (2 mm)
- **Top:** Orange foam (2 mm)
- **Legs:** Chartreuse MFC round rubber legs

TAKAPOPPER (GREEN/WHITE)

- **Hook:** #4-10 Daiichi 2720, TMC 8089, or Saber 7060
- **Thread:** White 140-denier UTC
- **Body:** Green foam (2 mm)
- **Belly:** White foam (2 mm)
- **Legs:** Green MFC round rubber legs
- **Flash:** Pearl Krystal Flash
- **Eyes:** 3-D molded eyes covered with Solarez Bone Dry UV resin
- **Tail:** Whiting Farms chartreuse dyed grizzly
- **Hackle:** Whiting Farms chartreuse dyed grizzly

TAKAPOPPER (YELLOW/WHITE)

- **Hook:** #4-10 Daiichi 2720, TMC 8089, or Saber 7060
- **Thread:** White 140-denier UTC
- **Body:** Yellow foam (2 mm)
- **Belly:** White foam (2 mm)
- **Legs:** Yellow/black MFC round rubber legs
- **Flash:** Pearl Krystal Flash
- **Eyes:** 3-D molded eyes covered with Solarez Bone Dry UV resin
- **Tail:** Whiting Farms yellow dyed grizzly
- **Hackle:** Whiting Farms yellow dyed grizzly

BASSOOKA (OLIVE/TAN)

- **Hook:** #4-8 Daiichi 2720 or Saber 7060
- **Thread:** White 140-denier UTC
- **Top:** Olive foam (2 mm)
- **Belly:** Tan foam (2 mm)
- **Legs:** Tan/black MFC barred round rubber legs

BASSOOKA (YELLOW/WHITE)

- **Hook:** #4-8 Daiichi 2720 or Saber 7060
- **Thread:** White 140-denier UTC
- **Top:** Yellow foam (2 mm)
- **Belly:** White foam (2 mm)
- **Legs:** Tan/black MFC barred round rubber legs

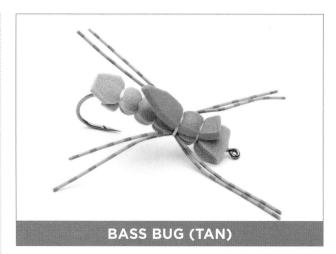

BASS BUG (TAN)

- **Hook:** #4-12 Daiichi 2720 or Saber 7060
- **Thread:** White 140-denier UTC
- **Body:** Tan foam (2 mm)
- **Legs:** Tan/brown MFC barred round rubber legs
- **Indicator:** Pink foam (2 mm)

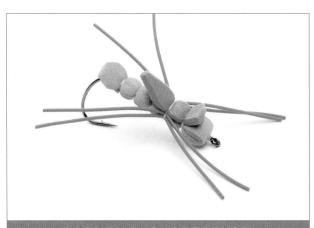

BASS BUG (CHARTREUSE)

- **Hook:** #4-12 Daiichi 2720 or Saber 7060
- **Thread:** White 140-denier UTC
- **Body:** Chartreuse foam (2 mm)
- **Legs:** Light green round rubber legs
- **Indicator:** Pink foam (2 mm)

FORK TAIL (TAN)

- **Hook:** #4-12 Daiichi 2720 or Saber 7060
- **Thread:** White 140-denier UTC
- **Body:** Tan foam (2 mm)
- **Legs:** Tan/black barred round rubber legs
- **Indicator:** Red foam (2 mm)

FORK TAIL (METALLIC GREEN)

- **Hook:** #4-12 Daiichi 2720 or Saber 7060
- **Thread:** White 140-denier UTC
- **Body:** Metallic green foam (2 mm)
- **Legs:** Red round rubber legs
- **Indicator:** Red foam (2 mm)

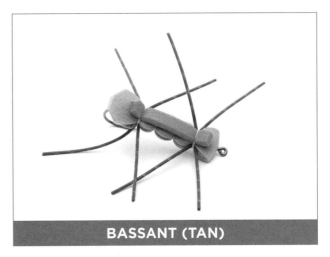

BASSANT (TAN)

- **Hook:** #4-12 Daiichi 2720 or Saber 7060
- **Thread:** White 140-denier UTC
- **Body:** Tan foam (2 mm)
- **Legs:** Wapsi barred orange and brown rubber legs
- **Indicator:** Pink foam (2 mm)

BASSANT (DARK GREEN)

- **Hook:** #4-12 Daiichi 2720 or Saber 7060
- **Thread:** White 140-denier UTC
- **Body:** Dark green foam (2 mm)
- **Legs:** Yellow/green Hareline barred round rubber legs
- **Indicator:** Yellow foam (2 mm)

-3-

CADDIS SERIES

I love to fish dry flies, so it seems logical I'd focus my creative energies toward coming up with adult caddis patterns. Caddis is one of the major insects that hatch in the waters of Colorado. One of the first caddis patterns I wanted to learn to tie was Al Troth's Elk Hair Caddis. As I started to tie this pattern, one problem I had was tying in the hackle so that the barbs of the hackle would face to the rear of the hook. I always started by tying in the hackle by its tip with the dull side facing up, dubbing a body, and tying in the elk hair. No matter how I tied in the hackle, there was a 50/50 chance the hackle would face the wrong direction—toward the hook eye.

Early in my demonstration tying days, I had the great fortune of tying next to Al Troth—talk about being intimidated. As the day wore on I got to know Al Troth and found him to be a man of kindness, willing to share, and with a great sense of humor. I gathered up the nerve to ask him how he tied his Elk Hair Caddis. What followed was a generous outpouring of his knowledge about fly tying, how he tied his patterns, and how to tie them correctly. I learned not only how to tie the Elk Hair Caddis but also several of his patterns. Several of his tying techniques have served me well.

Mr. Troth starts off tying his flies by gathering all the materials needed to tie a particular pattern. On this occasion, all of his hackle for the Elk Hair Caddis was presized and set aside; he had a board he had drilled out to accommodate about 50 spent .22 caliber shells that he had flared open slightly on the opening of the shell. He used this board with the shells as his hair-stacking device; he cut and stacked the whole board with elk hair and then tapped it lightly on the tabletop and stacked all the elk hair at once.

He used fine copper wire that he had precut to the exact size he needed for the size hook he was using. He used spar

Horned Caddis

varnish instead of head cement, and dubbing, which I don't recall but might have been rabbit, and, of course, he had hooks laid out in the size he needed.

He started the pattern by attaching his thread back from the hook eye, taking several wraps to secure the thread, then tied in the copper wire with several wraps to secure the wire and wrapped thread in touching wraps back to the hook bend opposite the barb. He then placed a small amount of varnish on his thread, and then applied his dubbing; he then wrapped the dubbed thread forward, creating a slightly tapered effect, to within one to two eye widths back from the eye of the hook.

He next tied in the hackle by the butt of the feather two eye widths back from the eye of the hook. He proceeded to wrap the hackle in evenly spaced wraps in a reverse palmer style to the hook bend in a clockwise fashion. He allowed the hackle pliers to hang down, holding the hackle at the bend of the hook opposite the barb. Next, he wrapped the wire counter to the direction he had tied in the hackle, around the hackle stem, and continued to wrap in evenly spaced wraps to one to two eye widths back from the hook eye. Then he tied off the wire and trimmed the excess. He told me that he tied many of his patterns using the concept of step tying, which meant that he tied in the wire first, then tied in the dubbed body, then tied in the hackle, whip-finished the thread, and trimmed the thread. After this was accomplished, he set the fly aside. After he tied the number of step-tied flies he required for an order, he would add the elk hair wing to each of the step-tied flies, trim the wing, and whip-finish the fly. He gathered the elk hair and put the hair into the shells tip first until he filled all the shells. He then tapped the board to stack all of the hair evenly in the shell; this stacked all the hair at once instead of individually. He then grasped one of the shells by lifting the shell in his

41

Large, skittering caddis may be found in lakes and provide excellent fishing. Caddis will skitter on the surface of the lake, giving their wings time to form and dry out or while they are laying eggs. When fishing an egg-laying caddis female, I will add about 12 to 18 inches of weight in front of the caddis and allow the flies to be pulled under the surface. I generally use a standard dry caddis pattern and coat it with Shimizaki Dry Shake; when it is pulled under the surface, the thin layer of desiccant creates bubbles on the wing that mimic air trapped by the fibers on the wing of the caddis.

left hand and pointing the base of the shell to his left. He would grasp the elk hair to be facing toward the rear of the hook. He measured the elk hair to the proper length and grasped the hair tightly with his left hand as he placed it on top of the body; with his right hand he tied in the elk hair. He whip-finished the fly and trimmed the tying thread, then took a sharp razor to cut the elk hair at an angle he wanted. A little varnish and the job was finished.

Look for areas that have different types of holding water. I look for areas where there might be a riffle leading into a pool, rock formations in the stream flow, banks that have hiding places for trout, and quiet pools where caddis might hang out to feed. TOM FLANAGAN PHOTO

A beautiful Rocky Mountain National Park cutthroat trout, which took a caddis adult pattern, showing its spawning colors. ISRAEL PATTERSON PHOTO

He told me that using this type of procedure of tying in materials in steps rather than completing an entire pattern aided in his tying a greater number of flies in a shorter period of time.

Key Materials for Caddis Patterns

HOOKS

For tying dry caddis patterns, I've found a variety of hook styles to be useful because of their function. I like to use Daiichi's 1260, 1100, 1222, 1110, 1280; Tiemco's 2312, 100, 5212, 900BL, 2302; and Dai-Riki's 280-285. For tying nymphs I favor using Daiichi's 1250, 1160, 1150, 1130, 1120, 1530, 1550 and Dai-Riki's 125, 135.

FOAM

I have a collection of 2 mm and 3 mm craft foams in a variety of colors from my local arts and crafts store and various fly shops that I visit. I love the foam sheets plus the various

The Blue River below Green Mountain Reservoir and upstream from Jurassic Park, home to big browns who often fall prey to a well-presented caddis pattern. TOM FLANAGAN PHOTO

foam cutters that River Road Creations produces. I also use foams that I find in electronic equipment packaging; they come in various-size thickness from very thin to 1 mm.

WINGS

My favorite wing materials for tying caddis dry flies is deer hair, especially the deer hair from Blue Ribbon Flies in West Yellowstone, Montana. Blue Ribbon Flies has a great selection of deer hair and any other hair for the fly tier, and you can order online. I also have had great luck with the top-notch products from Nature's Spirit, from various types of hairs to a whole host of different bird feathers. I like using Montana Fly Company's Widow's Web yarn for many of the wings I create for my dry caddis patterns; I often couple the yarn with deer hair. I have also found that white polyester macramé yarn, when brushed out, makes great high-floating wings and indicator posts.

BODIES

I like to make my dry caddis dubbed bodies with Superfine, Fly Rite, and Water's Edge Hydro dubbing made by Jason Haddix; I also like to use goose biots. I like to use the dubbings because I can make any size body configuration, and they come in a variety of colors. I have, however, tied most of my bodies with a Superfine caddis green color that I've found most productive. The goose biots make beautiful segmented bodies.

THREADS

I use Veevus, UNI, UTC, Danville, and Semperfli Nano threads for most of my tying needs. Veevus and Semperfli's Nano threads are very strong and less likely to break, and are small in diameter, which helps me make a more well-crafted fly.

Designing the Breadcrust Wannabe

The only reason I wanted to design my own version of Ed Rocca's Bread Crust (Pat Dorsey took over Ed Rocca's business about twenty years ago when Ed retired) was simply due to my frustration with the process of securing the right tail feather of the grouse (which are becoming seemingly harder to come by) and the time it takes to process the feather so that you can tie with it. I'd rather purchase the flies than to tie them myself, so I decided to see if I could create an alternative. What makes it difficult to prepare the feathers is that you have to collect grouse tail feathers in the brown phase, then trim the fiber to stubs close to the stem. Then you must split the tail quills in half lengthwise, remove the pith of the feather, and soak the quills to soften them up before tying in the material for the pattern. I'd rather buy the flies from Pat Dorsey, but with his busy schedule as a top-notch guide and all the orders he has for his tying business, I don't know how he has time to tie this pattern.

What I set out to do was create a pattern that was visually similar to the Bread Crust. One of the outstanding characteristics of the Bread Crust is the raised ribbed created by trimming the feather's individual fibers to get a stumpy effect. Getting the ruffed effect is a tall task to replicate, but I was determined to come up with a facsimile that just might work. I decided to use medium brown D-Rib to give the appearance of the grouse stem paired with a trimmed dun hackle stem.

I built up an underbody with wraps of lead wire about half the length of the hook shank, then used wool yarn to give it a tapered body. Next, I attached the D-Rib and the trimmed hackle stem at the hook bend opposite the barb. I wrapped the D-Rib in touching wraps to two eye widths back from the hook eye, then tied off the D-Rib and trimmed the excess material. I wrapped the ostrich herl or trimmed hackle stem in the grooves created by wrapping the D-Rib and tied off and trimmed the excess stem in front of the D-Rib. I finished the fly by adding a few wraps of Whiting Farms grizzly hen hackle as a soft-hackle. The result was a fair representation of the Bread Crust. Until I master tying the Bread Crust in the proper manner, I'll have to be satisfied with the few fish I catch with this variation.

BREADCRUST WANNABE CADDIS PUPA (BROWN)

- **Hook:** #12-16 Daiichi 1260 or TMC 2312
- **Thread:** Black 8/0 Veevus, UNI, or Semperfli Nano
- **Weight:** 6 to 8 wraps of lead wire appropriate to hook size. You can use a brass or tungsten bead if you want to make a bead-head version of this pattern.
- **Underbody 1:** Lead wire overwrapped to form a robust body shape, then covered with tying thread
- **Underbody 2:** Gray ostrich herl
- **Rib:** Medium brown D-Rib
- **Hackle:** Whiting Farms grizzly hen

TYING THE BREADCRUST WANNABE CADDIS PUPA

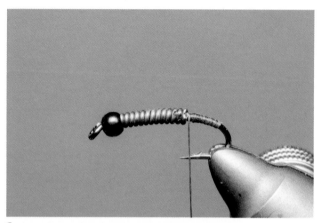

1. Attach bead to hook and slide to the hook eye. Wrap lead wire six to eight wraps around the hook shank. Next, wrap thread behind the lead wire. Wrap thread to the hook bend even with the barb; if preferred, take a couple of wraps of thread down the hook bend.

2. Tie in ostrich herl by its tip at the rear end of the lead wire, and then wrap thread over the herl back to the rear of the hook.

3. Prepare the D-Rib material by cutting a short slant to the tag end of the ribbing. Tie in the tip of the ribbing directly behind the weight and wrap the thread over the rib to the rear of the hook, even with the ostrich herl. Wrap thread forward to the front edge of the lead wire.

4. Wrap the D-Rib in touching wraps forward to one bead width back from the bead; tie off and trim excess D-Rib.

5. Wrap the ostrich herl forward in between the wraps of the D-Rib to the front edge of the lead wire; tie off and trim excess herl.

6. Tie in grizzly hen hackle with the shiny side facing forward; this will cause the feather to either be perpendicular to the hook shank or cupped slightly back toward the rear of the hook in a soft-hackle style.

7. Wrap the hen hackle forward to behind the bead; tie off and trim excess hen hackle.

8. Fold the hen hackle fibers back and take several wraps of thread back over the fibers, which will cause the fibers to bend back. Whip-finish and trim.

9. The Wannabe Breadcrust pattern represents a case-building caddis larva, which creates a shelter made out of various material found along the streambed.

Designing the Split Wing Caddis

Craig Mathews is one of my favorite fly tiers, and the Split Wing Caddis is my variation on his X-Wing Caddis. Tim England used to be the illustrator for *Fly Rod & Reel* magazine, and he had illustrated a new pattern designed by Craig called the X-Wing Caddis. I decided to tie up a half dozen for a fishing trip on the upper reaches of the Poudre River with Tim. As the day turned to dusk, we encountered a caddis hatch of substantial proportions. I shared the patterns I tied, which were only a few, with Tim. Within a short period I had only one X-Wing Caddis left.

I had great success fishing this pattern during that caddis hatch, but with the number of fish I caught, and only having one pattern remaining, I noticed the deer hair started to thin out and the wing became much sparser with each fish caught. Since I only had one of the patterns, I was forced to re-dress the fly with each fish caught. But with each fish caught, the X-Wing Caddis seemed to become more effective. I had an epiphany at the end of the day: If I tied the same pattern with a sparser wing, it might prove to be more effective. For my next attempt at the fly, I cut the center section of the deer hair, creating a split-wing version of the X-Wing Caddis. I've tied the pattern the same way, using a sparse amber Antron yarn for the shuck and caddis green Superfine Dubbing with Nature's Spirit mule deer hair, as one of my main caddis patterns. I also tie the Split Wing Caddis in several colored bodies using gray, cream, and rust to represent the more common coloration of the caddis.

TAK'S SPLIT WING CADDIS

- **Hook:** #14-16 Daiichi 1260
- **Thread:** Olive dun 8/0 UNI
- **Shuck:** Amber Antron yarn fibers
- **Body:** Caddis green Superfine Dubbing
- **Wing:** Nature's Spirit mule deer hair with center section cut out to form a split wing
- **Note:** Other hooks that are good for this fly are the Daiichi 1220, 1222; Tiemco 101, 2302; and Dai-Riki 280.

TYING TAK'S SPLIT WING CADDIS

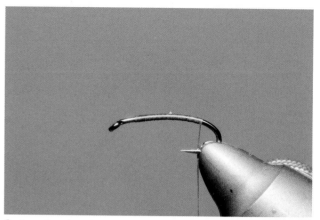

1. Attach tying thread to hook shank behind the hook eye. Wrap thread in touching wraps to the hook bend opposite the barb.

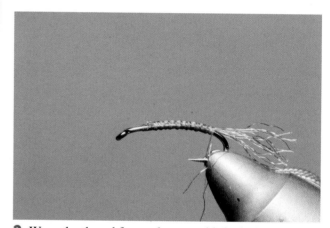

2. Wrap the thread forward to two-thirds the length of the hook shank. Tie in the Antron yarn fibers and wrap the thread over the fibers to the hook bend opposite the barb.

3. Dub on a sparse amount of dubbing to the thread. Wrap the dubbed thread forward to two eye widths back from the hook eye; add additional dubbing if needed.

4. Cut a small bunch of deer hair about half the size of the diameter of a pencil and stack the hair. Measure the deer hair so that it is half the length of the hook shank; trim the butt end of the hair.

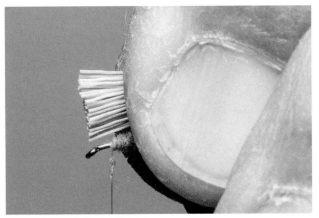

5. Line up the butt ends of the hair even with the front edge of the hook eye.

6. Tie in the deer hair, then, holding on to the deer hair and not allowing it to spin around, make several tight wraps with the tying thread to secure the deer hair to the hook.

7. Using a half-hitch tool, wrap thread around the tool then push the deer hair back and slip a half-hitch knot in front of the hair to force the deer hair to flare up. Whip-finish and trim tying thread.

8. Rotate the fly and trim the excess hair parallel to the hook shank as shown.

9. Cut the center section of the wing out to form a split wing. Trim the bottom of the fly parallel to the hook shank. Turn the fly over and apply a small amount of head cement at the junction of the deer hair and the body to help secure the deer hair wing. The completed Split Wing Caddis represents a "stillborn" caddis that has been trapped in its nymphal shuck with wings formed and in a spent position.

Designing the Triple Wing Caddis

With the effectiveness of the Takahopper, my version of Ed Shenk's Letort Hopper and Horned Caddis, I wanted to create a caddis pattern incorporating the wing materials (River Road Creations River Wing, white polyester yarn, and Nature's Spirit bleached deer hair) of those patterns—the result, the Triple Wing Caddis. The body can also incorporate other materials such as biots, stripped quill, and various types of dubbing to give the pattern flexibility to achieve the effect the tier desires. River Road Creations mottled wing material is ideal for forming the base wing of this pattern, and I cut the wing out in various sizes using the River Road Creations hopper wing cutter.

TAK'S OLIVE TRIPLE WING CADDIS

- **Hook:** #12-18 Daiichi 1220
- **Thread:** Black 8/0 UNI
- **Body:** Olive Superfine Dubbing
- **Top Wing:** Nature's Spirit bleached deer hair
- **Mid-Wing:** White poly yarn
- **Bottom Wing:** Speckled red-brown River Road Creations River Wing
- **Note:** Other hook models include Daiichi 1222, Tiemco 101, and Dai-Riki 300.

TYING TAK'S TRIPLE WING CADDIS

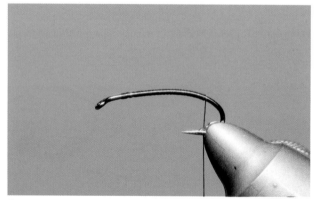

1. Attach the tying thread one-third back from the hook eye and trim excess thread. Wrap the tying thread in touching wraps back to the hook bend opposite the barb.

2. Dub the Superfine Dubbing sparsely onto the thread and make a 1-inch noodle of dubbing. I prefer to add a sparse amount of dubbing when making dubbing noodles; by doing so, I can create a sparser or a denser dubbed body by adding more dubbing or taking tighter wraps. You can always add more dubbing. Wrap the dubbing forward in touching wraps to two eye widths back from the hook eye.

3. Prepare the bottom wing material by either cutting out the wing shape using wing cutters or trimming a short length of wing material about as wide as the gape of the hook. Trim into a short point on one end of the wing, or however you want the rear end of the wing to look. Tie in the bottom wing, allowing the end of the wing to be equal to the hook bend; secure and trim off any excess material.

4. Prepare the mid-wing by cutting a 1½-inch length of yarn, then dividing it into fourths. I use polyester, Antron, Z-Lon, or MFC's Widow's Web for the mid-wing section. Attach the same length of yarn as the bottom wing; secure and trim the front end of the yarn equal to the rear of the hook eye.

5. Prepare the top wing material by cutting a small amount of deer hair (about half the diameter of a pencil) from the hide. Stack the deer hair so that the tips are even. Remove the deer hair from the stacker so that the butts are facing toward the rear and even with the other two wing materials. Once the deer hair is even with the other wings, grasp the rear portion of deer hair, set it on top of the hook shank, and measure the butt ends of the deer hair even with the hook eye. Trim off the butt ends. Tie in the deer hair at the one-third position on the hook shank, making sure that the butt ends are even with the front edge of the hook eye and tie-in, which should cause the deer hair to flare. Do not let go of the deer hair, as doing so might cause it to spin around the hook; hold it in place and make enough tight wraps to secure the hair in position on top of the hook. Whip-finish and trim excess thread.

6. The completed Triple Wing Caddis shows the versatility of creating the illusion of a caddis wing by combining wing materials.

Caddis
ADULTS

BIOT CADDIS (BLACK)

- **Hook:** #14-18 Daiichi 1220 or 1222 or TMC 101
- **Thread:** Black 8/0 UNI
- **Body:** Black biot tied with edge showing
- **Wing:** Nature's Spirit elk cow hair
- **Hackle:** Brown Whiting Farms saddle

BIOT CADDIS (GREEN)

- **Hook:** #14-18 Daiichi 1220 or 1222, TMC 101, or Dai-Riki 300
- **Thread:** Olive 8/0 UNI
- **Body:** Caddis green biot tied with edge showing
- **Wing:** Nature's Spirit elk cow hair
- **Hackle:** Brown Whiting Farms saddle

DESIGNING THE TAKAHOPPER

One of the first dry flies that I ever fished was Ed Shenk's Letort Hopper, and the pattern has brought many fish to hand—it is one of my favorite patterns to fish. During the 1970s I served in a Colorado Air National Guard unit stationed at Buckley Naval Air Station in Aurora, Colorado. The base had a small pond available to those stationed at the base to use in their off time. A friend of mine gave me a Letort Hopper, which was his fly of choice for that pond, and the pattern became my number one dry fly.

As I fished the Letort Hopper over the years, I found that its effectiveness lay in its ability to attract and entice trout into eating this pattern. What also became evident when fishing this pattern was that the underwing made of mottled oak turkey quills would often become shredded after repeated casting or when the trout's teeth separated the fibers of the wing. I would coat the turkey wing with a flexible covering, but in time it would still become shredded. In those days mottled oak turkey was a bit more costly than a regular turkey wing feather. I still have a few of the beautiful mottled oak turkey wing feathers left that I won't ever tie with; I just like to look at them. I determined in my mind that one of the trigger points of this pattern is the shape of the wing when viewed from the underside of the pattern. I decided that I would set out to find a substitute for the mottled oak turkey that wouldn't be so susceptible to disintegration.

In my quest I found a wing material that was mottled much like the original mottled oak turkey but came in a sheet that could be cut into the shape of underwing—Fishaus's mottled wing material. I was unable to get the wing material from Fishaus anymore, so I set out to look for a similar material. At JoAnn Fabrics I found a material called Pellon 808 that was durable yet lightweight enough for a wing. I found that I could use spray paint to mimic the mottled turkey by lightly pressing the button so that only a little air came out, causing a spotted application of the paint's pigment. I sometimes use a permanent marker to color the material. Once dry, the material can be cut into strips to form the underwing; I like to use River Road Creations hopper wing cutters for this process. River Road Creations produces a wing material that I like to tie with called River Wing, which comes in a variety of colors both plain and mottled. Montana Fly Company also makes mottled wing material that is really good. It's available in a variety of materials and colors.

The body on the original Letort Hopper calls for yellow rabbit dubbing. I like using rabbit but was looking for a slightly darker shade that would give a golden hue. I found the golden yellow color I was looking for in Flyrite's #9 Golden Yellow. The golden yellow is the main color I use for the Takahopper, but I've also started to use a tan Antron dubbing much like the dubbing Gary Lafontaine uses on his Caddis Emerger. I used the Pellon 808 cut out to the shape I wanted to replace the mottled oak turkey.

The final consideration for the Takahopper was the choice of top wing shape. The original patterns had deer hair spun around the hook shank much like the Muddler Minnow. I wanted to create a pattern that sat low on the surface of the water, so I decided to make a wing that did not spin around the hook shank, and I kept the hair on top of the shank.

Thus I had retooled the Letort Hopper into what is now known as the Takahopper, which was the name given to it by my fishing friends Jim Ferguson and Steve Solano, but the genesis was Ed Shenk's Letort Hopper.

I generally tie this pattern in size 14 to 16 and use it as a caddis pattern rather than the hopper.

BIOT CADDIS (BROWN)

- **Hook:** #14-18 Daiichi 1220 or 1222 or TMC 101
- **Thread:** Iron dun 8/0 UNI
- **Body:** Gray biot tied with edge showing
- **Wing:** Nature's Spirit elk cow hair
- **Hackle:** Dun Whiting Farms saddle

HORNED CADDIS (TAN)

- **Hook:** #14-18 Daiichi 1260 or TMC 2302
- **Thread:** Black 8/0 UNI
- **Body:** Olive Nature's Spirit stripped peacock herl
- **Wing:** Nature's Spirit bleached deer hair
- **Underwing:** White poly yarn
- **Horns:** Polyester tapered paintbrush fibers to match

HORNED CADDIS (BROWN)

- **Hook:** #14-18 Daiichi 1260 or TMC 2302
- **Thread:** Black 8/0 UNI
- **Body:** Brown Nature's Spirit stripped peacock herl
- **Wing:** Nature's Spirit bleached deer hair
- **Underwing:** White poly yarn
- **Horns:** Polyester tapered paintbrush fibers to match

HORNED CADDIS (OLIVE)

- **Hook:** #14-18 Daiichi 1260 or TMC 2302
- **Thread:** Black 8/0 UNI
- **Body:** Tan Nature's Spirit stripped peacock herl
- **Wing:** Nature's Spirit bleached deer hair
- **Underwing:** White poly yarn
- **Horns:** Polyester tapered paintbrush fibers to match

SPLIT WING CADDIS (VARIATION OF CRAIG MATHEWS X-WING CADDIS)

SPLIT WING CADDIS (CADDIS GREEN)

- **Hook:** #14-18 Daiichi 1260
- **Thread:** Olive dun 8/0 UNI
- **Shuck:** Amber Antron fibers
- **Body:** Caddis green Superfine Dubbing
- **Wing:** Nature's Spirit all-purpose deer hair with center section cut out

SPLIT WING CADDIS (OLIVE)

- **Hook:** #14-18 Daiichi 1260
- **Thread:** Olive dun 8/0 UNI
- **Shuck:** Amber Antron fibers
- **Body:** Olive Superfine Dubbing
- **Wing:** Nature's Spirit all-purpose deer hair with center section cut out

SPLIT WING CADDIS (BLACK)

- **Hook:** #14-18 Daiichi 1260
- **Thread:** Iron dun 8/0 UNI
- **Shuck:** Amber Antron fibers
- **Body:** Black Superfine Dubbing
- **Wing:** Nature's Spirit all-purpose deer hair with center section cut out

FOAM CADDIS

FOAM CADDIS (BLACK)

- **Hook:** #12-16 Daiichi 1220 or 1222 or TMC 101
- **Thread:** Black 8/0 UNI
- **Body/Head:** Black foam (2 mm)
- **Wing:** Nature's Spirit mule deer hair

FOAM CADDIS (TAN)

- ■ **Hook:** #12-16 Daiichi 1220 or 1222 or TMC 101
- ■ **Thread:** Black 8/0 UNI
- ■ **Body/Head:** Tan foam (2 mm)
- ■ **Wing:** Nature's Spirit mule deer hair

FOAM CADDIS (BRIGHT GREEN)

- ■ **Hook:** #12-16 Daiichi 1220 or 1222 or TMC 101
- ■ **Thread:** Black 8/0 UNI
- ■ **Body/Head:** Bright green foam (2 mm)
- ■ **Wing:** Nature's Spirit mule deer hair

12 O'CLOCK CADDIS

12 O'CLOCK CADDIS (CHARTREUSE)

- ■ **Hook:** #12-18 TMC 2302
- ■ **Thread:** Brown 8/0 UNI
- ■ **Underbody/Rib:** Tying thread
- ■ **Body:** Brown foam (2 mm) cut with River Road Creations grasshopper cutter
- ■ **Wing:** Natural deer hair
- ■ **Legs:** Natural/brown round rubber

12 O'CLOCK CADDIS (BLACK)

- ■ **Hook:** #12-18 TMC 2302
- ■ **Thread:** Brown 8/0 UNI
- ■ **Underbody/Rib:** Tying thread
- ■ **Body:** Black foam
- ■ **Wing:** Natural deer hair
- ■ **Legs:** White/black round rubber

12 O'CLOCK CADDIS (LIGHT TAN)

- **Hook:** #12-18 TMC 2302
- **Thread:** Brown 8/0 UNI
- **Underbody/Rib:** Tying thread
- **Body:** Light tan open-cell foam
- **Wing:** Natural deer hair
- **Legs:** Yellow/tan round rubber

TAK'S TRIPLE WING CADDIS SERIES

TRIPLE WING CADDIS (OLIVE)

- **Hook:** #12-16 Daiichi 1220 or 1222 or TMC 101
- **Thread:** Black 8/0 UNI
- **Body:** Olive Superfine Dubbing
- **Top Wing:** Nature's Spirit bleached deer hair
- **Mid-Wing:** White poly yarn
- **Bottom Wing:** River Road Creations speckled brown wing material

TRIPLE WING CADDIS (TAN)

- **Hook:** #12-16 Daiichi 1220 or 1222 or TMC 101
- **Thread:** Black 8/0 UNI
- **Body:** Tan Superfine Dubbing
- **Top Wing:** Nature's Spirit bleached deer hair
- **Mid-Wing:** White poly yarn
- **Bottom Wing:** River Road Creations speckled brown wing material

TRIPLE WING CADDIS (OLIVE BROWN)

- **Hook:** #12-16 Daiichi 1220 or 1222 or TMC 101
- **Thread:** Black 8/0 UNI
- **Body:** Olive Superfine Dubbing
- **Top Wing:** Nature's Spirit bleached deer hair
- **Mid-Wing:** White poly yarn
- **Bottom Wing:** River Road Creations speckled brown wing material

PUPAE AND LARVAE

DIAMOND CADDIS LARVA (OLIVE)

- **Hook:** #12-16 Daiichi 1120 or 1130 or TMC 101
- **Thread:** Olive 12/0 Veevus
- **Bead:** Black brass
- **Body:** Olive Midge Diamond Braid
- **Collar:** Peacock Ice Dub

DIAMOND CADDIS LARVA (ROOTBEER)

- **Hook:** #12-16 Daiichi 1120 or 1130 or TMC 2487
- **Thread:** Olive 12/0 Veevus
- **Bead:** Black brass
- **Body:** Rootbeer Midge Diamond Braid
- **Collar:** Peacock Ice Dub

WIRED CADDIS PUPA (CHARTREUSE)

- **Hook:** #12-16 Daiichi 1120 or 1130 or TMC 2487
- **Thread:** Black 16/0 Veevus
- **Body:** Chartreuse UTC wire
- **Legs:** Olive hare's ear dubbing loop
- **Wing Case:** Brown Swiss Straw covered with Solarez UV resin

WIRED CADDIS PUPA (TAN)

- **Hook:** #12-16 Daiichi 1120 or 1130 or TMC 2487
- **Thread:** Black 16/0 Veevus
- **Body:** Tan UTC wire
- **Legs:** Olive hare's ear dubbing loop
- **Wing Case:** Brown Swiss Straw covered with Solarez UV resin

WIRED CADDIS PUPA (GREEN)

- **Hook:** #12-16 Daiichi 1120 or 1130 or TMC 2487
- **Thread:** Black 16/0 Veevus
- **Body:** Green UTC wire
- **Legs:** Light hare's ear dubbing loop
- **Wing Buds:** Dun Medallion Sheeting
- **Wing Case:** Brown Swiss Straw covered with Solarez UV resin

GLITTER CADDIS LARVA (PEACOCK)

- **Hook:** #12-16 Daiichi 1120 or 1130 or TMC 2487
- **Thread:** Black 16/0 Veevus
- **Bead:** Black
- **Underbody:** Peacock Canadian Llama glitter thread
- **Dorsal Strip:** Brown Swiss Straw Strip covered with Solarez UV resin
- **Rib:** Small copper wire
- **Collar:** Black peacock Ice Dub

GLITTER CADDIS LARVA (GREEN)

- **Hook:** #12-16 Daiichi 1120 or 1130 or TMC 2487
- **Thread:** Black 16/0 Veevus
- **Bead:** Black
- **Underbody:** Green Canadian Llama glitter thread
- **Dorsal Strip:** Brown Swiss Straw strip covered with Solarez UV resin
- **Rib:** Small copper wire
- **Collar:** Olive Ice Dub

GLITTER CADDIS LARVA (OLIVE BROWN)

- **Hook:** #12-16 Daiichi 1120 or 1130 or TMC 2487
- **Thread:** Black 16/0 Veevus
- **Bead:** Black
- **Underbody:** Olive/brown Canadian Llama glitter thread
- **Dorsal Strip:** Brown Swiss Straw strip covered with Solarez UV resin
- **Rib:** Small copper wire
- **Collar:** Black peacock Ice Dub

GLITTER CADDIS PUPA (PEARL)

- **Hook:** #12-16 Daiichi 1120 or 1130 or TMC 2487
- **Thread:** Black 16/0 Veevus
- **Bead:** Black
- **Underbody:** Pearl Canadian Llama glitter thread
- **Dorsal Strip:** Brown Swiss Straw strip covered with Solarez UV resin
- **Rib:** Small copper wire
- **Collar:** Black peacock Ice Dub

THREAD CADDIS PUPA (TAN)

- **Hook:** #12-16 Daiichi 1150 or TMC 2487
- **Thread:** Black 16/0 Veevus
- **Underbody:** Tan sewing thread
- **Rib:** Tan sewing thread
- **Dorsal Strip:** Tan sewing thread colored with black Sharpie
- **Thorax/Legs:** Olive hare's ear dubbing loop
- **Wing Pad:** Brown Medallion Sheeting
- **Antennae:** Peacock fiber

THREAD CADDIS PUPA (GREEN)

- **Hook:** #12-16 Daiichi 1150 or TMC 2487
- **Thread:** Black 16/0 Veevus
- **Underbody:** Olive sewing thread
- **Rib:** Olive sewing thread
- **Dorsal Strip:** Olive sewing thread colored with black Sharpie
- **Thorax/Legs:** Olive hare's ear dubbing loop
- **Antennae:** Peacock fiber

BREADCRUST WANNABE CADDIS PUPA (BROWN)

- **Hook:** #12-16 Daiichi 1260 or TMC 2312
- **Thread:** Black 8/0 UNI
- **Underbody:** Gray ostrich herl
- **Rib:** Brown D-Rib
- **Hackle:** Grizzly hen

BREADCRUST WANNABE CADDIS PUPA (CHARTREUSE)

- **Hook:** #12-16 Daiichi 1260 or TMC 2312
- **Thread:** Chartreuse 8/0 UNI
- **Bead:** Canadian Llama black nickel
- **Underbody:** Gray ostrich herl
- **Rib:** Brown D-Rib
- **Hackle:** Grizzly hen

D-RIB CADDIS LARVA (CHARTREUSE)

- **Hook:** #12-16 Daiichi 1260 or TMC 2312
- **Thread:** Tan 70-denier UTC
- **Bead:** Canadian Llama black brass
- **Underbody:** Tying thread
- **Body:** Small tan D-Rib
- **Rib:** Chartreuse Life Cycle Dubbing (Nymph)
- **Collar:** Olive brown Ice Dub

BH BREADCRUST WANNABE CADDIS PUPA (BROWN)

- **Hook:** #12-16 Daiichi 1260 or TMC 2312
- **Thread:** Black 8/0 UNI
- **Bead:** Canadian Llama black nickel
- **Underbody:** Gray ostrich herl
- **Rib:** Brown D-Rib
- **Hackle:** Grizzly hen

DIAMOND BRAID CADDIS LARVA (TAN)

- **Hook:** #12-16 Daiichi 1260 or TMC 2312
- **Thread:** Tan 70-denier UTC
- **Bead:** Canadian Llama black brass
- **Underbody:** Tying thread
- **Body:** Pearl Diamond Braid
- **Rib:** Tan Life Cycle Dubbing (Nymph)
- **Collar:** Olive brown Ice Dub

DIAMOND BRAID LARVA (OLIVE BROWN)

- **Hook:** #12-16 Daiichi 1260 or TMC 2312
- **Thread:** Tan 70-denier UTC
- **Bead:** Black brass
- **Underbody:** Tying thread
- **Body:** Pearl Diamond Braid
- **Rib:** Olive brown Life Cycle Dubbing (Nymph)
- **Collar:** Olive brown Ice Dub

D-RIB CADDIS LARVA (YELLOW)

- **Hook:** #12-16 Daiichi 1260 or TMC 2312
- **Thread:** Tan 70-denier UTC
- **Bead:** Canadian Llama gold brass
- **Underbody:** Tying thread
- **Body:** Medium yellow D-Rib
- **Collar:** Dark olive brown hare's ear dubbing loop

DIAMOND BRAID LARVA (PEACOCK)

- **Hook:** #12-16 Daiichi 1260 or TMC 2312
- **Thread:** Tan 70-denier UTC
- **Bead:** Canadian Llama black brass
- **Underbody:** Tying thread
- **Body:** Peacock Diamond Braid
- **Collar:** Olive brown Ice Dub

D-RIB CADDIS LARVA (OLIVE BROWN)

- **Hook:** #12-16 Daiichi 1260 or TMC 2312
- **Thread:** Tan 70-denier UTC
- **Bead:** Canadian Llama black brass
- **Underbody:** Tying thread
- **Wing Case:** Dark dun Medallion Sheeting
- **Body:** Small olive brown D-Rib
- **Collar:** Peacock Ice Dub

BH D-RIB CADDIS PUPA (AMBER)

- **Hook:** #12-16 TMC 2488H
- **Thread:** Yellow 70-denier UTC
- **Bead:** Black brass
- **Underbody:** Tying thread
- **Body:** Small amber D-Rib
- **Wing Case:** Dark dun Medallion Sheeting
- **Wing Bud:** Dark dun Medallion Sheeting
- **Collar:** Olive hare's ear

GLITTER THREAD CADDIS LARVA (CHARTREUSE)

- **Hook:** #12-16 Daiichi 1120 or 1130 or TMC 2457
- **Thread:** Tan 70-denier UTC
- **Bead:** Gold brass
- **Underbody:** Tying thread
- **Body:** Small olive D-Rib
- **Collar:** Peacock brown Ice Dub

BH D-RIB CADDIS PUPA (OLIVE)

- **Hook:** #12-16 TMC 2488H
- **Thread:** Yellow 70-denier UTC
- **Bead:** Black brass
- **Underbody:** Tying thread
- **Body:** Small olive D-Rib
- **Wing Case:** Dark dun Medallion Sheeting
- **Wing Bud:** Dark dun Medallion Sheeting
- **Collar:** Olive hare's ear

-4-

GO2 SERIES

I purposely put off fishing Doug Prince's nymph for many years because of a mistaken and misguided lack of interest in fishing patterns that didn't represent actual insects. When I finally did fish a Prince Nymph, I couldn't believe the number of fish I caught. The Prince Nymph, in my estimation, is one of the best and most productive attractor nymphs ever designed, and it became one of my go-to patterns. I have fished it in a variety of sizes and configurations, both bead-head and non-bead-head types of flies. I've fished this pattern in every imaginable water condition, from lakes to streams, with good success. I developed a companion pattern I call the Go2 Caddis, which is tied in the same configuration but instead of the peacock body, I use chartreuse Midge Diamond Braid for the body. I chose this color to mimic the coloration of a caddis pupa found in the stream in my area.

I was diagnosed with a ruptured disc between vertebrae 3 and 4 with bone spurs pushing into my spinal cord in the spring of 1994, causing partial paralysis from my shoulder down, a condition that made fly tying difficult. I was faced with constant tingling in my fingers along with loss of feeling. The loss of feeling made it difficult to hold onto any materials that I was trying to tie onto the hook and it was frustrating to not be able to tie with a high degree of craftsmanship.

I wanted to tie some Prince Nymphs but found I had difficulties using the traditional materials to tie the pattern. I could not grasp the goose biots well enough to attach them to the hook in the proper position; every time I tried to do so, the biots would be out of position and uneven. I also discovered that tying on the partridge feather was becoming a problem for me. It was apparent that I would have to seek out an alternative material if I were to be successful tying one of my beloved Prince Nymphs.

Go2 Prince

I decided to try and find materials that would be easier for me to handle. As I experimented at my vise, selecting materials closely resembling the colors found on the Prince Nymph, I found a number of materials I could substitute without changing the overall color scheme of the pattern. The majority of the materials selected for exchange were readily available and much easier for me to handle.

The day I took the Go2 Prince out for a trial run was one of those days we are blessed with as fishermen. I hadn't had corrective surgery on my neck yet but needed to get out of the house to go fishing. I traveled to a favorite spot on the Poudre River called Diamond Rock Campground, which had fairly easy access to the river. I still had difficulty walking, so wading was going to be a challenge, and it took some time and care to get into position to fish a nice deep run next to a rock cliff.

On my first cast, I sent my nymph rig upstream next to a seam of fast, deep water next to a shallow, slower current. The flies hadn't drifted but a few feet when my strike indicator dove into the water and sped directly upstream. I gently raised my rod tip and was rewarded with a nice 14-inch rainbow. I quickly landed and released the fish, then made another cast in the same vicinity. Lo and behold, I had another take. Five more casts in a row netted the same result.

I was totally shocked that I had caught five rainbows in five casts; I surely thanked a higher being that day for allowing me to have such a memorable experience. I started fishing the Go2 Prince on every fishing trip and had good success with catch rates, which gave me confidence that I might have stumbled onto a good pattern.

All the Go2 patterns are simply attractor-style nymphs. One positive aspect of this pattern is the versatility of using a number of different tying materials to create a different look for the body of the fly. I've used colored wire, tubing, dubbings of different consistencies, various tying threads, stripped peacock herls, dyed peacock herls, and just about anything else I could think of. I also decided to use mercury glass beads in place of the brass beads; my friend Pat Dorsey has been highly successful in using mercury beads in his series of fly patterns.

Key Materials for Go2 Series

For the tail I selected Whiting Farms brown hen hackle as the material to replace the brown biots. I like the quality of the hen hackle fibers and found that I could bundle the fibers together and line them up well enough to create a well-defined tail.

I used the peacock herl for the abdomen as per the original. One of the triggers I feel that make this pattern so effective is the use of peacock herl. Peacock herl is one of those materials that trout seem to gravitate to, and many patterns incorporating this material stand a better chance of enticing the trout to actively take those patterns. Three strands of peacock, in my opinion, are just the right amount to create the body shape I'm looking for. I don't bother to align the butts of the peacock herl because I seldom

get near them, but I do trim the tips of the herl even. I then attach the tips at the midpoint of the hook and wrap my tying thread over the herls to the hook bend opposite the barb; when wrapping the herls forward, the individual fibers will be perpendicular or cup slightly toward the rear of the hook. If I tie the butt ends first, I find that the fiber of the herl cups forward, which I don't want to happen. I'd rather have the fibers leaning toward the bend of the hook.

I chose pearl Krystal Flash or pearl Flashabou tinsel to replace the oval gold tinsel. I decided to use pearl Krystal Flash because of my experience tying the Disco Midge Pupa. When a black thread underbody was used and the pearl Krystal Flash was wrapped to form the abdomen, it turned a greenish color, which gave a great contrasting color shift of flash to the peacock herl. The use of the pearl Krystal Flash was very successful for me when I fished this pattern.

As mentioned, the original brown partridge feather was difficult for me to hold onto even with hackle pliers. The position of the partridge feather as it was tied onto the hook shaft was difficult for me even before my neck injury. I selected a Whiting Farms midge saddle for the hackle. The selection of a saddle hackle was based on the fact that I had difficulty walking and was in pain. The saddle hackle was lying on my tying bench, so I decided to use it rather

Jim Browning netting the catch of the day on the Arkansas River tailwater, which harbors a fantastic caddis population. The Go2 series was not designed to be replicas of the insect but rather an attractor pattern.
JIM BROWNING PHOTO

Fishing a private section of the Dance Ranch on the Big Thompson River. ISRAEL PATTERSON PHOTO

than walk to my hackle storage drawer. I decided to add the hackle at the waist or midsection of the fly instead of behind the bead head. This was total serendipity: Using the stiffer hackle on a nymph pattern went against more conventional tying theory, but when fishing this pattern I found it to be a perfect marriage of materials. I've had individual tiers ask me why I use this saddle, and all I can tell them is it was by chance and not because I had an epiphany.

I selected white polyester yarn as a replacement for the white biots. I favored the use of polyester yarn because of its softer feel, and tying the wing at a slight rearward angle mimicked the angle of the white biots. Antron, Z-Lon, or Montana Fly Company's white Widow's Web is an acceptable alternative. I trim the tail even with the outward hook bend shank.

For the collar of the fly I thought of using peacock herl originally but decided to use olive brown (sometimes peacock) Ice Dub instead. I love the effect of using Ice Dub because the nature of the material breaks up the light reflected off its multifaceted surface.

I generally use a gold brass bead for most of my Go2 patterns, but feel free to use any color to match your overall color scheme. I tie most of my Go2 patterns in sizes from 14 down to 18 with corresponding beads sized to fit the hook. I use a 5/64 bead for a size 16 and 18 hook and a 3/32 bead for a size 14 hook.

GO2 PRINCE

- **Hook:** #14-16 Mustad 3399A or Dai-Riki 060
- **Bead:** Brass bead
- **Thread:** Olive 8/0 UNI
- **Tail:** Brown Whiting Farms hen hackle
- **Body:** 3 strands peacock herl
- **Rib:** Pearl Flashabou or Krystal Flash
- **Hackle:** Brown Whiting Farms saddle
- **Wing:** White poly yarn
- **Collar:** Peacock Ice Dub

TYING THE GO2 PRINCE

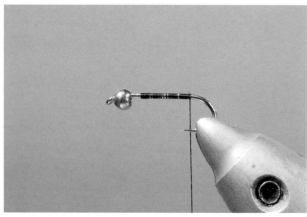

1. Slide the brass bead onto the hook and up to the hook eye. Attach the tying thread behind the bead and wrap thread to the hook bend opposite the barb.

2. Take a hen hackle and remove the fluff at the base of the stem, then hold the feather by its tip and stroke the feather toward the base, using your thumb and index finger, pushing the fiber perpendicular to the stem; this will be used as the tail.

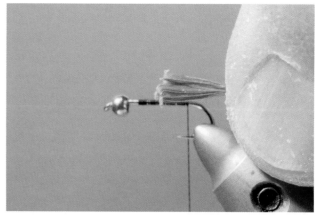

3. Select a small bunch of hen hackle fibers and position them with the tip facing toward the rear by holding the fibers in your right hand (vice versa if left-handed), then measure how long you want the tail to be. I like to tie my tails no longer than half the length of the hook shank.

4. Grasp the fibers with your left hand and place them on top of the hook shank so that they are parallel to the hook shank. Attach tailing material at a point opposite the barb and wrap thread to the midpoint of the hook.

5. Attach pearl Flashabou or Krystal Flash at the midpoint of the hook, then wrap thread over the Flashabou to the hook bend opposite the barb. Wrap thread back to the midpoint of the hook.

6. Take three strands of peacock herl and cut the tips even.

7. Attach the three strands of peacock herl by their trimmed top at the midpoint of the hook and wrap thread over the herl to the bend opposite the barb. Wrap thread forward to the midpoint of the hook.

8. Wrap the peacock herl forward to the midpoint of the hook and tie off.

9. Trim the peacock herl and wrap Flashabou forward in evenly spaced wraps (usually three to four wraps); tie off tinsel and trim excess.

10. Attach hackle at the front edge of the abdomen.

11. Make three consecutive wraps in the same place with the hackle. (I'll sometime even make a wrap of hackle behind the previous wrap.) Tie off and trim excess.

12. Moisten the end of the polyester yarn, then trim even.

13. Attach polyester yarn material in front of the hackle with the end of the yarn even with the front end of the brass bead, then wrap thread several times to secure.

14. Pull yarn back so that the ends of the yarn are on the top half of the bead. Wrap thread tight to the base of the poly yarn, which will force the butt ends of the yarn down to the bead hole with no tag end showing. Make even wraps over the yarn to the hackle base, forcing the yarn to slant at a 45-degree angle.

15. Dub the thread with peacock Ice Dub.

16. Form collar from the wing base to the bead; secure and whip-finish, then trim the thread.

17. Whip-finish behind the bead and trim excess thread.

18. The Go2 Prince, my variation of the Prince Nymph, using materials that replace the traditional materials for the most part.

Designing the Go2 Caddis

The success of the Go2 Prince prompted me to come up with a companion pattern I could fish in tandem. The waters I fish locally are premier caddis waters, so I decided I wanted to create a pattern incorporating the coloration of the caddis in these waters. The majority of the caddis I collected were green in body color, so I decided to make an abdomen with a green-colored material. I chose Midge Diamond Braid in chartreuse as the material for the body. I would tie the pattern the same as the original Go2 Prince except replace the peacock herl and pearl tinsel with the chartreuse Midge Diamond Braid. I fished the patterns exclusively for two years on the Big Thompson River with great success. I generally fish this tandem using the Go2 Prince as the point fly and the Go2 Caddis as the dropper.

CRYSTAL GO2 CADDIS

- **Hook:** #14-16 Mustad 3399A or Dai-Riki 060
- **Bead:** Mercury bead
- **Thread:** Olive 8/0 UNI
- **Tail:** Brown hen hackle
- **Body:** Chartreuse Hareline Midge Diamond Braid
- **Hackle:** Brown Whiting Farms saddle
- **Wing:** White poly yarn
- **Collar:** Peacock Ice Dub

TYING THE CRYSTAL GO2 CADDIS

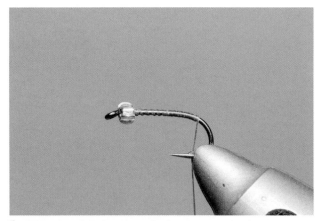

1. Slide the glass bead on the hook up to the hook eye. Attach the tying thread behind the bead and wrap thread to the hook bend opposite the barb.

2. Take a hen hackle and remove the fluff at the base of the stem, then hold the feather by its tip and stroke the feather toward the base, using your thumb and index finger, pushing the fiber perpendicular to the stem. Select a small bunch of the hen hackle fibers and pull off or trim with scissors. Position the tailing material with the tip facing toward the rear by holding the fibers in your right hand (vice versa if left-handed), then measure how long you want the tail to be. I like to tie my tails no longer than half the length of the hook shank. Grasp the fibers with your left hand and place them on top of the hook shank opposite the barb. Make sure that the tailing is not tied in facing in a slanted direction; you want the tail to be parallel to the hook shank. Attach tailing material and wrap thread to the midpoint of the hook.

Fishing my tandem fly patterns, the Go2 Prince and Go2 Caddis, near Deckers on the South Platte, which is a caddis-rich river. TOM FLANAGAN PHOTO

3. Attach chartreuse Midge Diamond Braid at the midpoint of the hook and wrap thread over the braid to the bend opposite the barb. Wrap thread forward to the midpoint of the hook, then wrap the braid to the midpoint of the hook and secure; this is the abdomen.

4. Trim the excess braid.

5. Attach hackle at the front edge of the abdomen.

6. Make three consecutive wraps in the same place with the hackle. (I'll sometimes even make a wrap of hackle behind the previous wrap.) Secure and trim excess.

7. Attach poly yarn material in front of the hackle. Wrap thread tightly to the base of the poly yarn and even over the yarn to force the yarn to slant at a 45-degree angle; secure and trim off excess yarn.

8. Dub the thread with peacock Ice Dub. Form collar from the wing base to the bead; secure and whip-finish, then trim the thread. Trim yarn wing as shown.

9. The Crystal Go2 Caddis utilizes chartreuse for the body, which mimics a wide range of coloration found in caddis nymphs in Colorado waters.

GO2 Nymphs

Note: Sizing for beads on the Go2 is as follows: 3/32 (14) and 5/64 (16-18). Hook options in addition to Daiichi 1550 include Daiichi 1560 and Tiemco (TMC) 3761 and 3769.

GO2 NYMPH (PRINCE)

- **Hook:** #14-18 Daiichi 1550
- **Bead:** Canadian Llama gold brass
- **Thread:** Olive 8/0 UNI
- **Tail:** Brown Whiting Farms hen hackle
- **Body:** Peacock herl
- **Rib:** Pearl Krystal Flash
- **Hackle:** Brown Whiting Farms saddle
- **Wing:** White poly yarn
- **Collar:** Mixture of muskrat dubbing, brown Ice Dub, peacock Ice Dub

GO2 NYMPH (CADDIS)

- **Hook:** #14-18 Daiichi 1550
- **Bead:** Canadian Llama gold brass
- **Thread:** Olive 8/0 UNI
- **Tail:** Brown Whiting Farms hen hackle
- **Body:** Chartreuse Hareline Midge Diamond Braid
- **Hackle:** Brown Whiting Farms saddle
- **Wing:** White poly yarn
- **Collar:** Mixture of muskrat dubbing, brown Ice Dub, peacock Ice Dub

GO2 NYMPH (GOLD-RIBBED HARE'S EAR)

- **Hook:** #14-18 Daiichi 1550
- **Bead:** Canadian Llama gold brass
- **Thread:** Olive 8/0 UNI
- **Tail:** Brown Whiting Farms hen hackle
- **Body:** Light hare's ear
- **Rib :** Fine gold oval tinsel
- **Hackle:** Brown Whiting Farms saddle
- **Wing:** White poly yarn
- **Collar:** Mixture of muskrat dubbing, brown Ice Dub, peacock Ice Dub

GO2 NYMPH (PHEASANT TAIL)

- **Hook:** #14-20 Daiichi 1550
- **Bead:** Canadian Llama gold brass
- **Thread:** Olive 8/0 UNI
- **Tail:** Pheasant tail fibers
- **Body:** Pheasant tail
- **Rib :** Fine copper wire
- **Hackle:** Brown Whiting Farms saddle
- **Wing:** White poly yarn
- **Collar:** Mixture of muskrat dubbing, brown Ice Dub, peacock Ice Dub

GO2 NYMPH (COPPER)

- **Hook:** #14-18 Daiichi 1550
- **Bead:** Canadian Llama copper brass
- **Thread:** Rust 8/0 UNI
- **Tail:** Brown Whiting Farms hen hackle
- **Underbody:** Tying thread
- **Rib :** Fine brown copper wire
- **Hackle:** Brown Whiting Farms saddle
- **Wing:** White poly yarn
- **Collar:** Copper or rust Ice Dub

GO2 NYMPH (GREEN WIRED)

- **Hook:** #14-18 Daiichi 1550
- **Bead:** Canadian Llama gold brass
- **Thread:** Black 8/0 UNI
- **Tail:** Brown Whiting Farms hen fibers
- **Body:** Green UTC wire
- **Hackle:** Brown Whiting Farms midge saddle
- **Wing:** White poly yarn
- **Collar:** Peacock Ice Dub

GO2 NYMPH (COPPER TOP)

- **Hook:** #14-18 Daiichi 1550
- **Bead:** Canadian Llama copper brass
- **Thread:** Rust 8/0 UNI
- **Tail:** Brown Whiting Farms hen hackle
- **Underbody:** Copper Flashabou
- **Rib :** Fine brown copper wire
- **Hackle:** Brown Whiting Farms saddle
- **Wing:** White poly yarn
- **Collar:** Copper Ice Dub

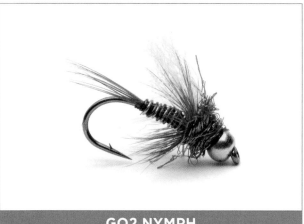

GO2 NYMPH (COPPER AND GOLD WIRED)

- **Hook:** #14-18 Daiichi 1550
- **Bead:** Canadian Llama gold brass
- **Thread:** Black 8/0 UNI
- **Tail:** Brown Whiting Farms hen fibers
- **Body:** Copper and gold UTC wire
- **Hackle:** Brown Whiting Farms midge saddle
- **Wing:** White poly yarn
- **Collar:** Peacock Ice Dub

GO2 NYMPH (BLUE WIRED)

- **Hook:** #14-18 Daiichi 1550
- **Bead:** Canadian Llama gold brass
- **Thread:** Black 8/0 UNI
- **Tail:** Brown Whiting Farms hen fibers
- **Body:** Blue UTC wire
- **Hackle:** Brown Whiting Farms midge saddle
- **Wing:** White poly yarn
- **Collar:** Peacock Ice Dub

GO2 NYMPH (BROWN BIOT)

- **Hook:** #14-18 Daiichi 1550
- **Bead:** Canadian Llama gold brass
- **Thread:** Black 8/0 UNI
- **Tail:** Brown Whiting Farms hen fibers
- **Body:** Brown goose biot
- **Hackle:** Brown Whiting Farms midge saddle
- **Wing:** White poly yarn
- **Collar:** Peacock Ice Dub

GO2 NYMPH (PURPLE BIOT)

- **Hook:** #14-18 Daiichi 1550
- **Bead:** Canadian Llama gold brass
- **Thread:** Black 8/0 UNI
- **Tail:** Brown Whiting Farms hen fibers
- **Body:** Purple goose biot
- **Hackle:** Brown Whiting Farms midge saddle
- **Wing:** White poly yarn
- **Collar:** Purple Ice Dub

GO2 NYMPH (CAHILL BIOT)

- **Hook:** #14-18 Daiichi 1550
- **Bead:** Canadian Llama gold brass
- **Thread:** Black 8/0 UNI
- **Tail:** Brown Whiting Farms hen fibers
- **Body:** Yellow goose biot
- **Hackle:** Brown Whiting Farms midge saddle
- **Wing:** White poly yarn
- **Collar:** Peacock Ice Dub

CO2 NYMPH (TAN BIOT)

- **Hook:** #14-18 Daiichi 1550
- **Bead:** Canadian Llama gold brass
- **Thread:** Black 8/0 UNI
- **Tail:** Brown Whiting Farms hen fibers
- **Body:** Tan goose biot
- **Hackle:** Brown Whiting Farms midge saddle
- **Wing:** White poly yarn
- **Collar:** Peacock Ice Dub

GO2 NYMPH (SILVER HOLOGRAPHIC)

- **Hook:** #14-18 Daiichi 1550
- **Bead:** Canadian Llama gold brass
- **Thread:** Black 8/0 UNI
- **Tail:** Brown Whiting Farms hen fibers
- **Underbody:** Tying thread
- **Rib:** Small silver holographic tinsel
- **Hackle:** Brown Whiting Farms midge saddle
- **Wing:** White poly yarn
- **Collar:** Peacock Ice Dub

GO2 NYMPH (PEARL HOLOGRAPHIC)

- **Hook:** #14-18 Daiichi 1550
- **Bead:** Canadian Llama gold brass
- **Thread:** Black 8/0 UNI
- **Tail:** Brown Whiting Farms hen fibers
- **Underbody:** Tying thread
- **Rib:** Small pearl holographic tinsel
- **Hackle:** Brown Whiting Farms midge saddle
- **Wing:** White poly yarn
- **Collar:** Peacock Ice Dub

GO2 NYMPH (PEARL BRAID)

- **Hook:** #14-18 Daiichi 1550
- **Bead:** Canadian Llama gold brass
- **Thread:** Black 8/0 UNI
- **Tail:** Brown Whiting Farms hen fibers
- **Body:** Pearl Hareline Midge Diamond Braid
- **Hackle:** Brown Whiting Farms midge saddle
- **Wing:** White poly yarn
- **Collar:** Peacock Ice Dub

GO2 NYMPH (PEACOCK BRAID)

- **Hook:** #14-18 Daiichi 1550
- **Bead:** Canadian Llama gold brass
- **Thread:** Black 8/0 UNI
- **Tail:** Brown Whiting Farms hen fibers
- **Body:** Peacock Hareline Midge Diamond Braid
- **Hackle:** Brown Whiting Farms midge saddle
- **Wing:** White poly yarn
- **Collar:** Peacock Ice Dub

GO2 CRYSTAL NYMPH (CADDIS)

- **Hook:** #14-18 Daiichi 1550
- **Bead:** Crystal glass
- **Thread:** Olive 8/0 UNI
- **Tail:** Brown Whiting Farms hen hackle
- **Body:** Chartreuse Hareline Midge Diamond Braid
- **Hackle:** Brown Whiting Farms saddle
- **Wing:** White poly yarn
- **Collar:** Mixture of muskrat dubbing, brown Ice Dub, peacock Ice Dub

GO2 NYMPH (ROOTBEER BRAID)

- **Hook:** #14-18 Daiichi 1550
- **Bead:** Canadian Llama gold brass
- **Thread:** Black 8/0 UNI
- **Tail:** Brown Whiting Farms hen fibers
- **Body:** Rootbeer Hareline Midge Diamond Braid
- **Hackle:** Brown Whiting Farms midge saddle
- **Wing:** White poly yarn
- **Collar:** Peacock Ice Dub

GO2 CRYSTAL NYMPH (PHEASANT TAIL)

- **Hook:** #14-20 Daiichi 1550
- **Bead:** Crystal glass
- **Thread:** Olive 8/0 UNI
- **Tail:** Pheasant tail fibers
- **Body:** Pheasant tail
- **Rib :** Fine copper wire
- **Hackle:** Brown Whiting Farms saddle
- **Wing:** White poly yarn
- **Collar:** Mixture of muskrat dubbing, Brown Ice Dub, peacock Ice Dub

GO2 CRYSTAL NYMPH (COPPER AND GOLD WIRED)

- **Hook:** #14-18 Daiichi 1550
- **Bead:** Crystal glass
- **Thread:** Black 8/0 UNI
- **Tail:** Brown Whiting Farms hen fibers
- **Body:** Copper UTC wire
- **Hackle:** Brown Whiting Farms midge saddle
- **Wing:** White poly yarn
- **Collar:** Peacock Ice Dub

GO2 CRYSTAL NYMPH (SILVER HOLOGRAPHIC)

- **Hook:** #14-18 Daiichi 1550
- **Bead:** Crystal glass
- **Thread:** Black 8/0 UNI
- **Tail:** Brown Whiting Farms hen fibers
- **Underbody:** Tying thread
- **Rib:** Silver holographic tinsel
- **Hackle:** Brown Whiting Farms midge saddle
- **Wing:** White poly yarn
- **Collar:** Peacock Ice Dub

GO2 CRYSTAL NYMPH (PEARL HOLOGRAPHIC)

- **Hook:** #14-18 Daiichi 1550
- **Bead:** Crystal glass
- **Thread:** Black 8/0 UNI
- **Tail:** Brown Whiting Farms hen fibers
- **Underbody:** Tying thread
- **Rib:** Small pearl holographic tinsel
- **Hackle:** Brown Whiting Farms midge saddle
- **Wing:** White poly yarn
- **Collar:** Peacock Ice Dub

GO2 CRYSTAL NYMPH (CHARTREUSE BIOT)

- **Hook:** #14-18 Daiichi 1550
- **Bead:** Crystal glass
- **Thread:** Black 8/0 UNI
- **Tail:** Brown Whiting Farms hen fibers
- **Body:** Chartreuse biot
- **Hackle:** Brown Whiting Farms midge saddle
- **Wing:** White poly yarn
- **Collar:** Peacock Ice Dub

GO2 CRYSTAL NYMPH (TAN BIOT)

- **Hook:** #14-18 Daiichi 1550
- **Bead:** Crystal glass
- **Thread:** Black 8/0 UNI
- **Tail:** Brown Whiting Farms hen fibers
- **Body:** Tan biot
- **Hackle:** Brown Whiting Farms midge saddle
- **Wing:** White poly yarn
- **Collar:** Peacock Ice Dub

GO2 GLITTER NYMPH (GREEN)

- **Hook:** #14-18 Daiichi 1550
- **Bead:** Canadian Llama copper brass
- **Thread:** Rust 8/0 UNI
- **Tail:** Brown Whiting Farms hen hackle
- **Underbody:** Tying thread
- **Rib:** Green Canadian Llama glitter thread
- **Hackle:** Brown Whiting Farms saddle
- **Wing:** White poly yarn
- **Collar:** Copper or rust Ice Dub

-5-

LEECH SERIES

One of my most memorable days fishing the San Juan River was catching a huge 26-inch-long rainbow trout in the Kiddie Pool section on a leech pattern dead-drifted along the near bank. When I started fishing the San Juan in the spring of 1991, the Kiddie Pool consisted of two deep channels running through its length. One channel was the near bank where the water was fairly deep right off the bank. If you weren't paying attention and stepped into the water off the bank, you'd be surprised at how deep the water was. Some will remember a large boulder in the middle of the run. The other deep run was along the upper portion of the Kiddie Pool on the far bank, much as it is today.

I was fishing the deeper run against the near bank with a strike indicator and a gray rabbit strip leech, dead-drifting it as it traveled down the current. The strike indicator took a violent dip into the water, and I was fast onto what I thought was a nice-size fish. I couldn't see the fish due to the off-colored water because Navajo Lake had turned over. As I allowed the fish to make its initial run, I started to apply a little rod pressure and then all hell broke loose.

I was fishing a 9-foot Sage RPL 3-weight fly rod with a 6X tippet tied to the leech, as I hadn't contemplated I would be catching a large trout that day using a leech pattern; I always use a 6X tippet when fishing midge pupae. In those days it was typical to have a fish try to spool you by making a long run downstream with you chasing after it, apologizing to all the fishermen who were fishing downstream from you. As I chased after the fish a good 50 yards downstream, I was able to turn its head using side rod pressure, but it kept up a good fight. At first I thought I'd foul-hooked the fish because it was pulling so hard; at that point I still had not seen the fish.

I was getting concerned that I'd been fighting the fish too much, so I started to use opposite rod pressure—every

Conehead Arizona Dubbing Leech

time it went one direction I'd apply pressure in the opposite direction. I was able to keep the fish swimming back and forth in front of me. It made a short run upstream, then turned around and started heading toward me. I thought I'd try and net it.

When that trout was in front of me and I had my net in the ready position, and I saw how big the trout was, I panicked; I'd never caught a trout that large. I tried to net the fish, but it wouldn't bend to fit into my net, which only had an opening of about 16 inches. It flopped out of the net and was back in the water. I thought for sure that I had lost this fish, but the stars were aligned that day—I still had the fish on.

The fish took another big turn toward me. I didn't know what to do, so I stuck the net in front of the trout and let it swim into the net, hoping to stop it. I immediately tucked the fly rod under my left arm that was also holding the net and grabbed the trout by its tail. I had finally landed the fish. Who would have thought that I could play and land a fish using 6X tippet material?

I didn't have a camera and asked if anyone would take a photograph for me. A nice elderly couple from Texas said they would as I started to revive the fish. They took the photograph and then I released the fish. I gave those folks around three dozen flies and my name and where they could send the photograph. Later they sent me the photograph and a thank-you note for the flies; they caught a majority of their fish with my flies during their trip.

I was so proud of that fish and made sure to put the photograph in a safe place so I could show it to my fishing friends. Guess what, I can't find the photograph. I was sure I knew where I put it, and maybe one day it will show up, but it really doesn't matter because I have the image of that beautiful rainbow in my mind's eye. Since that day, I always carry a box of leeches whenever I head out to fish.

Brian Yamauchi with a beautiful rainbow trout taken from North Delaney Butte Lake with his chironomid pupa.

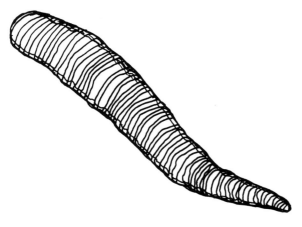

Leeches are commonly found in many of the streams and lakes in our region and should not be overlooked as a food source. Fish do like to eat leeches whenever they are present in the water. The patterns you select should incorporate materials that give undulating motion to the pattern. Leeches tend to change the length and shape of their bodies as they move from location to location. You should fish the leeches with a slow, steady motion and an occasional pause, and add weight ahead of the fly to impart an up-and-down motion to the fly.

In addition to the dubbing and picked-hair style of leeches, do not overlook rabbit and pine squirrel variations. The use of rabbit Zonker strips tied to the hook in the front behind the eye and at the hook bend with a thread underbody is one of the simplest patterns to tie. Don't let its simplicity fool you, though; this is a highly effective pattern. I choose not to add any weight to this pattern, preferring the near-neutral buoyancy to keep the fly in the "zone" for a longer period of time. If I require the leech to sink faster, I will add weight to the tippet in front of the leech to reach the desired depth. When fishing stillwaters, I like to use an intermediate fly line that has a slow sink rate; by using this type of line, I feel the flies I'm fishing are descending at a slower rate, thus keeping the flies in the zone longer. One of the rabbit strip leeches I tie uses a golden variant Zonker rabbit strip. My friend and guide Jude Duran would successfully use this colored rabbit strip leech to represent rehydrated moss that had dried on the streambed during low water and bleached out from exposure to the sun. As water levels rose, the dried-out moss rehydrated, providing a home for midge larvae. As the moss started moving downstream, I observed trout coming up and taking mouthfuls of the moss to dislodge the midge larvae and feed on them, an amazing event that I had never seen before. I fish this pattern dead-drift style using a strike indicator and vary the depth of the leech to the corresponding depth of the water when fishing streams.

Designing the Hot Head AZ Black/Red Leech

I was introduced to Arizona Dubbing years ago when I was having difficulties tying a mohair-style leech; my problem was that I would get the majority of the mohair yarn fiber trapped underneath each wrap, and it would take a lot of time to try and release those trapped fibers using a pick or a comb. I was also looking for a thicker-profile body than what I could achieve with mohair yarn. I wanted something else.

I watched a tying demonstration by Larry Walker, the inventor of the Dubbit tool. He dubbed some dubbing with his tool to make a body for the pattern he was tying. His demonstration opened up for me a whole new way of adding materials to a hook. At the time I was working at Rocky Mountain Fly Shop in Fort Collins, owned by my friend Steve Solano. He had ordered some of the Arizona Dubbing in the same colors the mohair yarn came in, and I knew instantly that I'd be a huge fan of this material. I realized that I could use a dubbing loop–type concept to create the spiky type of body that I had difficulty creating with the mohair yarn. I tie all of my mohair-style leeches with Arizona Simi-Seal Dubbing. John Rohmer has developed some highly effective colors for imitating leeches—can't wait to try some new colors.

In designing the Hot Head AZ Black/Red Leech pattern, I decided to use the dubbing to form the tail of the leech; I also use angora dubbing fibers as the tailing material in some of my leech patterns. With this pattern, I didn't want to use a dubbing loop to make the body of the leech, so I decided to dub the Arizona Dubbing as sparsely as I could to the tying thread, making a slender body, which I tied to the front of the hook behind the bead. I then used the dubbing loop to form a collar; I brushed out the mohair using Dennis Collier's dubbing brush to create the larger front-end profile of the pattern. I like to tie some of my leeches using a fluorescent orange bead, black brass bead, or gold brass bead, or sometimes I don't use a bead at all and make a head for the leech using thread.

HOT HEAD AZ SIMI-SEAL BLACK/ RED LEECH (VARIATION ON JOHN ROHMER'S LEECH)

- **Hook:** #8-12 Daiichi 1750
- **Bead (optional):** Fluorescent pink, orange, or red silver lined glass bead (optional)
- **Thread:** Black 140-denier UTC
- **Weight (optional):** Lead wire
- **Tail:** Black/red Arizona Simi-Seal Dubbing, Angora dubbing, or marabou
- **Flash (optional):** One strand of Krystal Flash on each side of the tail
- **Body:** Dubbed black/red Arizona Simi-Seal Dubbing
- **Collar:** Black/red Arizona Simi-Seal Dubbing using a dubbing loop
- **Throat:** Black 140-denier UTC
- **Note:** Brush out dubbing loop. Other hook models include Daiichi 1710 and 1720 and Tiemco 5262 and 5263.

TYING THE HOT HEAD AZ BLACK/RED LEECH

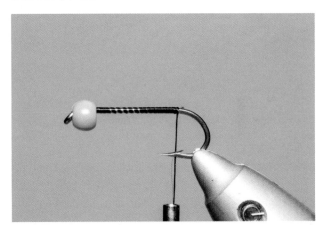

1. Slide on a bead if desired and push it to the eye of the hook. Attach tying thread behind the bead, then wrap thread to the hook bend opposite the barb; trim excess thread. If you want more weight to the pattern (optional), use lead wire directly in back of the bead; tie in the tying thread to hold the lead in place and wrap it back to the hook bend opposite the barb.

2. Tie in the Simi-Seal dubbing fibers or angora tailing material at the hook bend opposite the barb. Make several tight wraps forward, then fold over tailing material and wrap over material to secure the hook; this will form the tail.

3. Tie in a single strand of Krystal Flash, and then fold over to form one strand on each side of the tail. Tie thread over the flash to force it back alongside the tail.

4. Dub the thread with Arizona Simi-Seal and wrap a dubbed body forward to three eye widths back from the hook eye (two eye widths if using a bead).

5. Form a dubbing loop and insert Arizona Simi-Seal, spreading it out to form a dubbing brush. Twist the dubbing tool and fold fibers out of the way when twisting; I use the Collier's dubbing brush to tease the fibers from being trapped or to pull out the fibers. Wrap dubbing loop to the back of the bead or, if not using a bead, to one eye width back from the hook eye. Whip-finish and trim thread.

6. Brush the Simi-Seal out to form a dense collar; this gives the leech a large head flowing back to a slimmer body.

7. The Hot Head AZ Black/Red Leech, which mimics the coloration of leeches found in our waters.

Designing the Micro Pine Squirrel Leech

My Micro Pine Squirrel Leech is not a new pattern by any stretch of the imagination, but instead of pulling the squirrel forward over a dubbed body like John Barr's Slumpbuster, I wrap the squirrel Zonker strip around the hook shank tightly to the hook eye. I have found the pattern to be highly effective in catching trout as well as warmwater fish. I tie some of my leech patterns without a bead head with equal success. The Micro Pine Squirrel Leech is a great pattern when you want to fish a leech for all types of water. I sometimes mix the colors of the leech by making the tail one color and the body a different color.

MICRO PINE SQUIRREL LEECH

- **Hook:** #8-12 Daiichi 1750
- **Bead (optional):** Black brass bead or your choice of color. You can tie the pattern without a bead as an option.
- **Thread:** Black 70-denier UTC or Danville 110
- **Under Tail (optional):** Purple Senyo's Laser Dub
- **Weight (optional):** Lead wire
- **Tail/Body/Collar:** Micro pine squirrel Zonker strip
- **Note:** Other hook models include Daiichi 1710 and 1720 and Tiemco 5262 and 5263.

TYING THE MICRO PINE SQUIRREL LEECH

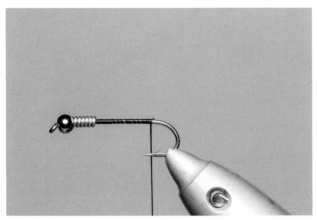

1. If using a bead, attach bead to the hook, slide to the eye of the hook, then make 6 to 10 wraps of lead and slide it to the bead. Wrap thread to the end of the lead wire and wrap to the hook bend opposite the barb; trim excess thread. Adding lead weight to the fly is optional.

2. Tie in the purple Senyo's Laser Dub for the tailing material at the hook bend opposite the barb. In the middle of the dubbing fibers, make several tight wraps forward, then fold over tailing material and wrap over the material to secure. Add flash if desired.

3. Tie in the micro pine squirrel, leaving a short section of the Zonker strip about the length of the body facing the rear, and secure with several tight wraps.

4. Wrap the Zonker strip in touching wraps toward the bead.

5. Wrap the Zonker strip to the bead, tie off with several wraps of thread, and trim thread. Whip-finish and trim excess thread.

6. The Micro Pine Squirrel Leech is one of my go-to patterns when fishing stillwaters and streams; the subtle movement of the squirrel gives a realistic impression of the leech itself.

I tie the Micro Pine Squirrel in as many of the colors available but have found the natural and black to be my favorite colors.

Leeches

HOT HEAD AZ SIMI-SEAL LEECH (CANADIAN OLIVE)

- **Hook:** #8-12 Daiichi 1750
- **Thread:** Black 140-denier UTC or 140-denier Danville
- **Bead:** Canadian Llama fluorescent orange brass
- **Tail:** Olive brown Angora goat
- **Flash:** Rust Krystal Flash
- **Body:** Canadian olive Arizona Simi-Seal Dubbing
- **Collar:** Canadian olive Arizona Simi-Seal using a dubbing loop

HOT HEAD AZ SIMI-SEAL LEECH (BLACK)

- **Hook:** #8-12 Daiichi 1750
- **Thread:** Black 140-denier UTC or 140-denier Danville
- **Bead:** Canadian Llama fluorescent orange brass
- **Tail:** Black Angora goat
- **Flash:** Black Krystal Flash
- **Body:** Black Arizona Simi-Seal Dubbing
- **Collar:** Black Arizona Simi-Seal using a dubbing loop

HOT HEAD AZ SIMI-SEAL LEECH (PURPLE)

- **Hook:** #8-12 Daiichi 1750
- **Thread:** Purple 140-denier UTC
- **Bead:** Canadian Llama fluorescent orange brass
- **Tail:** Claret Angora goat
- **Body:** Purple Arizona Simi-Seal Dubbing
- **Collar:** Purple Arizona Simi-Seal using a dubbing loop

HOT HEAD AZ SIMI-SEAL LEECH (CRAWDAD)

- **Hook:** #8-12 Daiichi 1750
- **Thread:** Black 140-denier UTC
- **Bead:** Canadian Llama fluorescent orange brass
- **Tail:** Light olive Angora goat
- **Body:** Crawdad Arizona Simi-Seal Dubbing
- **Collar:** Crawdad Arizona Simi-Seal using a dubbing loop

HOT HEAD AZ SIMI-SEAL LEECH (OLIVE)

- **Hook:** #8-12 Daiichi 1750
- **Thread:** Olive 140-denier UTC
- **Bead:** Canadian Llama fluorescent orange brass
- **Tail:** Olive Angora goat
- **Body:** Olive Arizona Simi-Seal Dubbing
- **Collar:** Olive Arizona Simi-Seal using a dubbing loop

CONEHEAD LEECH (BROWN BRICK) (VARIATION OF JOHN ROHMER'S SIMI-SEAL LEECH)

- **Hook:** #8-12 Daiichi 1750
- **Thread:** Black 140-denier UTC
- **Bead:** Canadian Llama black conehead bead
- **Tail:** Brown brick Arizona Simi-Seal Dubbing
- **Body:** Brown brick Arizona Simi-Seal or brown wool yarn
- **Collar:** Brown brick Arizona Simi-Seal using a dubbing loop

CONEHEAD LEECH (DARK OLIVE) (VARIATION OF JOHN ROHMER'S SIMI-SEAL LEECH)

- **Hook:** #8-12 Daiichi
- **Thread:** Black 140-denier UTC
- **Bead:** Canadian Llama black conehead bead
- **Tail:** Canadian dark olive Arizona Simi-Seal Dubbing
- **Body:** Canadian dark olive Arizona Simi-Seal or brown wool yarn
- **Collar:** Canadian dark olive Arizona Simi-Seal using a dubbing loop

CONEHEAD CANADIAN LEECH (ORANGE) (VARIATION OF JOHN ROHMER'S SIMI-SEAL LEECH)

- **Hook:** #8-12 Daiichi 1750
- **Thread:** Black or orange 140-denier UTC
- **Bead:** Canadian Llama black conehead bead
- **Tail:** Canadian orange Arizona Simi-Seal Dubbing
- **Body:** Canadian orange Arizona Simi-Seal or rust wool yarn
- **Collar:** Canadian orange Arizona Simi-Seal using a dubbing loop

RABBIT STRIP LEECH (VARIANT GOLD) (VARIATION OF JUDE DURAN'S RABBIT STRIP LEECH)

- **Hook:** #8-12 Daiichi 1750
- **Thread:** Wood duck 140-denier UTC
- **Tail/Body:** Hareline's variant gold Zonker rabbit strip
- **Underbody:** Tying thread
- **Head:** Tying thread

RABBIT STRIP LEECH (CHARCOAL)

- **Hook:** #8-12 Daiichi 1750
- **Thread:** Black 140-denier UTC
- **Tail/Body:** Charcoal Zonker rabbit strip
- **Underbody:** Tying thread
- **Head:** Tying thread

MICRO PINE SQUIRREL LEECH (BLACK)

- **Hook:** #8-12 Daiichi 1750
- **Thread:** Black 140-denier UTC
- **Tail/Body:** Black micro pine squirrel Zonker strip
- **Underbody:** Tying thread
- **Head:** Tying thread

MICRO PINE SQUIRREL LEECH (PURPLE)

- **Hook:** #8-12 Daiichi 1750
- **Thread:** Black 140-denier UTC
- **Tail/Body:** Purple micro pine squirrel Zonker strip
- **Underbody:** Tying thread
- **Head:** Tying thread

BEAD LEECH (BRONZE PEACOCK) (VARIATION OF JOHN ROHMER'S SIMI-SEAL LEECH)

- **Hook:** #8-12 Daiichi 1750
- **Thread:** 140-denier UTC, color to match overall color scheme
- **Bead:** Canadian Llama black conehead bead
- **Tail:** Bronze peacock Arizona Simi-Seal Dubbing
- **Body:** Bronze peacock Arizona Simi-Seal or brown wool yarn
- **Collar:** Bronze peacock Arizona Simi-Seal using a dubbing loop

PURPLE BUTT PINE SQUIRREL LEECH

- **Hook:** #8-12 Daiichi 1750
- **Thread:** Black 70-denier UTC or Danville 110
- **Bead:** Canadian Llama hot orange bead
- **Under Tail:** Purple Senyo's Laser Dub
- **Weight:** Lead wire (optional)
- **Tail/Body/Collar:** Natural micro pine squirrel Zonker strip

RED BUTT PINE SQUIRREL LEECH

- **Hook:** #8-12 Daiichi 1750
- **Thread:** Black 70-denier UTC or Danville 110
- **Bead:** Canadian Llama hot orange bead
- **Under Tail:** Red Senyo's Laser Dub
- **Weight:** Lead wire (optional)
- **Tail/Body/Collar:** Black micro pine squirrel Zonker strip

CHARTREUSE BUTT PINE SQUIRREL LEECH

- **Hook:** #8-12 Daiichi 1750
- **Thread:** Black 70-denier UTC or Danville 110
- **Bead:** Canadian Llama hot orange bead
- **Under Tail:** Olive Senyo's Laser Dub
- **Weight:** Lead wire (optional)
- **Tail/Body/Collar:** Micro pine squirrel Zonker strip

RUSTY PINE SQUIRREL LEECH

- **Hook:** #8-12 Daiichi 1750
- **Thread:** Black 70-denier UTC
- **Under Tail:** Rusty nail Senyo's Laser Dub
- **Weight:** Lead wire (optional)
- **Tail/Body/Collar:** Rust micro pine squirrel Zonker strip
- **Head:** Tying thread

-6-

MAYFLY SERIES

Thread Body Red Quill

One of my favorite forms of fly fishing is fishing a dry fly; I love to see a fish come up behind a dry fly and take it in with either a splashy take or a simple sucking in of the fly off the surface of the water. When I start to tie up a batch of dry flies, and more specifically mayflies, I center my tying efforts around trying to imitate Baetis, Pale Morning Duns, Tricos, and Green Drakes—and usually in that order.

My fly-fishing mentor Donn Johnson introduced me to the mayfly patterns of the Catskill fly tiers: Theodore Gordon, the Dettes, the Darbees, and Rube Cross. Donn tied in the Catskill style, making dry flies that were well crafted, slender, and visually pleasing to look at. I gained an appreciation for the Catskill style of tying sparse flies, and I try to reduce the amount of material used for the dry-fly patterns I tie.

Key Materials for Mayfly Series

HOOKS

I find that a good-quality hook is an important element of an effective dry-fly pattern. I favor using Daiichi 1220 and 1222 and Tiemco 100, 101, and 900 for my dry flies.

TAILING

Microfibetts, Antron yarns, Whiting Farms Coq de Leon hackle fibers, fibers from the spade hackle, elk hock hair, moose body hair, and tapered polyester paintbrush fibers are the main materials I use for creating tails and shucks for my dry flies.

ABDOMENS

Using tying thread can create the slender profile of a mayfly's abdomen similar to the Catskill-style flies. I often build up the underbody of the abdomen using tying thread to taper the body, then color the thread with a darker, contrasting color to mimic the segmentation of the abdomen of the mayfly. I cover the body with superglue, thinned-out head cement, or a light coating of the Solarez Bone Dry UV resin.

I also use stripped peacock herl to create a segmented body. I have found that Nature's Spirit and Spirit River produce a dyed peacock herl that is colorfast throughout the herl and retains its color even when stripped. To strip the herl of the fuzz, I use an eraser or my index finger and thumbnail to apply pressure, moving several times in the opposite direction from the tip of the herl to the base.

I have found dubbings like Superfine and Fine and Dry Dubbing and many fine-textured dubbings can produce the slender bodies that I favor for tying dry flies; I try to use as little dubbing as possible when making mayfly bodies. I also like to use Nature's Spirit and Spirit River's dyed peacock herls that I strip to make quill-style abdomens. It's important to put a coating on the quill to protect it; use a thinned-out head cement or a UV resin. I tie a good number of dry-fly abdomens using tying thread for an underbody, then I darken the thread by using a dark-colored permanent marker and cover with cement or resin to protect the thread.

WINGS

Perhaps my favorite style is a Compara-dun wing of deer hair, which I believe was based on Francis Betters's famous Haystack fly. I use good-quality deer hair for many of the wings for my dry flies, such as Nature's Spirit hair products.

Sometimes you have to stretch to get that perfect drift. Master fly tier and angler Chuck Esch keeps a low profile as he fishes the Cheesman Canyon section of the South Platte River. ISRAEL PATTERSON PHOTO

A beautiful brook trout falls prey to a small Baetis nymph.

I also like to make wings out of polyester yarns, Antron yarns, and various duck feather fibers. I love to tie Catskill-style dry flies using wood duck, gadwall, and teal body feathers and will often use CDC, mallard, and teal quill wings and Whiting Farms hen hackles for winging material. I'll use just about anything that I think will work to create a wing.

HACKLE

I use Whiting Farms neck and saddle hackle for most of my dry-fly hackles; I also like many of the hackles being produced by Keough Hackles and Metz Feathers. I never thought I'd see the day when you could hackle a dry fly using a saddle hackle, but Dr. Tom Whiting has developed some high-quality dry-fly-quality hackles using saddle hackles.

QUILL BODY DRY FLY

- **Hook:** #14-18 Daiichi 1220 or 1222 or Tiemco 100
- **Thread:** Olive 16/0 Veevus
- **Tail:** Dun tapered paintbrush fibers
- **Underbody:** Tying thread
- **Body:** Stripped Nature's Spirit or Spirit River dyed peacock herl
- **Wing:** White polyester yarn
- **Hackle:** Dun Whiting Farms saddle

TYING THE QUILL BODY DRY FLY

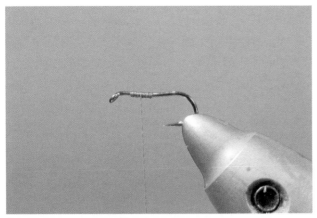

1. Attach tying thread one-third the distance back from the hook eye.

2. Tie the polyester yarn in the middle of the yarn.

3. Wrap the tying thread in front of and behind the wing post to secure into position. Wrap tying thread back to the hook bend opposite the barb.

4. Tie in two strands of tapered paintbrush fibers, then wrap thread over the tail material to behind the wing.

5. Trim off excess tail material.

6. Strip the fibers off the stem of the peacock herl by rubbing with an eraser or using your thumbnail to scrape off the fuzz (place stripped quill on a damp paper towel if the quill appears to be brittle; this will soften the quill).

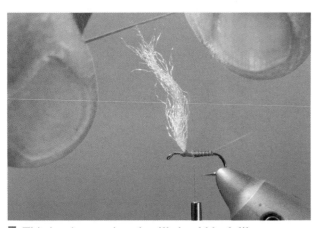

7. This is what a stripped quill should look like.

8. Place the tip end of the stripped quill behind the wing and tie in behind the wing base.

9. Wrap the tying thread over the quill back to the hook bend opposite the barb.

10. Wrap the quill forward in touching wraps to the base of the hook; tie off and trim excess quill.

11. Place a sparse coating of thinned-out head cement over the quill to protect it. Thinned-out head cement is less likely to crack when pressure from hemostats is applied.

12. Tie in one dun Whiting Farms saddle hackle, with the shiny side facing forward, behind the wing. Wrap the tying thread in front of the wing behind the eye.

13. Wrap hackle forward to one eye width back from the hook eye; tie off hackle.

14. Whip-finish, then trim thread.

15. The Quill-Body Dry Fly. I trim the wing to be slightly taller than the hackle or about the length of the thorax to the outside bend of the hook. The stripped-down dyed peacock herl makes an ideal quill-style body for dry flies.

Designing the Royal Poly Wing Humpy

I am also a fan of the attractor dry-fly styles, starting with Lee Wulff's famous Wulff's Royal Coachman, which does not necessarily resemble a mayfly of a specific species. This pattern incorporates peacock herl, red silk, white calf tail, and brown hackle; the result is a fish-catching pattern. The Humpy is another attractor pattern that I favor; I have tied a version of the Humpy that I call the Poly Wing Royal Humpy, which was developed by my friend Donn Johnson with a little input from me.

Donn wanted to create a pattern that would hold up to many fish and not fall apart; he set out to construct a high-floating dry fly in the style of a Humpy attractor pattern. He selected moose body hair for the tail, white polyester yarn for the back strap and wing, red thread for the body, and a brown hackle to complete his design. Donn found that the polyester yarn held up to repeated abuse by the trout's sharp teeth, the red body was an attractor color, and moose body hair made a sturdy tail.

We were successful the first day we ventured out to field-test this new pattern. We planned to fish the upper stretch of the Little South Fork of the Poudre River, which is approximately seven miles above the main Poudre River near Colorado State University Mountain Campus. We decided to set off in opposite directions and meet three hours later to compare our results. Our objective was to see how many fish we could catch on one fly. Upon meeting back at the car to compare notes, we found that Donn had caught well over forty trout and I had caught around twenty-five. All were caught on one fly, and the objective was to maintain the fly as best we could, but we were only to use one fly. To keep the pattern floating, I used Amadou, a fungi pad, to wick away moisture when the fly became waterlogged, then dipped the fly into Shimizaki Dry Shake to re-float the fly after blowing off any residual desiccant. The initial dry-fly dressing was Gink dry-fly floatant. What I learned from this experiment was how materials can be used to construct sturdy flies. I also learned that attractor fly patterns are effective for catching fish, and a well-tied fly often will hold up to repeated use.

ROYAL POLY WING HUMPY

- **Hook:** #14-18 Daiichi 1220 or 1222 or Tiemco 100
- **Thread:** Red 8/0 UNI
- **Tail:** Moose body hair
- **Underbody:** Tying thread
- **Overbody:** Light dun polyester yarn
- **Wing:** White polyester yarn
- **Hackle:** Brown Whiting Farms saddle

TYING THE ROYAL POLY WING HUMPY

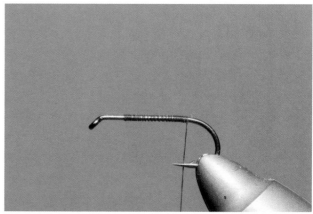

1. Attach tying thread one-third the distance back from the hook eye, then wrap tying thread back to the hook bend opposite the barb; trim off excess thread.

2. Stack four to six fibers from a moose belly hide and tie in the hair at the hook bend opposite the barb, with the tips of the hair extending the length of the hook shank beyond the hook bend—this will form the tail of the pattern. The tail should be the length of the abdomen. Wrap the tying thread over the moose belly hair in touching wraps to the midpoint on the hook shank; trim excess hair. Wrap tying thread to the midpoint of the hook.

3. Tie in the polyester yarn by the tag end with the yarn facing toward the rear of the hook, then wrap thread over the yarn to the hook bend opposite the barb; make sure to cover all the yarn.

4. Wrap the tying thread in touching wraps forward to the one-third position of the hook shank. Pull the yarn over the hook shank and tie in. Wrap the thread directly in front of the wing and tie in a small dam of thread immediately in front of the wing, forcing it to remain at a right angle to the shank. Wrap thread behind the yarn wing to the front edge of the body as shown; this space will provide a tie-in point for the hackle.

5. Tie in one brown Whiting Farms saddle hackle with the shiny side facing toward the hook eye at the front edge of the yarn body, then wrap thread to one eye width back from the eye of the hook.

6. Wrap the hackle in touching wraps to one eye width back from the hook eye, tie off hackle, trim the excess hackle, and whip-finish. Trim excess thread.

7. Trim the wing to length; I like it to be as long as from the thorax to the bend of the hook, or slightly longer in length than the hackle. The Poly Wing Royal Humpy is one of the great all-time attractor patterns.

Mayflies

POLY WING QUILL PMD

- **Hook:** #14-18 Daiichi 1220 or 1222 or TMC 100
- **Thread:** Light olive 8/0 UNI
- **Tail:** Dun tapered paintbrush fibers
- **Abdomen:** Light olive Nature's Spirit stripped peacock herl
- **Wing:** White polyester yarn
- **Hackle:** Medium dun Whiting Farms saddle

THREAD BODY PMD

- **Hook:** #14-18 Daiichi 1220 or 1222 or TMC 100
- **Thread:** Light olive 8/0 UNI
- **Tail:** Dun tapered paintbrush fibers
- **Abdomen:** Tying thread
- **Wing:** White polyester yarn
- **Hackle:** Medium dun Whiting Farms saddle

MALLARD WING PMD

- **Hook:** #14-18 Daiichi 1220 or 1222 or TMC 100
- **Thread:** Light olive 8/0 UNI
- **Tail:** Dun tapered paintbrush fibers
- **Abdomen:** Light pink Superfine Dubbing
- **Wing:** White polyester yarn with mallard flank feather fibers
- **Hackle:** Medium dun Whiting Farms saddle

POLY WING PMD HUMPY

- **Hook:** #14-18 Daiichi 1220 or 1222 or TMC 100
- **Thread:** Light olive 8/0 UNI
- **Tail:** Bleached moose body hair
- **Underbody:** Tying thread
- **Overbody:** Light dun polyester yarn
- **Wing:** White polyester yarn
- **Hackle:** Medium dun Whiting Farms saddle

POLY WING RED QUILL

- **Hook:** #14-18 Daiichi 1220 or 1222 or TMC 100
- **Thread:** Light olive 8/0 UNI
- **Tail:** Dun tapered paintbrush fibers
- **Abdomen:** Mahogany Nature's Spirit stripped peacock herl
- **Wing:** White polyester yarn
- **Hackle:** Medium dun Whiting Farms saddle

THREAD BODY PMD COMPARA-DUN

- **Hook:** #14-18 Daiichi 1220 or 1222 or TMC 100
- **Thread:** Tan 8/0 UNI
- **Tail:** Dun tapered paintbrush fibers
- **Abdomen:** Tying thread
- **Rib:** Tying thread colored with orange Sharpie
- **Wing:** Natural deer hair
- **Thorax:** Tying thread

THREAD BODY RED QUILL

- **Hook:** #14-18 Daiichi 1220 or 1222 or TMC 100
- **Thread:** Rust 8/0 UNI
- **Tail:** Dun tapered paintbrush fibers
- **Abdomen:** Tying thread
- **Rib:** Tying thread colored with black Sharpie
- **Wing:** White polyester yarn
- **Hackle:** Medium dun Whiting Farms saddle

RED QUILL SPINNER

- **Hook:** #14-18 Daiichi 1220 or 1222 or TMC 100
- **Thread:** Light olive 8/0 UNI
- **Tail:** Dun tapered paintbrush fibers
- **Abdomen:** Mahogany Nature's Spirit stripped peacock herl
- **Wing:** White polyester yarn
- **Thorax:** Rust Superfine Dubbing

-7-
CHIRONOMIDS (MIDGES) FOR STILLWATERS

Chironomids make up a large portion of the trout's diet throughout the year. (Midges and chironomids are the same thing.) I refer to midges found in stillwaters as chironomids and midges found in rivers and streams as midges.

The pupal stage plays a major role in what trout like to feed on the most, in my observations. Dr. Brian Chan, my entomology expert in *Modern Midges*, told me when chironomid/midge pupae are ascending to the surface to hatch, they do so by the thousands. This process begins at the bottom interface of the lake and continues to the surface. Trout can feed on these insects at any level of the water column under the relative safety of the water's depth; there is a greater chance to feed freely with reduced fear of predation from above. I've found the same situation in streams and rivers: The fish can swim in the current with their mouths open, taking in mouthfuls of these insects.

I concentrate my tying efforts on developing a variety of patterns that represent the pupa. The pupae have shiny, silvery bodies with distinct segmentation and prominent gills. Midges in stillwaters on average are much larger than those in rivers and range in color from black to grays, tans, and olives. I've tied the chironomid pupae in all the colors of the rainbow and with a wide variety of tying materials.

I started fishing chironomid pupae almost immediately when I started to study fly fishing in the lakes and reservoirs in the North Park area of Colorado and in southern Wyoming. I was totally ignorant and baffled as to what sort of food trout were feeding on in these waters. In my youth, when I'd fish with my grandfather and uncles, we'd always fish with night crawlers or salmon eggs. We caught

Bow Tie Buzzer

our share of fish, and I never thought about what other sorts of things trout might feed on.

Many years later I was invited on a fishing trip with my friend the late Steve Goto and Ken Iwamasa, a well-known artist, art professor, fly tier, and fisherman. As we set up our gear to go fly fishing, the only thing I could do was stand on the shoreline with fly rod in hand and look out over the water. I had absolutely no idea what to do. I finally put on a fly and began casting out into the water, hoping that I might catch something. I didn't catch a thing, which in some ways was a good thing, because I made up my mind that I was going to learn as much as I could about fly-fishing stillwaters.

While out on the lake, I'd find empty shucks floating in the surface film of the water. I collected samples of these shucks and put them in a glass bottle that I used to collect insects. I wondered what the adults looked like, so I set out to learn all I could about the insects. I learned that these insects are called chironomids, that trout loved to eat these insects, and that they provided a large volume of the trout's diet year-round. I learned that the chironomid has a complete life cycle consisting of egg, larva, pupa, and adult. Trout consume the larva, pupa, and adult year-round, and the pupae found in lakes are considerably larger in size than their counterparts in moving waters.

Upon closer inspection, I observed that the pupae coming to the surface to hatch into the adult form had shiny bodies. When all the factors for emergence are aligned and the time has come for its ascent to the surface, the pupa fills its body with a gaseous substance to aid in its travel upward. This process takes time, and the pupae may move up and down

Another above-average-size rainbow yields to Brian Yamauchi's Chironomid Pupa. Often pupal patterns with a distinct sheen work best, as the pupae fill their bodies with a gaseous substance as they hatch into adults.

Jim Kapral fishing the shallows of North Delaney Butte Lake with excellent results.

the water column for short distances until the time comes for their steady migration to the surface to hatch into adults, mate, lay eggs, and start the whole life cycle again. There are thousands if not millions of pupae rising to the surface en masse, which provide trout with easy feeding opportunities from the safety of depth in the water, anywhere from the surface to the bottom of the lake.

What caught my eye with the individual pupae I collected distilled down to four factors that I incorporate into my chironomid pupa designs. First, the gaseous substance that fills the body cavity of the pupae is highly reflective when sunlight reflects off their bodies in a silvery flash. Second, the segmentation of the abdomen is more widely spaced and of fewer number than other invertebrates I've observed. Third, the breathing structures located on the top and sides of the pupa's head are very apparent and possibly act as a trigger for trout. Fourth, the size of the pupae found in lakes is many times larger than the pupae I've collected in the rivers and streams I fish. With these four factors in mind, I set forth to replicate what I had observed in nature.

The first chironomid pupa pattern that I fished was one I had read about; it was a pattern of Gary Borger's called the Bow Tie Buzzer. I learned many years later that "buzzers" is a term used in the United Kingdom to refer to midges. The proportions used to tie this pupa were somewhat different than I'd seen in other fly patterns. It had a long abdomen and a round and short thorax made with white poly yarn tied in a spent-wing style and trimmed short to give the appearance of a bow tie. These same proportions are what I generally follow when tying midge pupae, regardless of their origination location.

In the design and construction of the pupa, I try to mimic components of the natural. I keep the abdomen somewhat

slender in shape, with wider segmentation and a shiny appearance, then add a shiny wing case to continue the chrome-like look. I make the thorax slightly longer than on the natural, usually measuring half the distance between the hook point and the eye; I do this to incorporate a wing bud. The last element, which I include on almost all the pupae I tie, is a breathing structure.

Key Materials for Stillwater Chironomids

I am always on the lookout for new materials and often discover a material that was originally designed for another purpose. An example would be using the silvery inside of a Cheetos bag, cutting it into narrow strips to use in the construction of abdomen segmentation. I use Oral-B Ultra or Super Dental Floss for most of the breathing structures (gills), but will use other materials like CDC, poly, or Antron yarns if I run out of the Oral-B.

ABDOMEN

I use several types of materials to reproduce the silver segmentation of the pupa. I love to tie with holographic tinsel in all colors and sizes. Having a selection of different colors on hand is advantageous when mimicking these types of bodies. I generally create an underbody of darker

The chironomid pupae found in stillwaters tend to be larger in size than their counterparts found in moving waters such as rivers and streams.

tying thread, using UTC threads in the 70- to 140-denier range. I've found that I can produce a smooth underbody by untwisting the tying thread; rotating the bobbin in a counterclockwise direction will untwist the thread, which facilitates the creation of a smooth body.

Nature's Spirit and Spirit River have produced a variety of dyed peacock herls. Strip the fuzz off the herl by using an eraser or your thumbnail and index finger to apply pressure, scraping off the fuzz by rubbing in the opposite direction of the way the fuzz is pointing. The stripped quills create an awesome segmented abdomen, and the colors remain consistent.

Pearl-colored and Mylar tinsels can also create the shiny segmentation. Once you have wrapped the tinsel on the hook, you can color it with a permanent marker in various colors to produce some interesting effects.

Stretch-type materials such as Spanflex also make wonderful segmented bodies; this material comes in a variety of colors that the fly tier will find useful. I like to use various types and sizes of tubing as another material to create great segmented bodies. I use Stretch Magic cord for one of the patterns I tie—Tak's Crystal Chironomid. I rely on one of the properties of clear tubing, which is that when wrapped around the hook shank, it will magnify whatever is underneath the tubing, which can create a whole host of effects.

One of the best chironomid pupa fly patterns I have ever seen was designed by my friend Brian Yamauchi. He used thin strips of natural latex to make an incredibly realistic pupa. You can see a photo of his chironomid pattern in my book *Modern Midges: Tying & Fishing the World's Most Effective Patterns*. I've seen Brian catching fish when other fly fishers struggled to get hook-ups. His pattern incorporates wing pads that mimic the naturals, and even includes eyes. I've been practicing my tying to try to replicate his highly effective patterns.

Small-diameter yarn and fine-textured dubbing can also produce the abdomen of the pupa. I like to use wire as ribbing to create the segmented effect. Charlie Craven has developed a series of midge pupae using a combination of colored wire to create the segmentation; I've had great success fishing his patterns, such as his Juju Midge. I have also used sewing threads to create the abdomens of my pupae, and wrote an article for *Fly Fisherman* about a thread midge pupa I used on the San Juan River.

Canadian Llama produces a glitter thread that I use to create pupae both for smaller and larger midges. Glitter thread comes in a wide variety of colors, and I'm still discovering how I can use this material in my fly tying.

WING CASE

I like to use UTC Ice Blue Pearl Tinsel in small and medium to imitate the shiny effect of the gaseous buildup in the pupa's body. I also use Pearl Tinsel and Mirage Tinsel to create similar types of effects.

WING BUDS

I favor using goose biots, which I tie in tip first, bringing them forward to create the wing pad. Spanflex, holographic tinsels, and Lite Bright fiber make effective wing buds, too.

GILLS

I use Oral-B Ultra Floss for the breathing gills on my flies almost exclusively, and if I can't find the Ultra Floss I'll use Oral-B Super Floss. CDC and various types of yarns can also be used to create gills.

THORAX

I tie most of my thoraxes using tying thread; however, I also like using Nature's Spirit and Spirit River dyed peacock herls to form the thorax, much like a Bow Tie Buzzer. I also use various types of dubbing in consistencies that range from fine to more texture in the dubbed body.

FLY COATINGS

I coat the exterior of the abdomen, thorax, and wing case with UV resins to create a transparent and protective coating to the fly. I use a thin resin to coat my abdomens, and a little thicker resin for building up the thorax of the pupa. I use Solarez Bone Dry UV resin because of its thin consistency; I also use Solarez Thin UV resin for the majority of my bodies and thorax as a covering. There are several other manufacturers of UV-type resins; Loon, Deerfield, and Bug Bond produce a range of resin types and consistencies.

Designing the Crystal Chironomid

The development of the Crystal Chironomid came from a number of observations I made while collecting the pupa stage of the chironomid (midge) in stillwaters. The most consistent characteristic of this developmental stage of the chironomid was the silvery or shiny appearance of the pupa. I felt this was one of the trigger points to consider while designing and tying up patterns to mimic this stage of development.

As the midge pupa prepares to ascend to the surface to hatch into the adult, it fills its body with a gaseous substance that aids in its travels to the surface. This gaseous substance results in the highly reflective, silvery quality of the pupa's body. This silvery appearance is what I wanted to re-create when I designed this pattern.

I selected clear Stretch Magic (.5 mm) for the creation of the midge's abdomen. I found wrapping a clear, tube-like material such as midge tubing, D-Rib, or Stretch Magic over any material used as the underbody magnified whatever the tubing was wrapped over. I experimented with wrapping tubing over a bare hook and found that the coloration of the hook was magnified; the end result was a silvery effect that mimicked the appearance of the natural.

In addition, I found that I could create a segmentation effect by coloring the Stretch Magic with a permanent marker, and wrapping in wide, evenly spaced wraps would produce a darker ribbed effect.

The next step in the design process was to come up with a thorax, wing buds, wing case, and breathing structure. I decided to use some of the techniques I learned from the fly tiers from the UK in tying this portion of the fly. I first chose a colored thread to match the overall color scheme of the pupa, then a goose biot for the wing pads, UTC Ice Blue Pearl Tinsel for the wing case (it produces a UV effect that aids in the silvery appearance), and Oral-B Ultra Floss for creating the breathing structure (gills) of the pupa.

To protect the materials, I use a coating of Solarez UV resins. I coat the abdomen with Solarez Bone Dry UV resin and the thorax with the Thin UV resin, except the gills. The Thin UV resin is a bit thicker in consistency than Bone Dry and helps me produce a more robust thorax. The UV resins create a transparent effect in the pattern that has proven highly effective.

CRYSTAL CHIRONOMID

- **Hook:** #14-16 Daiichi 1260 or 1760, Tiemco 2302 or 2312, or Dai-Riki 280 or 285
- **Thread:** 8/0 UNI or 70- or 140-denier UTC, color to match color scheme
- **Abdomen:** Clear Stretch Magic (.5 mm)
- **Rib:** Clear Stretch Magic (.5 mm) colored with a dark brown permanent marker
- **Thorax:** Tying thread
- **Wing Pads:** Orange, tan, or white goose biots tied in tip first
- **Wing Case:** UTC Ice Blue Pearl Tinsel
- **Gills:** Oral-B Ultra Floss

TYING THE CRYSTAL CHIRONOMID

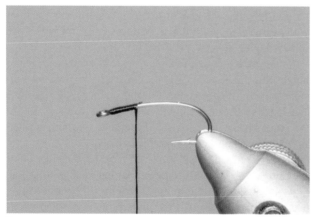

1. Attach thread behind the hook eye and wrap back one-third of the hook shank length toward the hook bend.

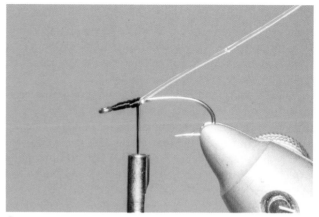

2. Tie in the tag end of the clear Stretch Magic and secure with several wraps of thread.

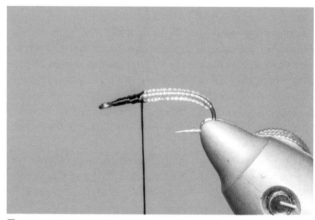

3. Wrap Stretch Magic in touching wraps to the hook bend, increasing pressure as you reach the midpoint of the hook. This will decrease the diameter of the Stretch Magic and create a tapered effect. Wrap the Stretch Magic forward in touching wraps to the original tie-in point. Tie off the material, secure, and trim excess material. Apply a thin layer of UV resin and cure with a UV light.

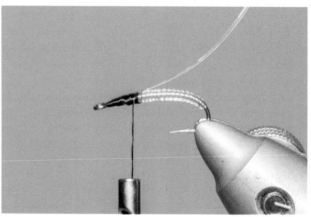

4. Attach a short length of UTC Ice Blue Pearl Tinsel onto the top half of the hook.

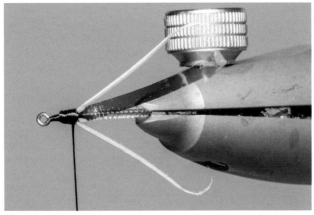

5. Attach biots by the tips to each side of the thorax, making sure that the biots are even on each side and that the tinsel and biots are even, then wrap thread to one eye width back from the eye.

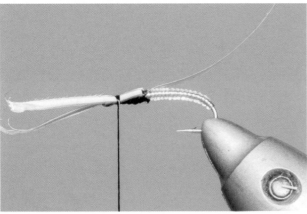

6. Pull each biot along the side and slightly to the top of the wing case; tie off and trim. Repeat process on the opposite side.

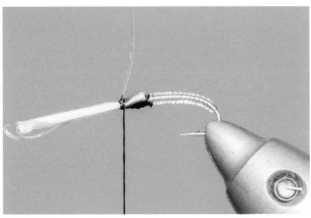

7. Pull the tinsel over the top of the thorax and tie off behind the eye; trim excess.

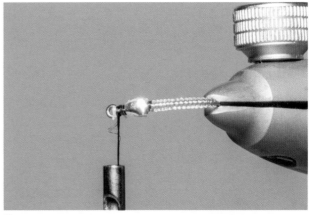

8. Wrap the thread to cover the butt ends of the biots and the tinsel in preparation for adding the breathing structure.

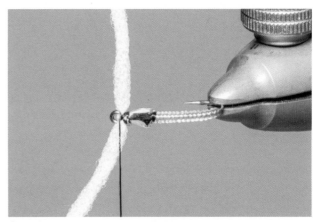

9. Cut a short length of Oral-B Ultra Floss and tie in spent-wing style using figure eight wraps on top of the hook shank behind the hook eye; pull Oral-B floss forward.

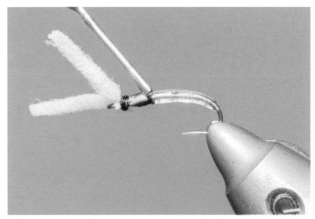

10. Apply a coating of Solarez Bone Dry UV resin to the abdomen, set UV resin, and then coat the thorax with Solarez Thin UV resin and set with a UV light. The Solarez Thin UV resin has a thicker viscosity than the Bone Dry that is almost like water, giving a thinner coating.

Jim Rose fighting a rainbow using a switch rod on a lake in southern Wyoming.

11. Whip-finish and trim thread. Pull gill perpendicular to the hook and trim short.

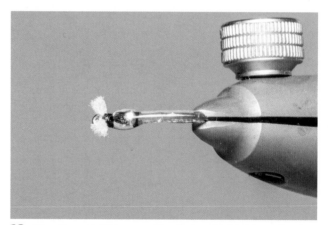

12. The Crystal Chironomid mimics the highly reflective abdomen caused by the trapped gas as the pupa fills its body prior to ascending to the surface to hatch.

Designing the Holographic Chironomid

I designed the Holo or Holographic Chironomid out of a need to try using the colored holographic tinsels that were showing up in the fly-tying materials world. I really like the prismatic reflective qualities of the holographic tinsels, which replicate the shiny effect of the gaseous substance found in the midge pupae. I thought that the holographic tinsels would contrast nicely with a dark underbody and mimic the widely spaced segmentation I observed in the naturals.

The very first chironomid pupa that I ever fished was a pattern I found in one of Gary Borger's books called a Bow Tie Buzzer; I immediately found success in fishing the pattern. I felt that using the holographic tinsel for the rib would replace the silver wire rib of the pupa. I then proceeded to tie up a variety of Holo Chironomids in all colors and sizes. I followed the premise of the Crystal Chironomid in general construction of the pattern.

I chose black, olive brown, dark gray, olive, and brown UTC thread in 140-denier for the abdomen and 70-denier for the thorax. UTC thread is easy to flatten out to create a smooth-looking body by unwinding the thread on the bobbin by twisting the bobbin counterclockwise. I continued to use Ice Blue, Mirage, and Pearl tinsels for what could be considered the wing case; my goal was to continue the shiny effect on the thorax. Goose biots in brown, tan, olive brown, and white were the first colors I tried, then I added orange and a whole host of other colored biots to see if I could catch fish with those colors. You can use other fly-tying materials to form the wing buds such as Spanflex, holographic tinsels, and Edge Brite. Oral-B floss remains my material of choice for the gill structure of the pupa, although I'll use polyester or Antron yarns or CDC Puffs to form the breathing gills, or I'll leave the gills off completely.

HOLOGRAPHIC CHIRONOMID PUPA (RED)

- **Hook:** #10-16 Daiichi 1260
- **Thread:** Black 140-denier UTC
- **Abdomen:** Tying thread
- **Rib 1:** Red holographic tinsel
- **Rib 2:** Small wire to match color scheme
- **Wing Case:** UTC Ice Blue Pearl Tinsel or Mirage Tinsel
- **Wing Buds:** Tan goose biots
- **Gills:** Oral-B Ultra Floss
- **Note:** Coat the entire fly with Solarez Bone Dry UV resin (body) and Thin UV resin (thorax) except the gills. Other hook models include Daiichi 1760; TMC 2302 and 2312; and Dai-Riki 280 and 285.

TYING THE HOLOGRAPHIC CHIRONOMID

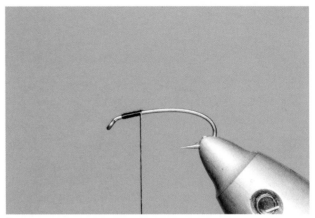

1. Attach thread behind the hook eye and wrap back toward the rear of the hook to a position approximately one-third the distance between the hook eye and the point.

2. Tie in the holographic tinsel by the tag end with several wraps of tying thread to secure firmly.

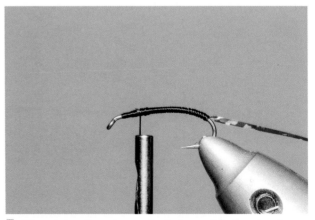

3. Wrap tying thread over the holographic tinsel and back to beyond the hook bend as desired, then wrap thread back to the original tie-in spot on the hook.

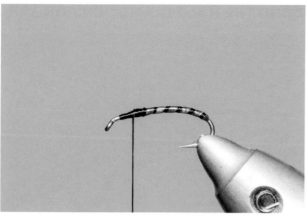

4. Wrap the holographic tinsel forward using wide, evenly spaced wraps; secure and trim excess. Cover the abdomen evenly with Solarez Bone Dry UV resin, then set with UV light.

5. Attach a 1-inch length of medium UTC Ice Blue Pearl Tinsel on top of the hook shank directly in front of the body.

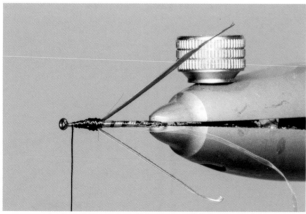

6. Attach the biots to the side of the thorax on each side of the hook by the tips (I generally will trim the very end point of the biot before tying in). Make sure the biots and tinsel are lined up evenly. Wrap the thread forward to the hook eye.

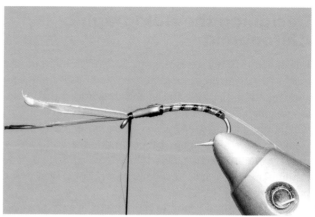

7. Fold the biots forward and crisscross behind the hook eye; secure and trim excess.

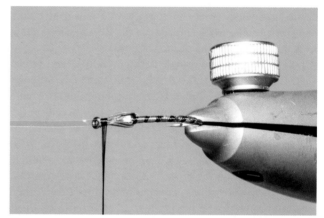

8. Fold the tinsel forward over the thorax; tie off and trim.

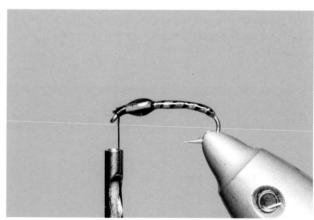

9. Wrap thread to cover up the butt ends of the biots and tinsel in preparation for the breathing structure. Apply Solarez Thin UV resin to make a thicker thorax, then set with UV light.

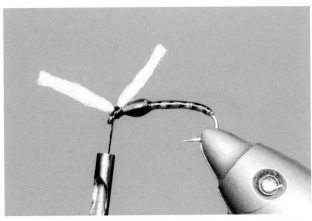

10. Attach a small length of Oral-B Ultra Floss behind the hook eye on top of the head, tie in the floss in the middle of the floss to form a spent wing, and figure-eight the tying thread over the floss to secure.

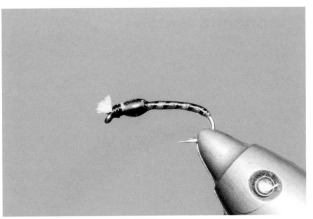

12. The Holographic Chironomid Pupa uses tinsel to create a wider-spaced segmentation found in chironomid pupae.

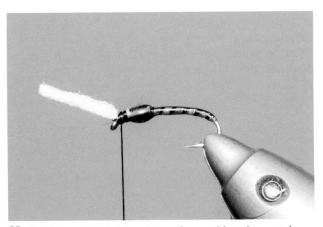

11. Fold the Oral-B Ultra Floss forward but do not trim. Wrap tying thread directly in front of the floss then back behind the floss; whip-finish and trim thread. Trim the Oral-B Ultra Floss short to form the breathing gills of the pupa.

Chironomid Pupae

BLACK BUZZER

- **Hook:** #10-16 TMC 2302 or Daiichi 1120
- **Thread:** Black 140-denier UTC
- **Body:** Tying thread
- **Rib:** Pearl Tinsel
- **Thorax:** Tying thread
- **Wing Case:** Mirage Tinsel
- **Wing Buds:** Orange goose biots
- **Gills:** Oral-B Ultra or Super Floss
- **Note:** Coat entire pattern except gills with Solarez UV resin.

BLUE BUZZER (BLUE)

- **Hook:** #10-16 TMC 2302 or Daiichi 1120
- **Thread:** Blue 140-denier UTC
- **Body:** Tying thread
- **Rib:** Pearl Tinsel
- **Thorax:** Tying thread
- **Wing Case:** Mirage Tinsel
- **Wing Buds:** Orange goose biots
- **Gills:** Oral-B Ultra or Super Floss
- **Note:** Coat entire pattern except gills with Solarez UV resin.

RED BUZZER

- **Hook:** #10-16 TMC 2457 or Daiichi 1120
- **Thread:** Red 140-denier UTC
- **Body:** Tying thread
- **Rib:** Pearl Tinsel
- **Thorax:** Tying thread
- **Wing Case:** Mirage Tinsel
- **Wing Buds:** Orange goose biots
- **Gills:** Oral-B Ultra or Super Floss
- **Note:** Coat entire pattern except gills with Solarez UV resin.

BRASSIE CHIRONOMID PUPA (MEDIUM COPPER)

- **Hook:** #12-18 Daiichi 1260 or TMC 2302
- **Thread:** Black 10/0 Veevus
- **Abdomen:** Red medium UTC wire
- **Wing Case:** Mirage Tinsel
- **Wing Buds:** Tan goose biot
- **Thorax:** Tying thread
- **Note:** Coat entire pattern except gills with Solarez UV resin.

BRASSIE CHIRONOMID PUPA (RED)

- **Hook:** #12-18 Daiichi 1260 or TMC 2302
- **Thread:** Black 10/0 Veevus
- **Abdomen:** Red medium UTC wire
- **Wing Case:** Mirage Tinsel
- **Wing Buds:** Tan goose biot
- **Thorax:** Tying thread
- **Note:** Coat entire pattern except gills with Solarez UV resin.

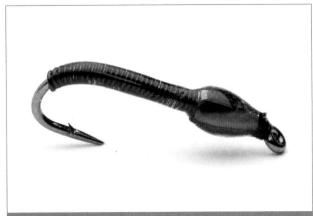

BRASSIE CHIRONOMID PUPA (MEDIUM BROWN)

- **Hook:** #12-18 Daiichi 1260 or TMC 2302
- **Thread:** Black 10/0 Veevus
- **Abdomen:** Brown medium UTC wire
- **Wing Case:** Mirage Tinsel
- **Wing Buds:** Tan goose biot
- **Thorax:** Tying thread
- **Note:** Coat entire pattern except gills with Solarez UV resin.

HOLO CHIRONOMID (MAROON)

- **Hook:** #12-18 Daiichi 1260 or TMC 2302
- **Thread:** Black 140-denier UTC
- **Underbody:** Tying thread
- **Rib 1:** Maroon holographic tinsel
- **Rib 2:** Fine gold UTC wire
- **Wing Case:** Mirage Tinsel
- **Wing Buds:** Light brown goose biot
- **Thorax:** Tying thread
- **Gills:** Oral-B Ultra Floss
- **Note:** Coat entire pattern except gills with Solarez UV resin.

HOLO CHIRONOMID (BLUE)

- **Hook:** #12-18 Daiichi 1260 or TMC 2302
- **Thread:** Black 140-denier UTC
- **Underbody:** Tying thread
- **Rib 1:** Blue holographic tinsel
- **Rib 2:** Fine silver UTC wire
- **Wing Case:** Mirage Tinsel
- **Wing Buds:** Light brown goose biot
- **Thorax:** Tying thread
- **Gills:** Oral-B Ultra Floss
- **Note:** Coat entire pattern except gills with Solarez UV resin.

HOLO CHIRONOMID (PURPLE)

- **Hook:** #12-18 Daiichi 1260 or TMC 2302
- **Thread:** Black 140-denier UTC
- **Underbody:** Tying thread
- **Rib 1:** Purple holographic tinsel
- **Rib 2:** Fine gold UTC wire
- **Wing Case:** Mirage Tinsel
- **Wing Buds:** Light brown goose biot
- **Thorax:** Tying thread
- **Gills:** Oral-B Ultra Floss
- **Note:** Coat entire pattern except gills with Solarez UV resin.

BUTTES CHIRONOMID PUPA (CHARTREUSE)

- **Hook:** #12-18 Daiichi 1120 or 1130 or TMC 2457
- **Thread:** Chartreuse 140-denier UTC
- **Underbody:** Tying thread
- **Rib 1:** Tan Spanflex
- **Rib 2:** Fine silver UTC wire
- **Wing Case:** UTC Ice Blue Pearl Tinsel
- **Wing Buds:** Tan goose biot
- **Thorax:** Tying thread
- **Gills:** Oral-B Ultra Floss
- **Note:** Coat entire pattern except gills with Solarez UV resin.

BUTTES CHIRONOMID PUPA (ORANGE)

- **Hook:** #12-18 Daiichi 1120 or 1130 or TMC 2457
- **Thread:** Red 140-denier UTC
- **Underbody:** Tying thread
- **Rib 1:** Orange Spanflex
- **Rib 2:** Fine gold UTC wire
- **Wing Case:** UTC Ice Blue Pearl Tinsel
- **Wing Buds:** Tan goose biot
- **Thorax:** Tying thread
- **Gills:** Oral-B Ultra Floss
- **Note:** Coat entire pattern except gills with Solarez UV resin.

BUTTES CHIRONOMID PUPA (AMBER)

- **Hook:** #12-18 Daiichi 1120 or 1130 or TMC 2457
- **Thread:** Tan 140-denier UTC
- **Underbody:** Tying thread
- **Rib 1:** Red/yellow Spanflex
- **Rib 2:** Fine gold UTC wire
- **Wing Case:** UTC Ice Blue Pearl Tinsel
- **Wing Buds:** Tan goose biot
- **Thorax:** Tying thread
- **Gills:** Oral-B Ultra Floss
- **Note:** Coat entire pattern except gills with Solarez UV resin.

FLASH BUZZER (ORANGE)

- **Hook:** #10-16 TMC 2302 or Daiichi 1260
- **Thread:** Black 140-denier UTC
- **Body:** Medium Mirage Tinsel colored with orange marker
- **Rib:** Black medium wire
- **Thorax:** Tying thread
- **Wing Case:** UTC Ice Blue Pearl Tinsel
- **Wing Buds:** Brown goose biots
- **Gills:** Oral-B Ultra or Super Floss
- **Note:** Coat entire pattern except gills with Solarez UV resin.

FLASH BUZZER (RED)

- **Hook:** #10-16 TMC 2302 or Daiichi 1260
- **Thread:** Black 140-denier UTC
- **Body:** Medium Mirage Tinsel colored with red marker
- **Rib:** Black medium wire
- **Thorax:** Tying thread
- **Wing Case:** UTC Ice Blue Pearl Tinsel
- **Wing Buds:** Brown goose biots
- **Gills:** Oral-B Ultra or Super Floss
- **Note:** Coat entire pattern except gills with Solarez UV resin.

FLASH BUZZER (MIRAGE)

- **Hook:** #10-16 TMC 2302 or Daiichi 1260
- **Thread:** Black 140-denier UTC
- **Body:** Medium Mirage Tinsel
- **Rib:** Black medium wire
- **Thorax:** Tying thread
- **Wing Case:** UTC Ice Blue Pearl Tinsel
- **Wing Buds:** Brown goose biots
- **Gills:** Oral-B Ultra or Super Floss
- **Note:** Coat entire pattern except gills with Solarez UV resin.

LATEX CHIRONOMID PUPA (BROWN)

- **Hook:** #12-16 Daiichi 1260 or TMC 2302
- **Thread:** Olive brown 140-denier UTC
- **Abdomen:** Latex strip colored with brown permanent marker
- **Rib:** Tying thread
- **Wing Case:** Mirage Tinsel
- **Wing Buds:** Light orange goose biot
- **Thorax:** Tying thread
- **Gills:** Oral-B Ultra Floss
- **Note:** Coat entire pattern except gills with Solarez UV resin.

LATEX CHIRONOMID PUPA (RED)

- **Hook:** #12-16 Daiichi 1260 or TMC 2302
- **Thread:** Red 140-denier UTC
- **Abdomen:** Latex strip colored with brown permanent marker
- **Rib:** Tying thread
- **Wing Case:** Mirage Tinsel
- **Wing Buds:** Light orange goose biot
- **Thorax:** Black 10/0 Veevus
- **Gills:** Oral-B Ultra Floss
- **Note:** Coat entire pattern except gills with Solarez UV resin.

MINI HOLLOW BOW TIE BUZZER (BLACK)

- **Hook:** #10-16 TMC 2457 or Daiichi 1120
- **Thread:** Black 70-denier UTC
- **Body:** Tying thread
- **Rib:** Silver holographic tinsel
- **Thorax:** Tying thread
- **Wing Case:** Pearl Flashabou
- **Wing Buds:** Orange goose biots
- **Gills:** Oral-B Ultra or Super Floss
- **Note:** Coat entire pattern except gills with Solarez UV resin.

LATEX CHIRONOMID PUPA (AMBER)

- **Hook:** #12-16 Daiichi 1260 or TMC 2302
- **Thread:** Olive brown 140-denier UTC
- **Abdomen:** Latex strip colored with amber permanent marker
- **Rib:** Tying thread
- **Wing Case:** Mirage Tinsel
- **Wing Buds:** Light orange goose biot
- **Thorax:** Tying thread
- **Gills:** Oral-B Ultra Floss
- **Note:** Coat entire pattern except gills with Solarez UV resin.

MINI HOLLOW BOW TIE BUZZER (RED)

- **Hook:** #10-16 TMC 2457 or Daiichi 1120
- **Thread:** Red 70-denier UTC
- **Body:** Tying thread
- **Rib:** Silver holographic tinsel
- **Thorax:** Tying thread
- **Wing Case:** Pearl Flashabou
- **Wing Buds:** Orange goose biots
- **Gills:** Oral-B Ultra or Super Floss
- **Note:** Coat entire pattern except gills with Solarez UV resin.

MINI HOLLOW BOW TIE BUZZER (BROWN)

- **Hook:** #10-16 TMC 2457 or Daiichi 1120
- **Thread:** Olive brown 70-denier UTC
- **Body:** Tying thread
- **Rib:** Silver holographic tinsel
- **Thorax:** Tying thread
- **Wing Case:** Pearl Flashabou
- **Wing Buds:** Orange goose biots
- **Gills:** Oral-B Ultra or Super Floss
- **Note:** Coat entire pattern except gills with Solarez UV resin.

MR. CHIRONOMID (OLIVE)

- **Hook:** #10-16 TMC 2457 or Daiichi 1120
- **Thread:** Black 70-denier UTC
- **Body:** Olive Hareline Synthetic Quill
- **Thorax:** Tying thread
- **Wing Case:** Mirage Tinsel
- **Wing Buds:** Brown goose biots
- **Gills:** Oral-B Ultra or Super Floss
- **Note:** Coat entire pattern except gills with Solarez UV resin.

MR. CHIRONOMID (TAN)

- **Hook:** #10-16 TMC 2457 or Daiichi 1120
- **Thread:** Black 70-denier UTC
- **Body:** Tan Hareline Synthetic Quill
- **Thorax:** Tying thread
- **Wing Case:** Mirage Tinsel
- **Wing Buds:** Brown goose biots
- **Gills:** Oral-B Ultra or Super Floss
- **Note:** Coat entire pattern except gills with Solarez UV resin.

MR. CHIRONOMID (YELLOW)

- **Hook:** #10-16 TMC 2457 or Daiichi 1120
- **Thread:** Black 70-denier UTC
- **Body:** Yellow Hareline Synthetic Quill
- **Thorax:** Tying thread
- **Wing Case:** Mirage Tinsel
- **Wing Buds:** Brown goose biots
- **Gills:** Oral-B Ultra or Super Floss
- **Note:** Coat entire pattern except gills with Solarez UV resin.

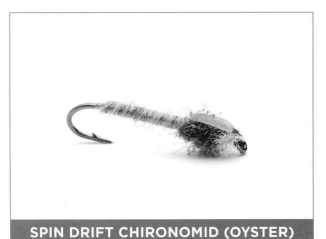

SPIN DRIFT CHIRONOMID (OYSTER)

- **Hook:** #12-16 Daiichi 1260 or TMC 2302
- **Thread:** Black 10/0 Veevus
- **Abdomen:** Oyster Spindrift yarn single strand
- **Rib:** Medium gold wire
- **Wing Case:** Latex strip colored with amber marker and coated with Solarez UV resin
- **Thorax:** Peacock herl
- **Gills:** Oral-B Ultra or Super Floss

SPIN DRIFT CHIRONOMID (CREAM)

- **Hook:** #12-16 Daiichi 1260 or TMC 2302
- **Thread:** Black 10/0 Veevus
- **Abdomen:** Cream Spindrift yarn single strand
- **Rib:** Medium black wire
- **Wing Case:** Latex strip colored with amber marker and coated with Solarez UV resin
- **Thorax:** Peacock herl
- **Gills:** Oral-B Ultra or Super Floss

SPIN DRIFT CHIRONOMID (BRACKEN)

- **Hook:** #12-16 Daiichi 1260 or TMC 2302
- **Thread:** Black 10/0 Veevus
- **Abdomen:** Bracken Spindrift yarn single strand
- **Rib:** Medium gold wire
- **Wing Case:** Latex strip colored with amber marker and coated with Solarez UV resin
- **Thorax:** Peacock herl
- **Gills:** Oral-B Ultra or Super Floss

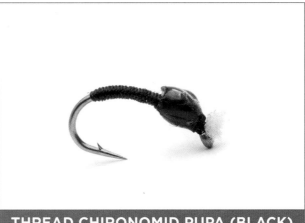

THREAD CHIRONOMID PUPA (BLACK)

- **Hook:** #12-16 Daiichi 1120 or 1130 or TMC 2457
- **Thread:** Black 10/0 Veevus
- **Abdomen:** Black Coats & Clark sewing thread
- **Wing Case:** Mirage Tinsel
- **Wing Buds:** Brown goose biot
- **Thorax:** Tying thread coated with Solarez UV resin
- **Gills:** Oral-B Ultra Floss

THREAD CHIRONOMID PUPA (SUMMER BROWN)

- **Hook:** #12-16 Daiichi 1120 or 1130 or TMC 2457
- **Thread:** Black 10/0 Veevus
- **Abdomen:** Summer Brown Coats & Clark sewing thread
- **Wing Case:** Mirage Tinsel
- **Wing Buds:** Brown goose biot
- **Thorax:** Tying thread coated with Solarez UV resin
- **Gills:** Oral-B Ultra Floss

RED BUTT CHIRONOMID (GREEN)

- **Hook:** #10-16 TMC 2457, Daiichi 1120 or 1130, or Dai-Riki 135
- **Thread:** Olive brown 70-denier UTC
- **Bead:** Pearl white glass
- **Body:** Clear Stretch Magic (.5 mm)
- **Rib:** Clear Stretch Magic (.5 mm) colored with green marker
- **Thorax:** Tying thread
- **Wing Case:** Latex colored with brown marker
- **Wing Buds:** Rust goose biots
- **Butt:** Colored with red Sharpie
- **Note:** Coat with Solarez UV resin.

THREAD CHIRONOMID PUPA (RED)

- **Hook:** #12-16 Daiichi 1120 or 1130 or TMC 2457
- **Thread:** Black 10/0 Veevus
- **Abdomen:** Red Coats & Clark sewing thread
- **Wing Case:** Mirage Tinsel
- **Wing Buds:** Brown goose biot
- **Thorax:** Tying thread coated with Solarez UV resin
- **Gills:** Oral-B Ultra Floss

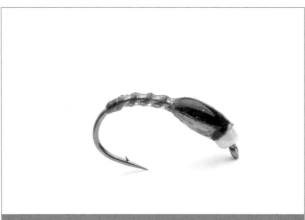

RED BUTT CHIRONOMID (RED)

- **Hook:** #10-16 TMC 2457 or Daiichi 1120
- **Thread:** Olive brown 70-denier UTC
- **Bead:** Pearl white glass
- **Body:** Clear Stretch Magic (.5 mm)
- **Rib:** Clear Stretch Magic (.5 mm) colored with red marker
- **Thorax:** Tying thread
- **Wing Case:** Latex colored with brown marker
- **Wing Buds:** Rust goose biots
- **Butt:** Colored with red Sharpie
- **Note:** Coat with Solarez UV resin.

RED BUTT CHIRONOMID (ORANGE)

- **Hook:** #10-16 TMC 2457 or Daiichi 1120
- **Thread:** Olive brown 70-denier UTC
- **Bead:** Pearl white glass
- **Body:** Clear Stretch Magic (.5 mm)
- **Rib:** Clear Stretch Magic (.5 mm) colored with orange marker
- **Thorax:** Tying thread
- **Wing Case:** Latex colored with brown marker
- **Wing Buds:** Rust goose biots
- **Butt:** Colored with red Sharpie
- **Note:** Coat with Solarez UV resin.

C-THRU CHIRONOMID (RED)

- **Hook:** #12-18 Daiichi 1260 or TMC 2302
- **Thread:** Black 140-denier UTC
- **Underbody:** Clear Stretch Magic (.5 mm)
- **Rib:** Clear Stretch Magic (.5 mm) colored with red Sharpie
- **Wing Case:** Mirage Tinsel
- **Wing Buds:** Light orange goose biot
- **Thorax:** Tying thread
- **Note:** Coat with Solarez UV resin.

BOW TIE BUZZER (OLIVE) (VARIATION ON GARY BORGER'S BOW TIE BUZZER)

- **Hook:** #10-16 TMC 5262
- **Thread:** Olive 140-denier UTC
- **Tail:** Oral-B Ultra or Super Floss
- **Body:** Tying thread
- **Rib:** Silver wire
- **Thorax:** Peacock herl
- **Gills:** Oral-B Ultra or Super Floss

C-THRU CHIRONOMID (OLIVE BROWN)

- **Hook:** #12-18 Daiichi 1260 or TMC 2302
- **Thread:** Black 140-denier UTC
- **Underbody:** Clear Stretch Magic (.5 mm)
- **Rib:** Clear Stretch Magic (.5 mm) colored with olive brown permanent marker
- **Wing Case:** Mirage Tinsel
- **Wing Buds:** Light orange goose biot
- **Thorax:** Tying thread
- **Note:** Coat with Solarez UV resin.

C-THRU CHIRONOMID (YELLOW/ORANGE)

- **Hook:** #12-18 Daiichi 1260 or TMC 2302
- **Thread:** Black 140-denier UTC
- **Underbody:** Clear Stretch Magic (.5 mm) colored with amber permanent marker
- **Rib:** Clear Stretch Magic (.5 mm) colored with dark orange permanent marker
- **Wing Case:** Mirage Tinsel
- **Wing Buds:** Light orange goose biot
- **Thorax:** Tying thread
- **Note:** Coat with Solarez UV resin.

NAKED BUTT CHIRONOMID (BROWN)

- **Hook:** #10-16 Daiichi 1260, TMC 2302, or Dai-Riki 280
- **Thread:** Brown 140-denier UTC
- **Body:** Bare hook shank
- **Rib:** Brown UTC wire
- **Thorax:** Tying thread
- **Wing Case:** Mirage Tinsel
- **Wing Pads:** Small brown holographic tinsel
- **Gills:** Madeira Glamour Prism White
- **Note:** Coat with Solarez UV resin.

NAKED BUTT CHIRONOMID (FLUORESCENT ORANGE)

- **Hook:** #10-16 Daiichi 1260 or TMC 2302
- **Thread:** Cream 140-denier UTC
- **Underbody:** Bare hook shank
- **Rib:** Fluorescent orange UTC wire
- **Thorax:** Tying thread
- **Wing Case:** Mirage Tinsel
- **Wing Pads:** Small brown holographic tinsel
- **Gills:** Madeira Glamour Prism White
- **Note:** Coat with Solarez UV resin.

NAKED BUTT CHIRONOMID (COPPER)

- **Hook:** #10-16 Daiichi 1260 or TMC 2302
- **Thread:** Brown 140-denier UTC
- **Body:** Bare hook shank
- **Rib:** Copper UTC wire
- **Thorax:** Tying thread
- **Wing Case:** Mirage Tinsel
- **Wing Pads:** Small brown holographic tinsel
- **Gills:** Madeira Glamour Prism White
- **Note:** Coat with Solarez UV resin.

GLITTER CHIRONOMID PUPA (GOLDEN BROWN)

- **Hook:** #16-22 Daiichi 1260 or TMC 2302
- **Thread:** Black 140-denier UTC
- **Underbody:** Tying thread
- **Rib:** Golden brown Canadian Llama glitter thread
- **Wing Case:** UTC Ice Blue Pearl Tinsel
- **Wing Buds:** Brown goose biot
- **Thorax:** Tying thread
- **Gills:** Oral-B Ultra Floss
- **Note:** Coat with Solarez UV resin.

GLITTER CHIRONOMID PUPA (RAINBOW)

- **Hook:** #16-22 Daiichi 1260 or TMC 2302
- **Thread:** Black 140-denier UTC
- **Underbody:** Tying thread
- **Rib:** Rainbow Canadian Llama glitter thread
- **Wing Case:** UTC Ice Blue Pearl Tinsel
- **Wing Buds:** Brown goose biot
- **Thorax:** Tying thread
- **Gills:** Oral-B Ultra floss
- **Note:** Coat with Solarez UV resin.

GLITTER MIDGE PUPA (PEARL)

- **Hook:** #16-22 TMC 2457
- **Thread:** White 140-denier UTC
- **Body:** Pearl Canadian Llama glitter thread
- **Wing:** Pearl glitter thread fibers
- **Thorax:** Black Superfine Dubbing

ICE DUB CHIRONOMID PUPA (BLACK)

- **Hook:** #16-22 Daiichi 1120 or 1130 or TMC 2457
- **Thread:** Black 10/0 Veevus
- **Abdomen:** Tying thread
- **Rib:** Silver wire
- **Wing Case:** Brown holographic tinsel coated with Solarez UV resin
- **Thorax:** Peacock Ice Dub
- **Gills:** Oral-B Ultra Floss

ICE DUB CHIRONOMID (CAMEL)

- **Hook:** #16-22 Daiichi 1120 or 1130 or TMC 2457
- **Thread:** Camel 8/0 UNI
- **Abdomen:** Tying thread
- **Rib:** Silver wire
- **Wing Case:** Brown holographic tinsel coated with Solarez UV resin
- **Thorax:** Peacock Ice Dub
- **Gills:** Oral-B Ultra Floss

ICE DUB CHIRONOMID PUPA (BLUE)

- **Hook:** #16-22 Daiichi 1120 or 1130 or TMC 2457
- **Thread:** White 70-denier UTC colored with blue marker
- **Abdomen:** Tying thread
- **Wing Case:** Brown holographic tinsel coated with Solarez UV resin
- **Thorax:** Peacock Ice Dub
- **Gills:** Oral-B Ultra Floss

STRETCHY CHIRONOMID PUPA (BROWN)

- **Hook:** #10-16 TMC 2457 or Daiichi 1120 or 1130
- **Thread:** Black 70-denier UTC
- **Body:** Tying thread
- **Rib:** Brown Spanflex or Sexi Floss
- **Thorax:** Tying thread
- **Wing Case:** Pearl Flashabou
- **Wing Buds:** Orange goose biots
- **Gills:** Oral-B Ultra or Super Floss
- **Note:** Coat with Solarez UV resin.

STRETCHY CHIRONOMID PUPA (RED)

- **Hook:** #10-16 TMC 2457 or Daiichi 1120
- **Thread:** Black 70-denier UTC
- **Body:** Tying thread
- **Rib:** Red Spanflex or Sexi Floss
- **Thorax:** Tying thread
- **Wing Case:** Pearl Flashabou
- **Wing Buds:** Orange goose biots
- **Gills:** Oral-B Ultra or Super Floss
- **Note:** Coat with Solarez UV resin.

STRETCHY CHIRONOMID PUPA (OLIVE)

- **Hook:** #10-16 TMC 2457 or Daiichi 1120
- **Thread:** Black 70-denier UTC
- **Body:** Tying thread
- **Rib:** Rust-brown Spanflex or Sexi Floss
- **Thorax:** Tying thread
- **Wing Case:** Pearl Flashabou
- **Wing Buds:** Orange goose biots
- **Gills:** Oral-B Ultra or Super Floss
- **Note:** Coat with Solarez UV resin.

BEND BACK CHIRONOMID (BLACK/RED)

- **Hook:** #12-16 Daiichi 1870
- **Thread:** Black 70- to 140-denier UTC
- **Body:** Tying thread
- **Rib:** Small red wire
- **Thorax:** Tying thread
- **Wing Case:** Mirage Tinsel
- **Wing Buds:** Brown Spanflex
- **Gills:** Oral-B Ultra Floss
- **Note:** Coat with Solarez UV resin.

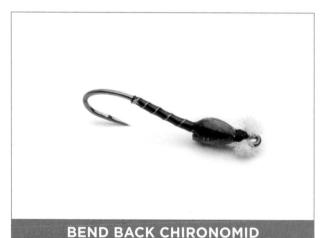

BEND BACK CHIRONOMID (BLACK/GOLD)

- **Hook:** #12-16 Daiichi 1870
- **Thread:** Black 70- to 140-denier UTC
- **Body:** Tying thread
- **Rib:** Small gold wire
- **Thorax:** Tying thread
- **Wing Case:** Mirage Tinsel
- **Wing Buds:** Brown Spanflex
- **Gills:** Oral-B Ultra Floss
- **Note:** Coat with Solarez UV resin.

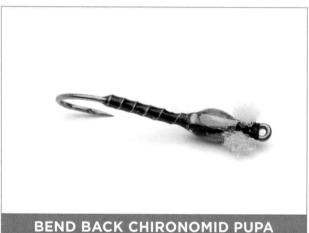

BEND BACK CHIRONOMID PUPA (BLACK/OLIVE)

- **Hook:** #12-16 Daiichi 1870
- **Thread:** Black 70- to 140-denier UTC
- **Body:** Tying thread
- **Rib:** Small olive wire
- **Thorax:** Tying thread
- **Wing Case:** Mirage Tinsel
- **Wing Buds:** Brown Spanflex
- **Gills:** Oral-B Ultra Floss
- **Note:** Coat with Solarez UV resin.

SPARKLE CHIRONOMID (SILVER)

- **Hook:** #12-16 Daiichi 1260 or TMC 2302
- **Thread:** Black 140-denier UTC
- **Bead:** White tungsten Canadian Llama
- **Underbody:** Silver tinsel
- **Rib:** Tying thread
- **Wing Case:** UTC Ice Blue Pearl Tinsel
- **Wing Buds:** White polyester yarn
- **Collar:** Olive brown Ice Dub
- **Gills:** Oral-B Ultra Floss
- **Note:** Coat with Solarez UV resin.

SPARKLE CHIRONOMID (GOLD)

- **Hook:** #12-16 Daiichi 1260 or TMC 2302
- **Thread:** Black 140-denier UTC
- **Bead:** White tungsten Canadian Llama
- **Underbody:** Gold tinsel
- **Rib:** Tying thread
- **Wing Case:** UTC Ice Blue Pearl Tinsel
- **Wing Buds:** White polyester yarn
- **Collar:** Olive brown Ice Dub
- **Gills:** Oral-B Ultra Floss
- **Note:** Coat with Solarez UV resin.

PAINTBRUSH LARVA

- **Hook:** #18-22 TMC 200R or Daiichi 1260
- **Thread:** Olive brown 70-denier UTC
- **Underbody:** Tying thread
- **Rib:** Dark olive paintbrush fiber
- **Head:** Tying thread

CARROT MIDGE PUPA

- **Hook:** #18-22 Daiichi 1260
- **Thread:** Orange 70-denier UTC
- **Underbody:** Tying thread
- **Rib:** Clear Stretch Magic (.5 mm)
- **Thorax:** Peacock Ice Dub
- **Bead:** Green glass

-8-

MIDGES FOR STREAMS AND RIVERS

High Post Midge

The day that really changed my fly fishing and fly tying was when I first fished the San Juan River over twenty-five years ago. What changed my fly fishing so drastically was that I didn't really have a clear idea of what a midge was and that what I was fishing was much too large.

I learned several important things: First, midges are not just smaller versions of the flies du jour. Second, midges are a separate species of insect, and the midges on the San Juan River are very small in size—if you wanted to catch fish, you would need to fish sizes starting from 22 down to 28. And third, fish feed heavily on these tiny insects all year long on the San Juan as well as in other tailwaters. I was highly motivated to learn all I could about midges and dedicated myself to studying this insect and to learning how to tie and fish this insect successfully.

My studies stimulated a desire to design a plethora of midge patterns in different shapes, colors, and sizes. I wanted to see how far I could push the envelope on design and use of fly-tying materials. I always try to find unconventional materials that I can use in tying my flies; I look at everything from the grass in Easter baskets to the silver lining of the bag holding Cheetos. My good friends Mark McMillian and Mark Tracy introduced me to the dollar stores and thrift shops, where a variety of items have the potential for use as fly-tying material.

Fishing midges in both moving waters (rivers and streams) and stillwaters (lakes and ponds) has become an integral portion of my fly fishing and fly tying. I generally use the term *chironomid* to represent the midges found in stillwaters and *midges* as the term for the insects found in rivers and streams; all midges are chironomids. Under closer inspection, both insects generally look the same no matter the size; however, I will make the thorax, wing pad, and breathing structure more pronounced in patterns that I design for lakes.

Midges can be tied in a variety of ways, and it is satisfying for me to design patterns that I can take out on the water to determine if the fish like them or not. There are thousands of species of midges worldwide, and coming up with midge patterns in different configurations usually results in success. I compiled my experimentation in a book called *Modern Midges: Tying & Fishing the World's Most Effective Patterns*. My goal was to show how fly tiers from around the world interpret the midge in its many forms. Many different patterns have been developed by fly tiers worldwide.

The fly patterns presented in this book illustrate the number of different materials that can be used to tie midges. Based on my observations regarding the proportion of the various anatomical parts of the midge pupa, I have come up with a few rules that I use when tying midge pupae for fishing in streams and rivers.

Studying the pupal stage of the midge, I observed that the majority of the abdomens of the insects I collected were roughly two-thirds to three-quarters the length of the pupa, and the thorax filled out the remainder. Therefore, many of the midge pupae I tie have an abdomen that corresponds to what I saw on the naturals. The same holds true for the large pupae found in lakes, but I often elongate the thorax to a third of the length when in reality the thorax is only

Spent midge adults adrift in the water's current.
BRIAN YAMAUCHI PHOTO

Beautiful rainbow trout that took a size 26 brown thread pupa on the Upper Flats of the San Juan River, a midge factory.

one-fourth the size of the pupa. The longer length of the thorax affords me a little more room to add wing buds and breathing gills; the abdomen is then two-thirds the length of the hook shank for the pupae I fish in lakes. Otherwise, the midge pupae I tie for the streams and rivers have abdomens that are two-thirds to three-quarters the length of the entire fly.

When viewing the midge pupa under magnification, I noticed that the segments of the abdomen were farther apart and fewer in number than in other orders of insects. I used this observation when tying up many of the midge patterns; instead of closer wraps for ribbing, I spaced them out. I don't necessarily do this for the entire midge pupa I tie; I sometimes make the ribbing much closer together and more in number.

The breathing structure of the midge pupa is an important element to add to patterns, and I tie a good number of pupae with the addition of gills. I am more apt to include the breathing gills on the midges I tie for stillwaters.

Tying midge pupae in colors other than the natural color schemes of brown, black, olive, cream, and olive brown is not a bad idea. I've designed many patterns using all the colors in the color spectrum and have found them to be effective in attracting the attention of trout. A great guide friend of mine, Bubba Smith of Fish Heads on the San Juan, once told me, "It ain't the arrow but the Indian," which I took to mean that it's often the skill level of the angler that catches fish and not the fly, although I still hold to Borger's size, shape, and color philosophy as an important factor in pattern design and presentation.

In some locations, the size of the midges being fished is an important element of catching fish in a given body of water. Case in point: I fished size 16-20 midge pupae when first learning to fish the San Juan nearly thirty years ago. When I changed the size down to 22-26, my fish-catching rate increased substantially.

I feel that the most important stages of the life cycle of midges are the larva, pupa, and at times the adult or a cluster of adults. In the morning I usually set up a rig using a midge larva as the point fly and a midge pupa as the dropper. My reasoning is based on the assumption that the larva is more active in the morning, thus more available to the fish. The hydraulics of the water often pushes the pupa higher in the water column; thus the pupa works well as the dropper. I personally fish the pupa stage almost exclusively when fishing midges.

The larva is the second stage of the midge's life cycle and is wormlike in appearance. The majority of midge larvae that I've observed are red in color due to their living in low-oxygen environments; thus the larvae store oxygen in the form of hemoglobin, which gives them their red coloration. Having said this, I also tie midge larvae in other colors such as clear, cream, tan, yellow, olive, and gray.

RED LACE LARVA

- **Hook:** #18-22 Tiemco 200R or Dai-Riki 270
- **Thread:** Red 70-denier UTC
- **Body:** Tying thread
- **Rib:** Clear Stretch Magic (.5 mm)
- **Head:** Tying thread
- **Note:** Coat the head with Solarez Bone Dry UV resin.

TYING THE RED LACE LARVA

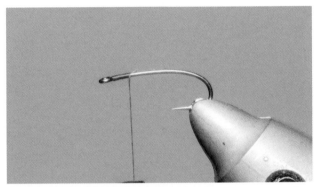

1. Attach tying thread behind the hook eye; secure and trim excess thread.

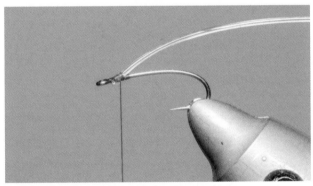

2. Tie in a 3-inch piece of clear Stretch Magic cord.

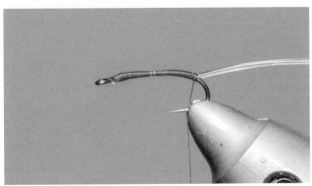

3. Take the bobbin and spin it counterclockwise to flatten out the thread; the un-spun thread will make a smooth transition layer. Wrap thread over the Stretch Magic in touching wraps toward the rear of the hook to the bend opposite the barb. Take care to cover all the Stretch Magic to form a solid color.

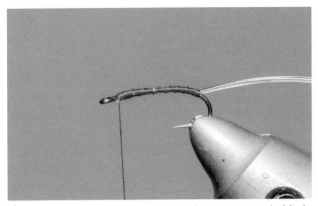

4. Wrap the thread forward in touching wraps to behind the hook eye.

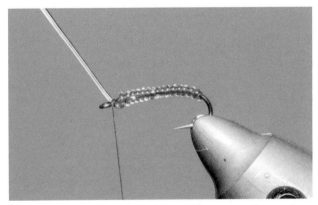

5. Wrap the Stretch Magic in touching wraps forward to the hook eye; secure and trim off the excess Stretch Magic. Wrap a small compact head and whip-finish, then trim excess thread. Coat the head with UV resin and set with UV light.

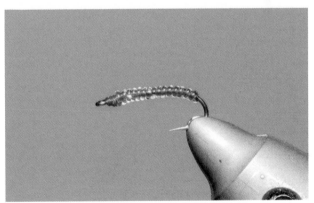

6. The Red Lace Larva mimics the coloration of larvae. I have found fishing the larva in the morning seems to work better, and I use a two-fly setup where I use the larva as the point fly and the midge pupa as the dropper. The hydraulics of water will push the pupa higher in the water column while the larva remains close to the streambed.

TWINKLE BROWN PUPA

- **Hook:** #18-24 Daiichi 1120
- **Thread:** Brown 16/0 Veevus
- **Body:** Brown Canadian Llama glitter thread
- **Thorax:** Tying thread colored with dark brown permanent marker and coated with UV resin
- **Flash:** Pearl Krystal Flash
- **Note:** Apply UV resin to the head of the fly. Other hook models include Daiichi 1130 and 1140; TMC 2487; and Dai-Riki 125.

TYING THE TWINKLE BROWN PUPA

1. Attach tying thread one eye width back from the hook eye; take several wraps to secure thread to hook and trim excess thread.

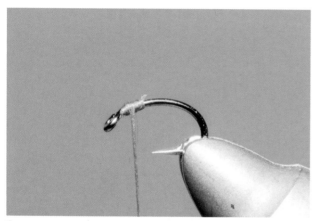

2. Attach tag end of Canadian Llama glitter thread to hook; trim excess if needed. Wrap tying thread over the glitter thread to the rear of the hook, continuing slightly down the hook bend as shown, then advance tying thread forward to one eye width back from the hook eye.

3. Wrap the glitter thread forward to one eye width back from the hook eye; tie off and trim excess.

4. Tie in a 1-inch strand of pearl Krystal Flash around the thread and fold the flash to the rear.

5. Trim the Krystal Flash to one-half the length of the body.

6. Build up a small, tapered thorax with thread, then whip-finish and trim thread. Apply a small amount of UV resin to cover the head and thorax and set with UV light.

7. The Twinkle Brown Pupa is one of many ways to design a midge pupa.

BIOT MIDGE ADULT

- ■ **Hook:** #20-26 Daiichi 1130
- ■ **Thread:** Black 16/0 Veevus
- ■ **Body:** Tying thread
- ■ **Rib:** Silver fine wire
- ■ **Wing:** White biot tied in tip first with curve up
- ■ **Hackle:** Black or grizzly Whiting Farms midge saddle
- ■ **Note:** Other hook models include Daiichi 1140 and 1180; Tiemco 2487, 2457, and 2488; and Dai-Riki 125.

TYING THE BIOT MIDGE ADULT

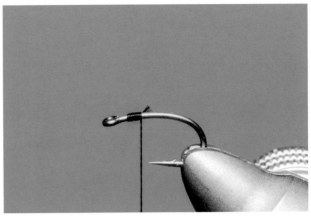

1. Attach tying thread one eye width the distance back from the hook eye.

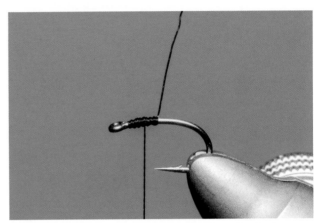

2. Tie in silver wire by the tag end. (The wire in the photograph looks black but is silver.)

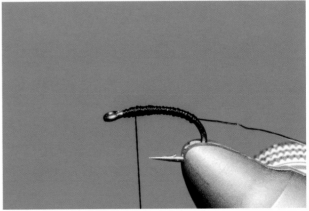

3. Wrap thread over the wire back to the hook bend opposite the barb, then wrap thread forward with touching wraps to the original tie-in point.

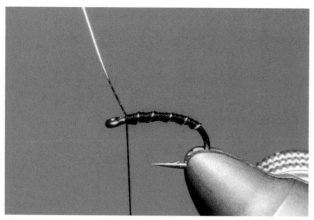

4. Wrap the wire forward in wide-spaced wraps, then tie off and trim excess wire.

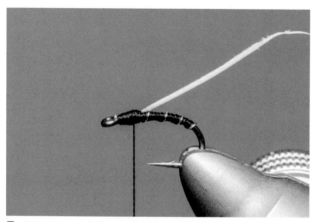

5. Select one white goose biot and trim the point off the tip of the biot. Tie in the tip of the biot so that the natural curve is facing up, away from hook shank. Trim the biot about two-thirds the length of the body.

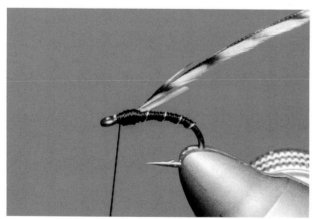

6. Tie on the hackle with the shiny side forward.

7. Make several wraps of the hackle, then tie off and trim excess hackle. Tie in a small head, whip-finish, and trim thread.

8. Rotate the hook over and trim the bottom of the hackle; this will allow the fly to sit flush in the surface film.

9. The Biot Midge Adult is a great pattern to replicate a freshly hatched adult midge resting on the surface of the water prior to taking flight.

Stream Midges

Note: Alternative hook models for Lil' Bop Pupa, Ultra Midge Pupa, Lil' Chiro Pupa, Flash Wing Midge Pupa, and Beadhead Stretch Lace Pupa include Daiichi 1560 or TMC 2488 or 2457.

LIL' BOP PUPA (BLACK)

- **Hook:** #18-26 Daiichi 1180
- **Thread:** Black 10/0 Veevus
- **Body:** Tying thread colored with black Chartpak marker
- **Rib:** Gold extra-fine Lagartun wire
- **Flash:** Pearl Krystal Flash
- **Thorax:** Tying thread colored with black Pantone marker
- **Coating:** Solarez thin UV resin

LIL' BOP PUPA (BROWN)

- **Hook:** #18-26 Daiichi 1180
- **Thread:** White 10/0 Veevus
- **Body:** Tying thread colored with sand Chartpak marker
- **Rib:** Gold extra-fine Lagartun wire
- **Flash:** Pearl Krystal Flash
- **Thorax:** Tying thread colored with dark brown Pantone marker
- **Coating:** Solarez thin UV resin

LIL' BOP PUPA (OLIVE)

- **Hook:** #18-26 Daiichi 1180
- **Thread:** Olive 10/0 Veevus
- **Body:** Tying thread colored with black Chartpak marker
- **Rib:** Gold extra-fine Lagartun wire
- **Flash:** Pearl Krystal Flash
- **Thorax:** Tying thread colored with tan Pantone marker
- **Coating:** Solarez thin UV resin

LIL' BOP PUPA (GRAY)

- **Hook:** #18-26 Daiichi 1180
- **Thread:** Gray 10/0 Veevus
- **Body:** Tying thread
- **Rib:** Gold extra-fine Lagartun wire
- **Flash:** Pearl Krystal Flash
- **Thorax:** Tying thread colored with gray Pantone marker
- **Coating:** Solarez thin UV resin

ULTRA MIDGE PUPA (LIGHT GRAY)

- **Hook:** #18-26 Daiichi 1180
- **Thread:** Gray 18/0 Nano Silk
- **Underbody:** Tying thread
- **Rib:** Clear Stretch Magic (.5 mm)
- **Wing Pad:** Tan goose biots
- **Thorax:** Tying thread
- **Gills:** Oral-B Ultra Floss

ULTRA MIDGE PUPA (YELLOW)

- **Hook:** #18-26 Daiichi 1180
- **Thread:** Yellow 16/0 Veevus
- **Underbody:** Tying thread
- **Rib:** Clear Stretch Magic (.5 mm)
- **Wing Pad:** Tan goose biots
- **Thorax:** Tying thread
- **Gills:** Oral-B Ultra Floss

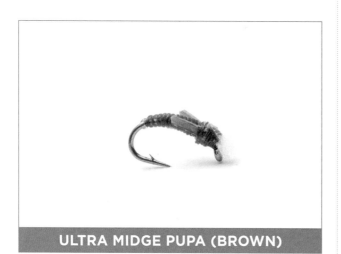

ULTRA MIDGE PUPA (BROWN)

- **Hook:** #18-26 Daiichi 1180
- **Thread:** Brown 18/0 Nano Silk
- **Underbody:** Tying thread
- **Rib:** Clear Stretch Magic (.5 mm)
- **Wing Pad:** Tan goose biots
- **Thorax:** Tying thread
- **Gills:** Oral-B Ultra Floss

ULTRA MIDGE PUPA (RUST)

- **Hook:** #18-26 Daiichi 1180
- **Thread:** White 16/0 Veevus colored with rust marker
- **Underbody:** Tying thread
- **Rib:** Clear Stretch Magic (.5 mm)
- **Wing Pad:** Tan goose biots
- **Thorax:** Tying thread
- **Gills:** Oral-B Ultra Floss

FLASH WING MIDGE PUPA (BLACK)

- **Hook:** #18-26 Daiichi 1180
- **Thread:** Black 18/0 Veevus
- **Body:** Black Canadian Llama glitter thread
- **Wing:** Pearl Krystal Flash
- **Thorax:** Black Superfine Dubbing

FLASH WING MIDGE PUPA (PEARL)

- **Hook:** #18-26 Daiichi 1180
- **Thread:** Black 18/0 Veevus
- **Body:** Pearl Canadian Llama glitter thread
- **Wing:** Pearl Krystal Flash
- **Thorax:** Black Superfine Dubbing

LIL' CHIRO PUPA

- **Hook:** #18-26 Daiichi 1180
- **Thread:** White 16/0 Veevus
- **Underbody:** Tying thread
- **Body:** Cream latex strip colored with tan Pantone marker
- **Thorax:** Tying thread colored with dark brown Pantone marker
- **Head:** Tying thread colored with tan Pantone marker
- **Note:** Coat body with thinned head cement.

UV LIGHT MIDGE PUPA

- **Hook:** #18-26 Daiichi 1140
- **Thread:** White 16/0 Veevus
- **Underbody:** Tying thread
- **Rib:** Pearl Krystal Flash
- **Wing Pads:** Orange goose biots
- **Wing Case:** UTC Ice Blue Pearl Tinsel
- **Thorax:** Tying thread colored with sand-colored Chartpak marker
- **Gills:** Oral-B Ultra Floss
- **Note:** Coat entire pattern except gills with Solarez Bone Dry UV resin.

ORANGE HOT PUPA

- **Hook:** #18-26 TMC 2488
- **Bead:** Orange mercury polyester
- **Thread:** Red 16/0 Veevus
- **Body:** Tying thread colored with orange Sharpie
- **Thorax:** Black Superfine Dubbing

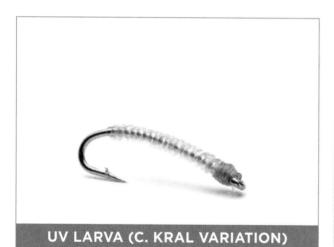

UV LARVA (C. KRAL VARIATION)

- **Hook:** #18-26 TMC 200R or Daiichi 1260 or 1270
- **Thread:** White 8/0 UNI
- **Underbody:** Tying thread with pearl UV Krystal Flash
- **Rib:** Clear Stretch Magic (.5 mm) or clear micro tube
- **Head:** Tying thread colored with tan permanent marker and coated with thinned head cement

BEADHEAD STRETCH LACE PUPA (CREAM)

- **Hook:** #18-26 Daiichi 1140
- **Bead:** Rootbeer polyester
- **Thread:** Cream 16/0 Veevus
- **Underbody:** Tying thread
- **Rib:** Clear Stretch Magic (.5 mm) or clear micro tube
- **Thorax:** Tying thread

C-THRU MIDGE

- **Hook:** #18-26 TMC 2488
- **Thread:** Light Cahill 8/0 UNI
- **Underbody:** Tying thread
- **Dorsal Line:** Rootbeer Krystal Flash
- **Rib:** Clear Stretch Magic (.5 mm) or clear micro tube
- **Head:** Tying thread colored with sand permanent marker

GUNMETAL PAINTBRUSH MIDGE

- **Hook:** #18-26 TMC 100
- **Thread:** Olive dun 8/0 UNI
- **Bead:** Blue gunmetal glass
- **Body:** Olive polyester paintbrush fiber
- **Thorax:** Peacock Ice Dub
- **Wing:** Pearl Krystal Flash

LACE LARVA (FLASHBACK)

- **Hook:** #20-24 TMC 200R or Daiichi 1260 or 1270
- **Thread:** Cahill 6/0 Danville
- **Body:** Tying thread
- **Rib:** Clear Stretch Magic (.5 mm)
- **Head:** Tying thread coated with UV resin

NUFF MIDGE PUPA

- **Hook:** #18-26 TMC 100
- **Thread:** Light Cahill 8/0 Danville
- **Underbody:** Tying thread
- **Dorsal line:** Two olive polyester paintbrush fibers
- **Rib:** Tying thread
- **Head:** Tying thread colored with tan permanent marker

LACE LARVA (RED)

- **Hook:** #18-22 TMC 200R or Daiichi 1260 or 1270
- **Thread:** Red 70-denier UTC
- **Body:** Tying thread
- **Rib:** Clear Stretch Magic (.5 mm)
- **Head:** Tying thread coated with UV resin

LACE LARVA (CREAM)

- **Hook:** #18-20 TMC 200R or Daiichi 1260 or 1270
- **Thread:** Light Cahill 8/0 Danville
- **Body:** Cream tying thread
- **Head:** Tying thread colored with tan marker and coated with UV resin

FLASH-WIRED MIDGE PUPA

- **Hook:** #16-20 Daiichi 1260 or TMC 2302
- **Bead:** White glass
- **Thread:** Tan 16/0 Veevus
- **Underbody:** Pearl Mirage Flashabou
- **Rib:** Small olive UTC wire
- **Tail:** White polyester yarn
- **Wing Buds:** Clear Medallion Sheeting, colored orange
- **Wing Case:** Clear Medallion Sheeting, colored brown
- **Thorax:** Olive brown Ice Dub

TRANSPARENT PUPA (TAN)

- **Hook:** #20-24 TMC 2487 or 2457
- **Thread:** White 16/0 Veevus
- **Underbody:** Tying thread colored with tan permanent marker
- **Body:** Clear Stretch Magic (.5 mm)
- **Rib:** Silver extra-small Lagartun wire
- **Head:** Tying thread colored with dark brown Pantone marker and coated with UV resin

TRANSPARENT PUPA (BROWN)

- **Hook:** #20-24 TMC 2487 or 2457
- **Thread:** White 16/0 Veevus
- **Underbody:** Tying thread colored with brown permanent marker
- **Body:** Clear Stretch Magic (.5 mm)
- **Rib:** Silver extra-small Lagartun wire
- **Head:** Tying thread colored with dark brown Pantone marker and coated with UV resin

GB BIOT PUPA (OLIVE)

- **Hook:** #20-24 TMC 2487 or 2457
- **Bead:** Rootbeer polyester
- **Thread:** White 16/0 Veevus
- **Body:** Olive Stalcup's goose biot
- **Thorax:** Rust Ice Dub
- **Wing Case/Breathing Tube:** White organza fibers

BEADHEAD LATEX PUPA (OLIVE)

- **Hook:** #18-22 TMC 2457
- **Thread:** White 16/0 Veevus
- **Bead:** Rootbeer glass
- **Body:** Latex strip colored with olive permanent marker and coated with thinned cement
- **Wing Buds:** Rust goose biots
- **Collar:** Rust Ice Dub

GB BIOT PUPA (BROWN)

- **Hook:** #20-24 TMC 2487 or 2457
- **Thread:** White 16/0 Veevus
- **Body:** Brown Stalcup's goose biot
- **Thorax:** Rust Ice Dub
- **Wing Case/Breathing Tube:** White organza fibers
- **Bead:** Rootbeer polyester

BEADHEAD LATEX PUPA (NATURAL)

- **Hook:** #18-22 TMC 2457
- **Thread:** White 16/0 Veevus
- **Bead:** Rootbeer glass
- **Body:** Natural latex coated with thinned cement
- **Wing Buds:** Rust goose biots
- **Collar:** Rust Ice Dub

BEADHEAD LATEX PUPA (ORANGE)

- **Hook:** #18-22 TMC 2457
- **Thread:** White 16/0 Veevus
- **Bead:** Rootbeer glass
- **Body:** Natural latex colored with orange marker and coated with thinned cement
- **Wing Buds:** Rust goose biots
- **Collar:** Rust Ice Dub
- **Gill:** Oral-B Ultra Floss

VICTOR PUPA (GOLDEN OLIVE)

- **Hook:** #18-24 TMC 2488
- **Thread:** White 16/0 Veevus
- **Bead:** Rootbeer clear glass
- **Body:** Golden olive Canadian Llama glitter thread
- **Rib:** Clear Stretch Magic (.5 mm)
- **Collar:** Rust Ice Dub

VICTOR PUPA (BLACK/WHITE)

- **Hook:** #18-24 TMC 2488
- **Thread:** White 16/0 Veevus
- **Bead:** Pewter brass
- **Body:** Pearl Canadian Llama glitter thread
- **Rib:** Clear Stretch Magic (.5 mm)
- **Collar:** Black peacock Ice Dub

ALIEN PUPA (RAINBOW)

- **Hook:** #18-24 TMC 2488
- **Thread:** White 16/0 Veevus
- **Bead:** Brown clear glass
- **Body:** Rainbow Canadian Llama glitter thread
- **Collar:** Peacock Ice Dub
- **Note:** Coat body with thinned head cement.

ALIEN PUPA (RUST)

- ■ **Hook:** #18-24 TMC 2488
- ■ **Thread:** White 16/0 Veevus
- ■ **Bead:** Rootbeer clear glass
- ■ **Body:** Rust Canadian Llama glitter thread
- ■ **Collar:** Peacock Ice Dub
- ■ **Note:** Coat body with thinned head cement.

ALIEN PUPA (PEARL)

- ■ **Hook:** #18-24 TMC 2488
- ■ **Thread:** White 16/0 Veevus
- ■ **Bead:** Rootbeer clear glass
- ■ **Body:** Pearl Canadian Llama glitter thread
- ■ **Collar:** Peacock Ice Dub
- ■ **Note:** Coat body with thinned head cement.

HANGING MIDGE (PEARL)

- ■ **Hook:** #16 TMC C230BL
- ■ **Thread:** Cream 16/0 Veevus
- ■ **Tail:** White poly yarn
- ■ **Body:** Tying thread
- ■ **Rib:** Pearl Krystal Flash
- ■ **Thorax:** Peacock herl
- ■ **Wing Bud:** Orange goose biots
- ■ **Wing Case:** Tan CDC
- ■ **Gill:** Tan CDC

HANGING MIDGE (GRAY)

- ■ **Hook:** #16 TMC C230BL
- ■ **Thread:** Gray 16/0 Veevus
- ■ **Tail:** White poly yarn
- ■ **Body:** Tying thread
- ■ **Rib:** Pearl Flashabou
- ■ **Thorax:** Peacock herl
- ■ **Wing Bud:** Orange goose biots
- ■ **Wing Case:** CDC colored with orange Sharpie
- ■ **Gill:** Tan CDC

CRYSTAL MIDGE PUPA (TAN/ORANGE)

- **Hook:** #18-24 Daiichi 1260 or 1270 or TMC 2302
- **Thread:** Cream 16/0 Veevus
- **Tail:** White poly yarn
- **Body:** Tying thread
- **Rib:** Pearl Krystal Flash
- **Thorax:** Tying thread colored orange
- **Wing Bud:** Orange goose biots
- **Wing Case:** UTC Ice Blue Pearl Tinsel
- **Gill:** White poly yarn
- **Thorax:** Colored orange
- **Coating:** Solarez Bone Dry UV resin

HIGH POST MIDGE (OLIVE)

- **Hook:** #18-26 TMC 2488
- **Thread:** Olive 16/0 Veevus
- **Tail:** Black Krystal Flash
- **Body:** Tying thread
- **Wing:** Black Antron fibers
- **Hackle:** Black Whiting Farms midge saddle hackle

HIGH POST MIDGE (BLACK)

- **Hook:** #18-26 TMC 2488
- **Thread:** Black 16/0 Veevus
- **Tail:** Black Krystal Flash
- **Body:** Tying thread
- **Wing:** Black Antron fibers
- **Hackle:** Black Whiting Farms midge saddle hackle

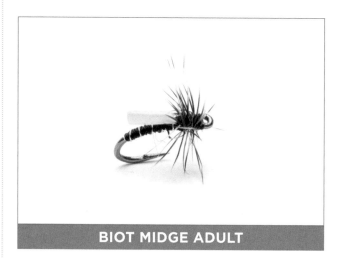

BIOT MIDGE ADULT

- **Hook:** #20-26 TMC 2488
- **Thread:** Black 16/0 Veevus
- **Body:** Tying thread
- **Rib:** Silver fine Lagartun wire
- **Wing:** White biot tied in tip first
- **Hackle:** Black or grizzly Whiting Farms midge saddle

STONEFLY SERIES

When I was working as a dishwasher for my dad in our Italian restaurant (yes, a Japanese American owning an Italian restaurant), the husbands of the waitresses who worked for my folks would often come in to visit their wives. I remember them talking about going fishing on the weekend; they often talked about the Salmonfly hatch on the famed Gunnison River.

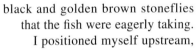

Golden Stonefly Nymph

I had absolutely no idea what they were talking about, and I was such a young kid that my folks often reminded me I was to be seen, not heard. I remember them saying the fish went crazy for these big flies and the fish they caught were large.

When I got older, other activities took the place of fishing; school sports and more hours spent helping my folks out at the restaurant left little time to go fishing except at local ponds where I could ride my bike. Eventually I forgot about the Salmonflies I had heard about as a young kid. When I graduated from high school and went to college, I fished as much as I could, but had to spend most of my time earning money for college and studying.

I was working on my master's degree when I became reacquainted with the Salmonfly, or as I learned later, the stonefly. Dave Vanloo and I had become good friends at the University of Northern Colorado, and we started to plan fishing trips on the weekends. We had heard the stoneflies were hatching on the Colorado River near the town of Hot Sulphur Springs, on the west side of the Continental Divide. We decided we'd make a day of driving over to Hot Sulphur Springs to camp out overnight and to fish the stonefly hatch; I still hadn't seen a stonefly yet.

We arrived at the river and found a place to camp, set up our tents, unfolded our sleeping bags, donned our fishing gear, and headed to the river. I knew that this stonefly hatch was similar to the legendary hatches in Montana, with large black and golden brown stoneflies that the fish were eagerly taking.

I positioned myself upstream, above the bridge next to the hotel in Hot Sulphur Springs, and was standing in the river when I noticed these gigantic bugs crawling up my waders.

I didn't have a stonefly pattern except for a weighted black Woolly Bugger, but decided to give it a try. I cast the fly slightly upstream, threw a mend in the line, and followed the drift downstream with my fly rod tip. As soon as the fly reached the end of the drift, I slowly started to lift the fly line out of the water for a re-cast; that's when the fish took my Woolly Bugger. I was rewarded with several nice-size rainbows that fell for my black Woolly Bugger.

While standing in the water I noticed some of the huge bugs flying around; I later learned that these were the adult stoneflies. I noted that they were not very adept in flight, and many dropped into the river. I watched as these adults struggled on the surface of the water, then suddenly disappeared into what looked like a toilet bowl flushing, as trout after trout sucked in these struggling insects. Since then I've put a considerable amount of study into all phases of the stonefly's life cycle.

To understand the stoneflies, I started to collect the nymphs in the streams I fished. I made a collecting net by attaching a door screen between two wooden dowels. My fishing partner would position himself above me, then kick up a rock in the streambed to dislodge any insects from the bottom, which would be trapped in the net downstream. We'd lift the net up and see what we collected. Collecting the insects made us more aware of what trout were feeding on and helped us understand better what flies we should be using to catch trout. A former student of mine suggested that I buy some collection bottles from the science department at Colorado State University to store what we had

A brown trout caught on the Big Thompson River goes back in the water after falling prey to a Golden Stonefly nymph. ISRAEL PATTERSON PHOTO

collected. He told me to make a preservative solution consisting of 50 percent water and 50 percent cheap vodka.

I collected several species of stoneflies, which were later identified as golden stonefly nymphs and black stonefly nymphs, and incorporated what I observed into the patterns I developed. My objective in designing stonefly nymphs is to construct them in such a manner as to give an impressionistic appearance rather that a full realistic rendition.

As a fly tier, I am continually looking for any type of material that I might use in the construction of the flies I tie. This is also true when looking for materials to tie stoneflies. Almost all the patterns I've tied have been nymphs; I seldom have encountered the adult, either because I'm not there for the hatch or because they hatch in the dark; I've seen evidence of the hatch by the empty nymphal shucks on the rocks. If fishing an adult pattern, I rely on a large yellow Stimulator and an adult tied out of foam.

Key Materials for Stoneflies

TAILING

My favorite materials to use for the tails of the nymph are goose biots or peccary hairs. The ease of tying with biots is evidenced by the number of patterns I've seen using biots for the tail. Ease of application is the main reason I use biots as my primary tailing material for stonefly nymphs. I had a good friend who liked to cement several strands of Microfibetts together to make his stonefly tails. When I can get my hands on a nice piece of peccary hair that is

not too dried out or with split fibers, I'll use the hair as tailing material.

DORSAL COVERING

Masking tape and brown Swiss Straw are the materials I use for making the dorsal covering and wing pads of the stonefly nymph. I discovered masking tape as a possible material for tying flies when I used it to secure my illustration board or drawing paper to the drawing board. When using permanent markers, I would sometimes continue the color off the illustration board or drawing, and I noticed that the markers' color pigment would not penetrate the surface of the masking tape, and repeated coatings with the markers would often result in a mottled effect.

I thought I'd experiment using masking tape as a body material for stoneflies. I took a strip of masking tape about 10 inches in length and folded the tape in half, putting the glued surfaces together. I then cut a long, tapered strip matching the width I wanted for the dorsal topping of the stonefly, with a wider, tapered end to be used for the wing case later in the tying process. I used a brown Marks-a-Lot to color the top of the masking tape (any permanent marker will work), allowed the marker to dry, which took seconds, and then dabbed the marker on the colored surface to create a mottled effect. I set this piece aside until I was ready to tie the nymph (I made several of these colored strips of masking tape for later use).

I also like to use any number of the vinyl-type materials available for fly tying to create the dorsal top of the abdomen and wing case, such as Thin Skin's Mottled Oak and

Quick release back into the water. Stonefly nymphs are present year-round and are available to a feeding trout looking for a larger meal. ISRAEL PATTERSON PHOTO

Mottled Bustard, Gator, and Fly Specks. Scud Back and Nymph Skins are materials that can also be used to create the dorsal top.

ABDOMEN UNDERBODIES

Using lead wire or lead-free wire underneath the abdomen helps add weight to get the stonefly pattern down deep. I often use a fine-diameter yarn to create a tapered underbody on which I'll add other materials to form the abdomen of the nymph. I flatten the underbody with pliers to create an oval cross-section prior to tying in the body materials. If using dubbing for the underbody, I prefer a coarse type of nymph dubbing in the coloration of the stoneflies I'm trying to imitate. I often make my own dubbing with acrylic yarn in the colors I want or by mixing different colors of yarn to create the color I want. A coffee grinder works well to blend up my dubbings; I cut the yarn into short pieces and pulse in short bursts in the grinder to create the

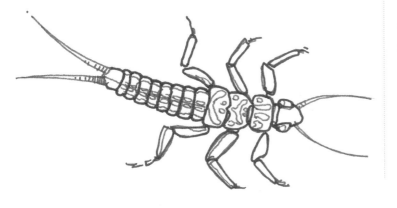

dubbing. I try to make a dubbing that is free of any pilling or those nasty little balls of yarn.

RIBBING

The ribbing of the stonefly nymph is an important aspect in the construction of the abdomen of the nymph. Ribbing materials such as D-Rib, Stretch Rib, standard tubing, oval gold tinsel, and copper wire colored in gold, brown, or black will create the appearance of a ribbed or segmented abdomen. I've been tying a new stonefly nymph using Cousin Iridescent Cord in gold with green highlights to create the abdomen of the stonefly nymph; Hareline's Diamond Braid is a good choice for this application, too.

Tubing materials that are either hollow or have a D-type cross-section are also great materials to create the segmented look; hollow tubing will compress to a flat shape when wrapped around the underbody and create the visual effect of a segmented body.

WING CASES

The wing cases I tie are simple: I often use the same materials that I used to create the dorsal covering and pull the material over to form a basic wing case. I like using Swiss Straw, turkey quill sections, various types of Thin Skin such as Gator and Mottled Bustard and Oak, masking tape, and Scud Back strips. Permanent markers give me the colors I want—usually in the brown, tan, and black color range—which covers most of the stonefly colors I fish in my region. Coating the wing case with UV resin gives it a more finished appearance.

There are many types of premade stonefly wing cases on the market that will give the stoneflies a more realistic look.

THORAX

All the thoraxes that I use in my designs follow the same coloration as the abdomen, but I apply it a tad bit heavier. I look for nymph dubbing in the golden stonefly nymph colors for the majority of my nymphs, using a light dun-colored ostrich herl for the gill structure of the nymph, which I palmer wrap through the dubbed thorax. I'll use a coarser, darker dubbing material for the larger, darker stonefly of the Pteronarcys family.

LEGS

I use Whiting Farms saddle hackles in colors such as brown, yellowish brown, black, and tan when creating legs by palmer wrapping the hackle through the thorax. The Coq de Leon saddle hackle from Whiting Farms makes a good mottled leg as well as their mottled Brahma hen back feathers. Whiting Farms dyed Euro saddle hackles create a wonderful mottled leg appearance. I like to use the hackles for the legs following Joe Brooks's stonefly in the round. Round rubber legs, MFC's mottled Sexi Floss, and goose biots make wonderful legs; I use and intersperse all these materials on the various patterns that I have developed.

HEAD

The head of a stonefly nymph is large and can be easily represented by using the same materials as for the wing case or by dubbing to create the impression of a larger head. The addition of antennae will enhance a more realistic appearance, but the majority of the stonefly nymphs I tie do not have antennae mostly because I am a lazy fly tier.

SPARKLE STONEFLY NYMPH

- ■ **Hook:** #8-12 Daiichi 1730
- ■ **Thread:** Yellow 3/0 Monocord
- ■ **Bead:** Black conehead bead sized to fit hook
- ■ **Weight:** Lead wire (.015)
- ■ **Tail:** Tan goose biots
- ■ **Underbody:** Tan nymph dubbing
- ■ **Abdomen:** Gold/green Cousin Iridescent Cord or Hareline's Diamond Braid
- ■ **Wing Case:** Brown mottled turkey
- ■ **Thorax:** Tan Life Cycle Dubbing
- ■ **Legs:** Tan round rubber
- ■ **Gills:** Light dun ostrich herl

TYING THE SPARKLE STONEFLY NYMPH

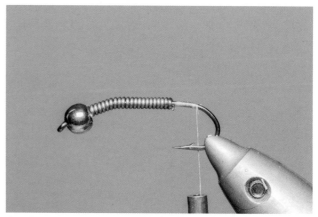

1. Add a conehead (or round) bead onto the hook and slide to the hook eye. Wrap the lead wire toward the bend of the hook to opposite the barb but slightly forward, saving space to tie in the tail. Slide the lead wire forward tightly to the back of the bead. Tie thread behind the bead and wrap thread back to the hook bend opposite the barb.

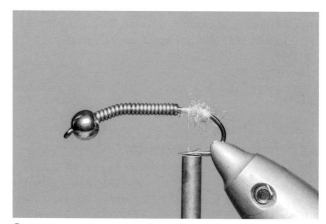

2. Dub a small amount of dubbing a form a small ball at the end of the abdomen, opposite the barb of the hook.

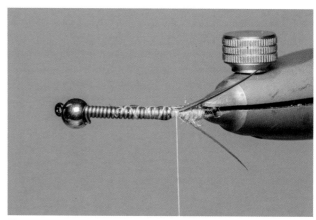

3. Tie in a goose biot, with the concave side facing the hook, directly in front of the dubbed ball; repeat on the opposite side. I make the tail about the length of the body or half the hook shank length.

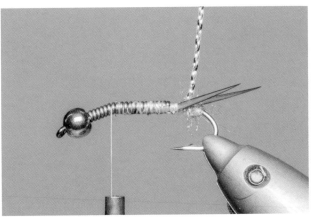

4. Wrap tying thread to the midpoint of the hook. Tie in the braid on the side of the hook shank and wrap thread over the braid back to the tail.

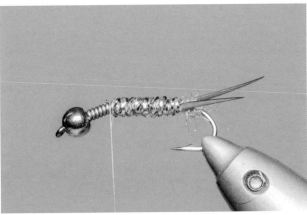

5. Wrap the braid forward with touching wraps to just beyond the midpoint of the hook shank. I like to tie my stonefly nymph to be 50 percent abdomen and 50 percent thorax and wing case.

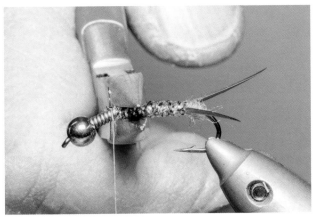

6. Flatten the abdomen with pliers to form an oval-shaped cross-section of the body.

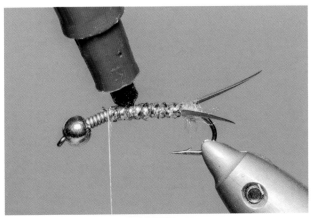

7. Color the top or dorsal side of the braided abdomen with a brown permanent marker.

8. Tie in the turkey quill wing materials; the wing case should be the same width or slightly larger than the width of the abdomen.

9. Tie in the ostrich herl.

10. Dub the thread with the tan nymph dubbing and wrap dubbing forward to the midpoint between the abdomen and the bead.

11. Tie in two pieces of round rubber on each side of the thorax.

12. Wrap dubbing in between the legs and the remaining space of the thorax to the bead.

13. Wrap ostrich herl in evenly spaced wraps to the bead; tie off and trim excess herl.

14. Fold the turkey quill over the thorax to form the wing case; tie off behind the bead and trim excess quill. Whip-finish and trim excess thread.

15. Trim rubber legs to desired length.

Fishing stonefly nymphs on the North Branch of the Poudre River in Cherokee Park. ISRAEL PATTERSON PHOTO

16. Coat wing case with Solarez Thin UV resin and set.

17. The Sparkle Stonefly Nymph was designed to fish off-colored waters where the extra flash on the abdomen might catch a fish's attention.

TAK'S MASKING TAPE STONEFLY NYMPH

- **Hook:** #8-12 Daiichi 1730
- **Thread:** Yellow 3/0 monocord
- **Bead (optional):** Gold brass bead or conehead bead
- **Weight:** Lead wire sized to fit hook size
- **Tail:** Tan goose biots
- **Abdomen:** Masking tape colored with brown permanent marker
- **Underbody:** Tan Life Cycle Dubbing
- **Rib:** Brown medium copper wire
- **Wing Case:** Masking tape
- **Thorax:** Tan Life Cycle Dubbing
- **Legs:** Brown Whiting Farms saddle hackle
- **Gills:** Light dun ostrich herl
- **Antennae:** Yellow Chinese boar fibers

TYING TAK'S MASKING TAPE STONEFLY NYMPH

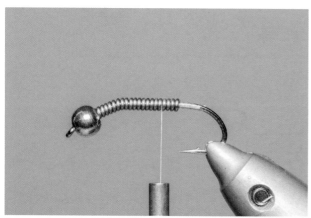

1. Add bead or conehead bead onto the hook and slide to the hook eye. Wrap the appropriate-size lead wire toward the bend of the hook opposite the barb but slightly forward, saving space to tie in the tail, masking tape, and butt end of the abdomen. Slide the lead wire forward tightly to the back of the bead. Tie thread behind the bead and wrap thread back to the hook bend opposite the barb.

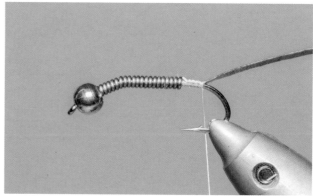

2. Measure a 10-inch piece of masking tape and fold it in half; glue sides together, making it as smooth as possible and with the edges of the tape even. Cut the masking tape lengthwise in an elongated "V" with the larger width approximately the width you plan for the wing case. This section of masking tape will be used for the dorsal covering, starting with the narrowest width at the tail. Color the masking tape with a brown permanent marker, such as a Marks-a-Lot or Sharpie. Cut the narrow end of the masking tape a fraction larger than the width of the hook shank. Tie in the narrow end of masking tape with the colored side facing the hook shank (the tape will be folded over, exposing the colored side).

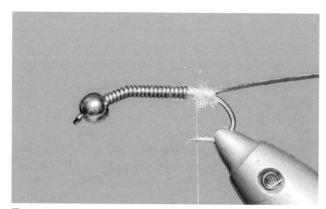

3. Dub a small amount of dubbing to form a small ball at the end of the abdomen, opposite the barb of the hook.

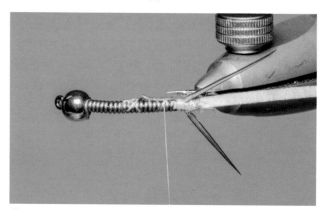

4. Tie in a goose biot, with the concave side facing the hook, directly in front of the dubbed ball; repeat on the opposite side. I make the tail about the length of the body or half the hook shank length.

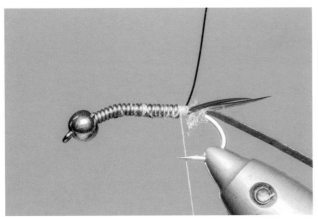

5. Tie in the wire in front of the tails on the far side of the hook.

6. Dub the abdomen and wrap the dubbing forward to just past the midpoint of the hook shank.

7. Fold masking tape over the top of the dubbed body and secure at the midpoint.

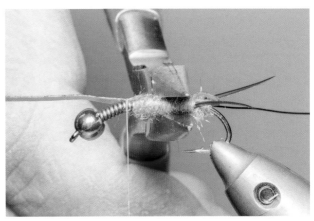

8. Flatten the abdomen with pliers to form an oval-shaped cross-section of the body.

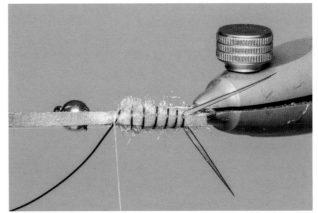

9. Wrap the wire forward with evenly spaced wraps—but not too closely; I make six to seven wraps to create the segmented body. Tie off and trim excess wire.

10. Fold the masking tape perpendicular to the hook shank and wrap tying thread directly in front of the masking tape.

11. Tie in the saddle hackle and ostrich herl.

12. Dub the tying thread with the dubbing for the thorax.

13. Wrap dubbing to the bead.

14. Wrap the ostrich herl in evenly spaced wraps to behind the bead; tie off and trim excess ostrich herl. The herl will form the gills of the stonefly nymph.

15. Wrap the saddle hackle in between the ostrich herl to behind the bead; tie off and trim excess hackle. The hackle will form the legs of the stonefly nymph.

16. Fold the remaining masking tape over the thorax to form the wing case; tie off then trim the tape. Whip-finish and trim excess thread. Dab the wing case and dorsal covering with the permanent marker to create a mottled effect if desired.

17. Trim excess masking tape and add dubbing in front of the wing case behind the bead.

18. Dab color on the masking tape with brown permanent marker to add mottled effect. The wing case is colored in the first phase of the tying process; however, you can dab the marker to enhance the mottled effect.

19. The Masking Tape Stonefly Nymph mimics the darker dorsal segmentation of the stonefly nymph.

Stonefly Nymphs

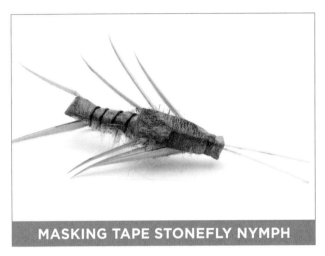

MASKING TAPE STONEFLY NYMPH

- **Hook:** #8-12 Daiichi 1730
- **Thread:** Yellow 3/0 monocord
- **Weight:** Lead wire (.015)
- **Tail:** Tan goose biots
- **Abdomen:** Masking tape colored with brown permanent marker
- **Underbody:** Tan Life Cycle Dubbing
- **Rib:** Brown medium copper wire
- **Wing Case:** Masking tape
- **Thorax:** Tan Life Cycle Dubbing
- **Legs:** Tan goose biots
- **Antennae:** Yellow Chinese boar fibers

STONEFLY NYMPH

- **Hook:** #8-12 Daiichi 1730
- **Thread:** Yellow 3/0 monocord
- **Weight:** Lead wire (.015)
- **Tail:** Tan goose biots
- **Abdomen:** Tan Life Cycle Dubbing
- **Rib:** Brown dyed Stretch Magic
- **Wing Case:** Tan/black Thin Skin Gator
- **Thorax:** Tan Life Cycle Dubbing
- **Legs:** Whiting Farms dark Coq de Leon hen feather
- **Antennae:** Yellow Chinese boar fibers

RUBBER-LEGGED STONEFLY NYMPH

- **Hook:** #8-12 Daiichi 1730
- **Thread:** Yellow 3/0 monocord
- **Weight:** Lead wire (.015)
- **Tail:** Brown goose biots
- **Underbody:** Golden Stonefly nymph dubbing
- **Abdomen:** Tan/black Thin Skin Gator
- **Rib:** Small gold wire
- **Wing Case:** Tan/black Thin Skin Gator
- **Thorax:** Golden stonefly dubbing
- **Legs:** Wapsi brown/gold round rubber legs

BLACK STONEFLY NYMPH

- **Hook:** #8-12 Daiichi 1730
- **Thread:** Black 140-denier UTC
- **Weight:** Lead wire (.015)
- **Tail:** Black goose biots
- **Abdomen:** Clear Scud Back
- **Underbody:** Black wool yarn
- **Rib:** Brown medium copper wire
- **Dorsal/Wing Case:** Brown/black Thin Skin Gator
- **Thorax:** Black Life Cycle Dubbing
- **Legs:** Black round rubber

HEN LEGGED GOLDEN STONEFLY NYMPH

- **Hook:** #8-12 Daiichi 1730
- **Thread:** Yellow 3/0 monocord
- **Weight:** Lead wire (.015)
- **Tail:** Brown goose biots
- **Underbody:** Golden stonefly nymph dubbing
- **Abdomen:** Tan/black Thin Skin Gator
- **Rib:** Medium brown wire
- **Wing Case:** Tan/black Thin Skin Gator
- **Thorax:** Golden stonefly dubbing
- **Legs:** Whiting Farms dark Coq de Leon hen feather

GOLDEN STONEFLY NYMPH

- **Hook:** #8-12 Daiichi 1730
- **Thread:** Yellow 3/0 monocord
- **Weight:** Lead wire (.015)
- **Tail:** Tan goose biots
- **Rib:** Small or medium brown D-Rib
- **Underbody:** Tan Life Cycle Dubbing
- **Dorsal Strip:** Masking tape colored with brown permanent marker
- **Wing Case:** Mottled wing material
- **Thorax:** Golden stonefly dubbing
- **Legs:** Whiting Farms dyed golden olive grizzly
- **Note:** Coat wing case and head with UV resin.

CDL GOLDEN STONEFLY NYMPH

- **Hook:** #8-12 Daiichi 1730
- **Thread:** Yellow 3/0 monocord
- **Weight:** Lead wire (.015)
- **Tail:** Tan goose biots
- **Rib:** Small or medium brown D-Rib
- **Underbody:** Tan Life Cycle Dubbing
- **Wing Case:** Mottled wing material
- **Dorsal Strip:** Masking tape colored with brown permanent marker
- **Thorax:** Golden stonefly dubbing
- **Legs:** Whiting Farms dark Coq de Leon hen feather
- **Note:** Coat wing case and head with UV resin.

BH BLACK STONEFLY NYMPH (GOLDEN)

- **Hook:** #8-12 Daiichi 1730
- **Thread:** Black 3/0 monocord
- **Bead:** Black
- **Weight:** Lead wire (.015)
- **Tail:** Black round rubber
- **Rib:** Medium black D-Rib
- **Underbody:** Tan Life Cycle Dubbing
- **Wing Case:** Black Swiss Straw
- **Thorax:** Gold/cream Woolly Bugger chenille
- **Legs:** Black round rubber
- **Antennae:** Black round rubber

GATOR CASE STONEFLY NYMPH

- **Hook:** #8-12 Daiichi 1730
- **Thread:** Yellow 3/0 monocord
- **Weight:** Lead wire (.015)
- **Tail:** Tan goose biots
- **Rib:** Small or medium brown D-Rib
- **Underbody:** Golden stonefly dubbing
- **Wing Case:** Tan/black Thin Skin Gator
- **Thorax:** Golden stonefly dubbing
- **Legs:** Whiting Farms dyed golden olive grizzly saddle
- **Antennae:** Yellow Chinese boar hair
- **Note:** Coat wing case and head with UV resin.

BH SWISS STRAW GOLDEN STONEFLY NYMPH

- **Hook:** #8-12 Daiichi 1730
- **Thread:** Yellow 3/0 monocord
- **Bead:** Gold
- **Weight:** Lead wire (.015)
- **Tail:** Tan goose biots
- **Rib:** Small or medium brown D-Rib
- **Underbody:** Tan Life Cycle Dubbing
- **Wing Case:** Brown Swiss Straw
- **Thorax:** Golden stonefly dubbing
- **Legs:** Whiting Farms dark Coq de Leon hen feather
- **Note:** Coat wing case and head with UV resin.

BH SPARKLE STONEFLY NYMPH

- **Hook:** #8-12 Daiichi 1730
- **Thread:** Yellow 3/0 monocord
- **Bead:** Gold brass bead
- **Weight:** Lead wire (.015)
- **Tail:** Tan goose biots
- **Abdomen:** Hareline's Bonefish Diamond Braid or gold/green Cousin Iridescent Cord
- **Underbody:** Tan nymph dubbing
- **Wing Case:** Brown mottled turkey
- **Thorax:** Tan Life Cycle Dubbing
- **Legs:** Tan round rubber

BH SWISS STRAW BROWN STONEFLY NYMPH

- **Hook:** #8-12 Daiichi 1730
- **Thread:** Yellow 3/0 monocord
- **Bead:** Gold
- **Weight:** Lead wire (.015)
- **Tail:** Brown goose biots
- **Underbody:** Tan nymph dubbing
- **Rib:** Medium copper wire
- **Wing Case/Dorsal Strip:** Brown Swiss Straw
- **Thorax:** Tan Life Cycle Dubbing
- **Gills:** Light dun ostrich herl
- **Legs:** Brown round rubber
- **Note:** Coat wing case and head with UV resin.

BH LATEX STONEFLY NYMPH

- **Hook:** #8-12 Daiichi 1730
- **Thread:** Yellow 3/0 monocord
- **Bead:** Gold brass bead
- **Weight:** Lead wire (.015)
- **Tail:** Tan goose biots
- **Abdomen:** Latex colored with golden brown permanent marker
- **Underbody:** White small-diameter yarn
- **Wing Case:** Turkey tail section
- **Thorax:** Tan Life Cycle Dubbing
- **Gills:** Light dun ostrich herl
- **Legs:** Whiting Farms dark Coq de Leon hen feather

BH UV STONEFLY NYMPH

- **Hook:** #8-12 Daiichi 1730
- **Thread:** Black 140-denier Danville
- **Bead:** Black nickel Canadian Llama
- **Weight:** Lead wire (.015)
- **Tail:** Dark brown goose biots
- **Underbody:** Black Spirit River UV dubbing
- **Rib:** Medium black tubing
- **Wing Case:** Turkey tail
- **Thorax:** Black Spirit River UV dubbing
- **Legs:** Black round rubber
- **Note:** Coat wing case and head with UV resin.

BH GATOR GOLDEN STONEFLY NYMPH

- **Hook:** #8-12 Daiichi 1730
- **Thread:** Yellow 140-denier Danville
- **Bead:** Black nickel Canadian Llama
- **Weight:** Lead wire (.015)
- **Tail:** Dark brown goose biots
- **Underbody:** Tan nymph dubbing
- **Rib:** Brown copper wire
- **Wing Case/Dorsal Strip:** Brown Thin Skin Gator
- **Thorax:** Tan nymph dubbing
- **Legs:** Brown Whiting Farms saddle hackle

BH PTERONARCY STONEFLY NYMPH

- **Hook:** #8-12 Daiichi 1730
- **Thread:** Yellow 140-denier Danville
- **Bead:** Black nickel Canadian Llama
- **Weight:** Lead wire (.015)
- **Tail:** Dark brown goose biots
- **Underbody:** Black wool yarn
- **Rib:** Brown medium tubing
- **Wing Case/Dorsal Strip:** Black Swiss Straw
- **Thorax:** Cream Wapsi Woolly Bugger chenille
- **Legs/Antennae:** Black round rubber
- **Collar:** Orange Ice Dub

BH NASTY GOLDEN STONEFLY NYMPH

- **Hook:** #8-12 Daiichi 1730
- **Thread:** Yellow 140-denier Danville
- **Bead:** Gold Canadian Llama
- **Weight:** Lead wire (.015)
- **Tail:** Tan goose biots
- **Underbody:** Cream wool yarn
- **Rib:** Gold wire
- **Wing Case/Dorsal Strip:** Black Thin Skin Mottled Oak
- **Thorax:** Cream Woolly Bugger chenille
- **Legs:** Yellow/black round rubber
- **Collar:** Brown Whiting Farms Coq de Leon hen hackle
- **Throat:** Cream nymph dubbing

-10-
STREAMER SERIES

Most of my streamer experience comes from fishing them in stillwaters. Early on in my river streamer education, forays with Keven Evans and Vince Wilcox helped shed light on how successful fishing streamers can be in moving water, and I eventually gained the confidence to experiment on my own. I fished a lake in Wyoming and caught several fish with small minnows filling up their gullet. That gave me the incentive to try and tie up some minnow-type

Mini Rainbow Minnow

patterns. I tied up a few streamer patterns and thought I'd give it a try. What amazed me as I fumbled along, trying to swing a streamer in deep pools, was witnessing a trout following my streamer as I retrieved it from a downstream presentation. The trout never took the fly due to my mishandling of the retrieve, but this incident had me hooked.

I had tied some of the more traditional streamer patterns, such as the Mickey Finn and the Muddler Minnow, but the first pattern that I developed

Chuck Esch and Jon Quillian discuss strategies for fishing the South Platte River. ISRAEL PATTERSON PHOTO

Andy Barkley prepares to return his catch to the waters of Grey Reef. ISRAEL PATTERSON PHOTO

is one that I eventually called Tak's Streamer, which has a yarn body and Zonker wing. As with all the patterns I design, I first wanted to get a close look at what I was trying to imitate, so I started collecting minnows that I could easily capture with the aquarium net I carry around. I observed that the minnows were very fast and adept at evading my net, and often all I could see was their big eyes and a glimpse of the flash from their sides. The Takaminnow came next, which had a Mylar body to capture the essence of the shiny, pearl-colored bodies of the minnows that I was collecting, and also a Zonker strip wing, which I didn't tie down in the rear for added action.

For warmwater species, fishing streamers is sometimes the only thing that will produce results, and I have developed a few simple variations that have served me well, including the Simple T Streamer and the Strip Teaser, both of which are Clouser-style flies designed to sink quickly, ride hook up, and jig on the retrieve.

Designing the Ghost Streamer

The Ghost Streamer is my riff on the tried and true beadhead Woolly Bugger. It incorporates materials that provide a silhouette of a minnow, reflecting the whitish side of the fish and creating a pulsing and pushing action as

it moves through the water. Oversize schlappen wrapped over an Estaz Chenille body provides additional movement and bulk to the fly when it is stripped through the water. I borrowed the mallard topping from Scott Stisser's D-style flies, where he folds a bronze mallard feather and places it along the top of the fly body to create a flattened look.

I also wanted to ensure that the fly would travel through the water in an upright fashion when pulled and not twist to its side when stripped. I like to use deer hair for many of the hopper and caddis patterns that I tie and remembered Al Troth using deer hair to tie his highly effective sculpin streamer pattern, so I thought I'd try it out on this pattern. I feel that the deer hair helps the fly move through the water in an upright manner much like Galloup's Zoo Cougar, provides more bulk on the front end of the fly, adds an unusual appearance to the streamer, and attracts fish.

Later, I developed the Sparkle Bugger, which is another Woolly Bugger variation. Instead of Estaz and schlappen, I use a product called Eyelash Yarn, which I discovered at our local Hobby Lobby. The yarn is made up of a flashy tinsel interspersed with threadlike material banded together on a small-diameter core similar in structure to UV Polar Chenille. It comes in many different color combinations.

GHOST STREAMER

- **Hook:** #12-16 Daiichi 700
- **Thread:** White 150-denier UTC
- **Bead:** Canadian Llama's nickel metal sized to match hook or conehead with eyes
- **Tail:** White blood marabou with a few strands of pearl Krystal Flash
- **Body:** Medium pearl Estaz Chenille
- **Hackle:** Whiting Farms white schlappen
- **Rib:** Silver wire
- **Back:** Mallard flank feather
- **Topping:** Natural deer hair
- **Collar:** Pearl Ice Dub
- **Weight:** Lead or substitute wire sized to match hook

TYING THE GHOST STREAMER

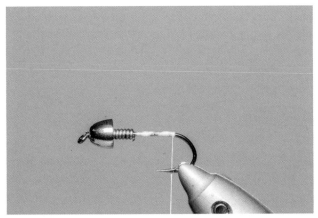

1. Attach bead to the hook and slide to the hook eye. Attach an appropriate-size lead wire behind the bead and wrap to the midpoint of the hook, then slide the lead forward to fit snuggly behind the bead. Attach tying thread behind the lead wire and wrap in spiral wraps to the hook bend opposite the barb. Trim excess thread.

2. Prepare a marabou feather by trimming the stem to half the length of the feather; I slip the tips of my scissors between the herls of the marabou to cut the stem. Measure the tip of the marabou feather to extend the length of the hook shank beyond the hook bend. Grasp the marabou feather and place on top of the hook shank. Tie in the marabou with several tight wraps, then wrap the tying thread forward in spiral wraps to the rear of the lead.

3. Trim excess marabou. Tie in two strands of pearl Krystal Flash to each side of the tail about the length of the tail.

4. Prepare the Estaz by pulling some of the material from the tag end, then tie in the Estaz by the tag end directly in front of the tail.

5. Tie in the silver wire at the hook bend and advance the thread to the bead.

6. Wrap Estaz to the bead.

7. Prepare the schlappen by trimming some of the fibers at the base of the stem, then tie in the feather at the leading edge of the Estaz. Tie the schlappen feather so that the shiny side of the feather is facing toward the hook eye.

8. Wrap the schlappen in evenly spaced wraps back toward the hook bend at the base of the marabou tail. When you reach the hook bend, secure the feather with the wire, then proceed to wrap the wire in evenly spaced wraps over the feather stem to secure the feather to the hook. (I sometimes will attach the schlappen feather with pair of old English-style hackle pliers and allow to hang down.) Grasp the wire and wrap over the schlappen feather to trap the stem and then wrap forward in evenly spaced wraps to the bead; tie off and trim excess wire.

9. Fold the front edge of the schlappen feather back toward the rear of the hook and wrap several wraps of thread over the fibers to force them to fold backwards, much like you would a wet-fly hackle.

Jim Browning releases another fine example of a brown trout caught on a streamer. JIM BROWNING PHOTO

10. Prepare the mallard flank feather by removing all of the down from the stem. Place the flank feather over the top of the body (the flank feather should be as long as the fly body) and tie it in at the front edge of the body. Dub on a small amount of pearl Ice Dub and form a collar behind the bead.

11. Prepare and stack the deer hair. The amount of hair varies with the size of the hook; use an amount equal to one-half to one-quarter the size of a pencil diameter. Measure the deer hair to one-half the length of the body and trim the butts even. Tie in the deer hair causing the butt ends to flare; hold the hair in place while tightening the tying thread, and do not allow hair to spin around the hook. Whip-finish and trim excess thread.

Designing the Mini Minnow

I developed the Mini Minnow series to imitate the forage fish—fathead minnows—I had seen in the mouths of fish I caught in some of the lakes and rivers I fish in Wyoming and Colorado: Lake John, Delaney Butte, and Lake Hattie, and the Grey Reef, Little Snake, and North Platte Rivers. These baitfish have pearlescent sides, dark greenish-olive backs, and big silver eyes with black pupils.

I had the opportunity of tying across the aisle from Enrico Puglisi, and from time to time I'd watch him tying his fabled saltwater baitfish patterns. He tied his patterns by taking some of his body material, such as EP Fibers, and pulling out the amount he needed, then pulling slightly on both ends of the fibers to create a tapered end. He would attach the fibers to his hook in the middle, take several wraps to secure them, and then fold them over to create a baitfish shape to his pattern. He would continue tying, adding various colors for the baitfish he was imitating. This gave me the basis for how I might create my Mini Minnow.

What I needed to create was about one-tenth the size of the patterns Puglisi tied, so I went searching for suitable materials. His EP Fibers were too rigid for the pattern I had envisioned in my mind; I wanted to create a very small minnow pattern.

For my needs, Senyo's Laser Dub was perfect for the body. When applied to the shank in the same manner as Enrico Puglisi's, it provides the impression of a minnow body with iridescent scales. What I liked about the dubbing was the crinkly nature of the material, the soft texture, and its ability to keep its shape when tied onto the hook and folded back to form the body. Brushing out the dubbing helped blend the colors together and form the shape I desired.

These fish move fast in the water, and when chased by a predator, I think that the shape, color, and eyes of the fish are the most outstanding features, so this pattern has prominent 3-D eyes coated with a UV resin for durability.

I fished the prototype pattern in both lakes and streams, and not only targeted trout but also warmwater species. I had great success with the pattern, which prompted me to try to mimic other colors of minnow; I came up with a rainbow fry, brown fry, shad fry, and fathead minnow, which I suspect was what I saw the first time.

I've been fishing this pattern off and on for the past ten years, mostly in lakes, for trout as well as for warmwater species such as crappie, bluegill, and largemouth and smallmouth bass.

The Mini Minnow was tied using a UV resin head and 3-D molded eyes, but recently I've been tying the pattern and omitting the use of the UV resin and have started using Flymen Fish Masks, which slide easily over the hook eye to form the head; I add 3-D molded eyes, which come in a package, then cover the eyes with Solarez Bone Dry UV resin. I often put a small amount of gel superglue on the thread of the head before attaching the Fish Mask; tie a

small dam of thread behind the eye if you need added security to hold the head in place. The Fish Mask is convenient to use and cuts down the tying time considerably. I have also created a Rainbow Mini Minnow and am looking to develop a Brown Trout version.

MINI MINNOW (VARIATION OF ENRICO PUGLISI'S STYLE)

- **Hook:** #8-10 Dai-Riki 930 or 7057 Salmon Egg
- **Thread:** White 70-denier UTC
- **Dorsal:** Olive Arizona Simi-Seal Dubbing
- **Body:** White Senyo's Laser Dub
- **Belly:** White Senyo's Laser Dub
- **Eyes:** Pearl 3-D molded eyes
- **Head:** UV resin colored with olive marker or Flymen's Fish Mask with eyes

TYING THE MINI MINNOW

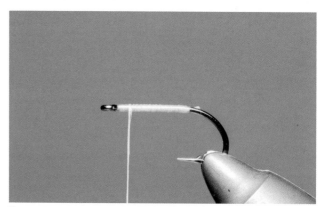

1. Attach tying thread behind the hook eye and wrap to the midpoint of the hook shank; trim excess thread.

2. Grasp a small amount of white Senyo's Laser Dub and pull fibers apart slightly to form a tapered piece of Laser Dub at both ends of the yarn. Position the dubbing lengthwise along the top of the hook shank in the middle of the bundle of dubbing and tie in with several wrap at the one-fourth position, then fold dubbing over and make two wraps folding the dubbing rearward; this will form the top half of the body.

3. Turn the hook upside down so that the point is facing up. Repeat the same procedure as for the top of the body to form the belly of the minnow.

4. Turn the hook so that the body is facing up. Take a very small amount of olive Arizona Simi-Seal, pull it apart slightly, and then tie in on top of the hook shank to form the dorsal section. Fold the dubbing over to form the dorsal top of the minnow.

5. Wrap the thread over the front edge of the minnow with enough wraps to sweep all of the body toward the rear. Form a small head and then whip-finish and trim excess thread.

6. Place a small amount of gel superglue on the side of the head and place a 3-D molded eye between the hook eye and the body; repeat the process on the opposite side of the hook. Apply UV resin to form the head; I prefer to use Solarez Thin, which has enough viscosity to form a head. Put enough UV resin on the head to form a small bubble-type head. Set with UV light.

7. Rotate the hook and apply a small amount of a thin UV resin to form a small underside of the head.

8. Set UV resin with UV light. Color top of head with olive permanent marker.

9. The Mini Minnow gives the profile of the basic shape of a minnow with a darker dorsal back, a light transparent body, and well-defined eyes to give this pattern the fleeting glimpse of a fleeing minnow. I would suggest using Flymen's Fish Mask in place of the molded 3-D eyes and UV resin head as an alternative.

Streamers

GHOST STREAMER (CHARTREUSE/BLACK)

- **Hook:** #6-12 Daiichi 1720
- **Thread:** Black 140-denier Danville
- **Bead:** Nickel metal
- **Tail:** Chartreuse marabou
- **Tail Highlights:** Pearl Krystal Flash
- **Body:** Black Estaz Chenille
- **Hackle:** Black saddle hackle
- **Underwing:** Natural mallard flank feather
- **Wing:** Black deer hair
- **Collar:** Black Ice Dub

GHOST STREAMER (OLIVE BROWN)

- **Hook:** #6-12 Daiichi 1720
- **Thread:** Brown 140-denier Danville
- **Bead:** Gold metal
- **Tail:** Olive dyed grizzly marabou
- **Tail Highlights:** Olive Krystal Flash
- **Body:** Olive brown Estaz Chenille
- **Hackle:** Brown schlappen hackle
- **Underwing:** Brown mallard flank feather
- **Wing:** Brown deer hair
- **Collar:** Olive brown Ice Dub

GHOST STREAMER (BROWN)

- **Hook:** #6-12 Daiichi 1720
- **Thread:** Brown 140-denier Danville
- **Bead:** Gold metal
- **Tail:** Olive dyed grizzly marabou
- **Tail Highlights:** Rootbeer Krystal Flash
- **Body:** Olive brown Estaz Chenille
- **Hackle:** Brown saddle hackle
- **Underwing:** Brown mallard flank feather
- **Wing:** Brown deer hair
- **Collar:** Olive brown Ice Dub

MINI RAINBOW MINNOW

- **Hook:** #10-12 Dai-Riki 950
- **Bead:** Mercury
- **Thread:** White 140-denier UTC
- **Body:** White Senyo's Laser Dub
- **Dorsal:** Custom Blend Dragon Dub
- **Side:** Pink Senyo's Laser Dub
- **Lateral Line:** Pearl hareline chironomid braid
- **Eyes:** 3-D molded eyes
- **Head:** Cover with thin Clear Cure Goo
- **Marker:** Black Sharpie

LATERAL MINI RAINBOW MINNOW

- **Hook:** #8-10 Dai-Riki 950 or 930
- **Thread:** White 140-denier UTC
- **Body:** White Sanyo's Laser Dub
- **Dorsal:** Custom Blend Dragon Dub
- **Side:** Sanyo's Laser Pink Dubbing
- **Lateral Line:** Pearl hareline chironomid braid
- **Eyes:** Metz 1/8 molded eyes
- **Head:** Cover with UV resin
- **Marker:** Black and light blue Sharpie

MINI ALVIN MINNOW

- **Hook:** #10-12 Dai-Riki 950
- **Bead:** Mercury
- **Thread:** White 140-denier UTC
- **Body:** White Senyo's Laser Dub
- **Dorsal:** Custom Blend Dragon Dub
- **Side:** Brown Senyo's Laser Dub
- **Lateral Line:** Pearl hareline chironomid braid
- **Eyes:** 3-D molded eyes
- **Head:** Cover with thin UV resin
- **Marker:** Black Sharpie

SIMPLE T STREAMER

- **Hook:** #4-10 Daiichi 1750
- **Thread:** White 140-denier UTC
- **Eyes:** Pearl white Spirit River Real Eyes Plus
- **Body:** Pearl Krystal Flash
- **Belly:** Minnow body Senyo's Laser Dub
- **Dorsal:** Olive Senyo's Laser Dub

SIMPLE T STREAMER (RAINBOW)

- **Hook:** #4-10 Daiichi 1750
- **Thread:** White 140-denier UTC
- **Eyes:** Pearl white Spirit River Real Eyes Plus
- **Body:** Pearl Krystal Flash
- **Belly:** Minnow body Senyo's Laser Dub
- **Mid:** Hot pink Senyo's Laser Dub
- **Dorsal:** Olive Senyo's Laser Dub

SPARKLE STREAMER (HOLOGRAPHIC GOLDIE)

- **Hook:** #4-8 Daiichi 1750
- **Thread:** White 70-denier UTC
- **Bead:** Gold conehead
- **Tail:** White marabou
- **Body:** Holographic gold and white Eyelash Yarn
- **Hackle:** White Nature's Spirit schlappen feather
- **Collar:** Pearl Ice Dub

SPARKLE STREAMER (HOLOGRAPHIC FIREWORKS)

- **Hook:** #4-8 Daiichi 1750 or 1710, TMC 3761 or 5262, Mustad 9672, or Dai-Riki 730
- **Thread:** Black 70-denier UTC
- **Bead:** Black nickel conehead
- **Tail:** Black marabou
- **Body:** Fireworks Eyelash Yarn
- **Hackle:** Black Nature's Spirit schlappen feather
- **Collar:** Black Ice Dub

SPARKLE BUGGER (CHARTREUSE LIME)

- **Hook:** #4-8 Daiichi 1750
- **Thread:** White 70-denier UTC
- **Bead:** Gold conehead
- **Tail:** Chartreuse marabou
- **Body:** Green Eyelash Yarn
- **Hackle:** Yellow/grizzly Whiting Farms hen saddle feather
- **Collar:** Chartreuse Ice Dub

SPARKLER BUGGER (BLACK)

- **Hook:** #4-8 Daiichi 1750
- **Thread:** Black 70-denier UTC
- **Bead:** Black conehead
- **Tail:** Black marabou
- **Body:** Black Eyelash Yarn
- **Hackle:** Black Nature's Spirit schlappen feather
- **Collar:** Black Ice Dub

STREAKER STREAMER (OLIVE)

- **Hook:** #4-10 Daiichi 1750
- **Thread:** White 140-denier UTC
- **Bead:** Silver conehead
- **Tail:** 5 strands pearl Krystal Flash
- **Lateral Line:** 5 strands pearl Krystal Flash wrapped along hook shank
- **Top:** Olive Emulator Tinsel
- **Belly:** Pearl Emulator Tinsel

STRIP TEASE STREAMER (OLIVE)

- **Hook:** #4-10 Daiichi 1780
- **Thread:** White 140-denier UTC
- **Eyes:** Pearl white Spirit River Real Eyes Plus
- **Belly:** Minnow body Senyo's Laser Dub
- **Dorsal:** Olive/black barred rabbit Zonker strip

STRIP TEASE STREAMER (SALT N PEPPER)

- **Hook:** #4-10 Daiichi 1780
- **Thread:** White 140-denier UTC
- **Eyes:** Pearl white Spirit River Real Eyes Plus
- **Belly:** Minnow body Senyo's Laser Dub
- **Dorsal:** Black and white barred rabbit Zonker strip

TAKAMINNOW (BARRED OLIVE)

- **Hook:** #8-10 TMC 5262 or Mustad 9672
- **Thread:** White 140-denier UTC
- **Bead:** Gold metal
- **Body:** Pearl Mylar braid
- **Wing:** Olive barred Zonker strip
- **Throat:** Tying thread colored with red permanent marker

TAKAMINNOW (BARRED NATURAL)

- **Hook:** #8-10 TMC 5262 or Mustad 9672
- **Thread:** White 140-denier UTC
- **Bead:** Silver metal
- **Body:** Pearl Mylar braid
- **Wing:** White barred Zonker strip
- **Throat:** Tying thread colored with red permanent marker

TAKAMINNOW (BARRED CHARTREUSE)

- **Hook:** #8-10 TMC 5262 or Mustad 9672
- **Thread:** White 140-denier UTC
- **Bead:** Gold metal
- **Body:** Gold Mylar braid
- **Wing:** Olive barred Zonker strip
- **Throat:** Tying thread colored with red permanent marker

-11-
STILLWATER SERIES

The first time I fished a lake with a fly rod, I just stood there looking out over the water with not a clue as to what to do. My lack of knowledge of fly fishing stillwaters motivated me on a lifelong quest to learn as much as I can about how to fish stillwaters—from entomology to fly-fishing techniques and presentation.

Static Damsel Nymph

The big questions from the beginning revolved around location of the fish and how to catch them. In chapter 14 I share some lake fly-fishing techniques and explain what I have learned concerning basic entomology, equipment, and strategies that will help the beginning fly fisher when fishing stillwaters.

In this chapter I will explain what I've learned about the basic foods that are important for stillwater trout based on my fishing experiences in Colorado, Wyoming, and to a lesser extent Utah and Montana. From reading and talking with many anglers around the country, I learned that their experiences are similar to mine, and I suspect that this basic information holds true for much of the stillwaters we fish. I know one thing for certain: I've only scratched the surface of my understanding of fishing lakes, reservoirs, and ponds.

Damsels

Damsel nymphs have three large, caudal-like tails (gills), a long segmented abdomen approximately two-thirds the length of the hook shank, six legs, a thorax that equals one-third of its total length, a head slightly larger than the width of the thorax, and prominent eyes.

From around mid-May into July is prime time for damsels on local stillwaters. As soon as the water starts to warm, they begin their migration toward shore, where they climb onto weed tops or reeds—anything sticking out of the water—to hatch. I've often been out on the water in my belly boat and have had the nymph crawl up onto the surface of the boat. I've sat mesmerized watching the whole hatching process take place, often forgetting to fish. The nymph will crawl out of its shuck and sit there pumping blood into its wing and other body parts; it's amazing to watch the wings take shape. During this migration, trout will often key in to the nymphs and can be caught with damsel nymph patterns at all water levels.

When the nymphs swim, they have a distinct side-to-side movement that propels them through the water. This movement is best duplicated with the use of marabou or rabbit for the most part, combined with a jerky type of retrieve. Fishing the damsel nymphs with either a floating line or an intermediate line can provide some of the best action for the early parts of summer.

Another interesting trait that damsel nymphs exhibit is a distinct pause for short periods of time before continuing on their journey to shore. Instead of trying to create movement, I wanted to design a damsel nymph at rest that I could fish with the vertical approach. In the vertical approach I will present the damsel nymph hanging in the water column straight down from a strike indicator. As the water settles, I give the line a short jerk with my fly rod tip then stop; after a few seconds I'll start a slow hand-over-hand retrieve, then stop and start the process over again. This quick jerk starts up the movement to put the damsel

Brian Yamauchi's cutthroat trout displays the colors of the mating season. This beautiful "cutty" fell victim to a damsel nymph while chasing it toward shore.

nymph that was resting in the water column to shore to hatch into an adult. I mention this technique later in my stillwater fishing techniques chapter and call it the Bow Tie Boogie, which I use for chironomid fishing as well as with any other insects found in lakes.

The Static Damsel Nymph is built on Daiichi's Swimming Nymph hook, which has an upturned bent hook shank that suggests the possible posture that a damsel at rest might take. It has a slim abdomen of sewing thread and Swiss Straw wing case. I unfold the Swiss Straw so that it is flat and lightly spray it with Scotch 77 spray glue, then fold the Swiss Straw in half. Gluing the Swiss Straw makes the material a little stiffer and easier to cut a strip out for the wing case. You can also unfold the Swiss Straw and fold it over but not glue the pieces together, or you can use Medallion Sheeting; this material makes a suitable substitute for the wing case. I like to use various materials for the eyes including bead chain, plastic molded eyes, and glass beads attached to monofilament line with burnt ends, to name a few. The bead chain adds the element of weight that will help the damsel sink in the water. I use hair or partridge feathers to effect a leg and various types of dubbing for the thorax.

You can also do very well fishing adult damsel patterns, though the fishing is not nearly as consistent as it is with the nymphs. The adult damsels may be caught in the surface film and the trout will often cruise around picking off the trapped damsels. I usually spot fish swimming around taking these hapless adults and will determine which direction they are feeding, then cast in front of them and let the fly lie still with an occasional twist. Hold on, because the trout take these insects with distinctive rise forms. I use a floating fly line with 12-foot leaders in the 3X to 4X range but have often had to switch to a larger-diameter leader to reduce the breakoffs.

DESIGNING THE BIG-EYED DAMSEL

While fishing Spinney Mountain Reservoir in Colorado's South Park system of stillwaters, which also include Antero and Eleven Mile Reservoirs, I noticed the damsel nymphs in those waters appeared to have larger eyes than most of the damsel nymphs I'd seen in the waters of northern Colorado. I don't know why these damsel nymphs were so much more anatomically different than their cousins farther north or if it was just my imagination, but I wasn't going to let my misconceptions lessen my chances at hooking up fish in those environs. I decided to create a damsel pattern that incorporated the use of larger eyes just in case there was some validity to the differences I saw. The pattern proved to be effective in all the lakes I fish; I do tie damsels with smaller eyes but always have a half dozen of the larger-eyed damsel in my fly box. This style of damsel is also a fish catcher in warmwater lakes.

For this pattern, I use marabou for the tail and stripped peacock herls from Nature's Spirit coated with a UV resin for durability. You can also substitute three ostrich herls to give a more realistic look to the damsel nymph's paddle-like tail. I take an eraser or use my thumbnail to remove the fibers from the herl, rubbing the stem of the herl from the tip to the base. The thorax is made from any coarse nymph-type dubbing that soaks up water and helps sink the fly. I sometimes use knitting yarns in the olive color range to give me the color I'm looking for. I'll cut the yarn into small lengths and then blend it in my coffee grinder in small batches. You can also add other materials to the mix to create some interesting effects.

For the legs, I use hare's ear in a dubbing loop. I like the way the fur moves in the water, giving the impression of legs being held to the side and underside of the damsel's body while being pulled through the water. When at rest or during a pause in the retrieve, the fur will relax and go back to its original position.

Author with a rainbow caught close to shore at South Delaney Butte Lake during one of those late spring or early summer cold spells. Caught this little fellow on a damsel with Callibaetis nymph as the dropper on a two-fly rig. JIM KAPRAL PHOTO

BIG-EYED DAMSEL NYMPH

- **Hook:** #12-16 Daiichi 1770 or Tiemco 400T
- **Thread:** Olive 6/0 Danville, 6/0 UNI, or 70-denier UTC
- **Tail:** Olive grizzly marabou
- **Underbody:** Tying thread
- **Rib:** Olive Nature's Spirit stripped peacock herl
- **Wing Case:** Light olive Swiss Straw or Medallion Sheeting
- **Thorax:** Olive Nymph Life Cycle Dubbing
- **Legs:** Olive hare's ear in dubbing loop
- **Eyes:** Black bead chain

TYING THE BIG-EYED DAMSEL NYMPH

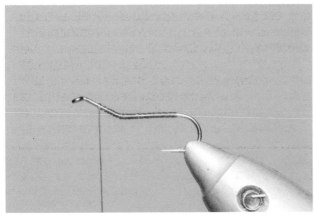

1. Attach tying thread to the hook behind the hook eye and wrap back one-third the distance from the eye.

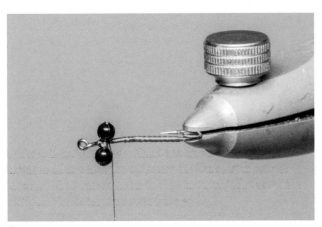

2. Attach the bead chain eyes about one eye width back from the hook eye with a figure eight wrap.

3. Wrap tying thread to the rear of the hook opposite the barb. Tie in marabou about half the length of the hook shank, making the tying wraps touching and tight. Stroke the marabou stem so that it creates a slim feather and pull forward to the midpoint of the hook.

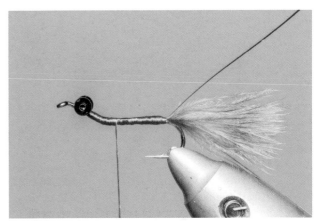

4. Wrap the tying thread forward to the midpoint of the hook over the marabou, covering it up completely. Tie off marabou and trim excess. Tie in the stripped peacock herl, and then wrap the thread over the stripped herl and back to the hook bend opposite the barb.

5. Wrap the tying thread forward to the bend at the midpoint of the hook. Wrap the stripped herl forward to the midpoint of the hook in evenly spaced wraps to form the segmentation of the abdomen; tie off the stripped herl.

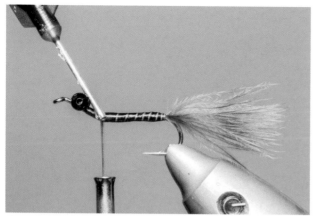

6. Trim the excess stripped quill, apply UV resin to the abdomen, and set with UV light.

7. Dub the tying thread with the nymph dubbing and advance the dubbing to the back end of the bead chain eyes.

8. Attach the tag end of the Swiss Straw behind the bead chain eyes with the Swiss Straw facing forward over the hook eye. Wrap tying thread directly in front of the bead chain eyes, covering the Swiss Straw. Continue wrapping the tying thread to the hook eye then back to in front of the bead chain eyes.

9. Create a dubbing loop in front of the bead chain eyes; wrap the thread around the dubbing loop to close off the end of the loop closest to the hook. Using hare's ear dubbing, insert small bunches of dubbing about ½ inch long and spread out the fibers. Next, twist the dubbing loop to form a dubbing brush; comb out the trapped fibers.

10. Wrap the dubbing brush in front of the bead chain eyes and then behind the eyes to form the legs; tie off and trim excess.

11. Fold Swiss Straw back over the eye and tie off with several wraps of tying thread behind the bead chain eyes. Whip-finish the wing case directly behind the eyes and trim excess thread. Trim the wing case material the desired length for the upper wing case.

DESIGNING THE FEATHER DAMSEL ADULT

Back in the late '70s and early '80s, I started fishing North Delaney Butte Lake in early July after the July 4th celebration. Back then the lake was not well-known and we would often be the only fishermen on the lake. We used to see hundreds of rise forms out in the lake at around 9 a.m. and we'd kick out in our float tubes to get in among those rising fish. The fish were rising to the surface to take hatched *Callibaetis* mayflies and trapped damsel adults on the surface film of the lakes.

I decided I needed to have several damsel adult patterns for these feeding fish. This pattern was developed at the tying desk; when I was tying dry flies and needed to prepare a hackle, I'd always peel off the fuzz on the base of the hackle stem. When I was finished stripping the fuzz off the base of the hackle, I looked at the stripped feather and thought, "Wow, this looks like the rear end of an adult damsel." I colored that stem with a light blue permanent marker, and thus was born the abdomen of the adult damsel.

One of my favorite tactics when fishing an adult damsel was to position myself out into the lake, in the shallow part no more than 12 feet or so deep. I would spot a cruising trout sipping drowned damsels on the surface of the water and would cast my dry damsel pattern about 5 feet in front of the trout's line of feeding. Then, ever so slightly, I would jiggle the damsel to make it look like it was struggling and to catch the trout's attention. If I was fortunate enough to attract the attention of the trout and the trout took the fly with relish, I sometimes broke off the damsel using 3X tippet because the take was so savage. The majority of the damsels I see are a light blue color, but I have also seen a few tan, red, and rust-colored adults.

FEATHER DAMSEL ADULT

- **Hook:** #10-14 TMC 100
- **Thread:** White 8/0 UNI colored with a light blue permanent marker, or any color close to the coloration of the damsels in your area
- **Body:** Whiting Farms grizzly rooster hackle cape with all fibers stripped from stem and colored with light blue marker; select one of the larger hackles from the top or back of the neck
- **Thorax:** Light blue dubbing (handmade from light blue acrylic yarn)
- **Wing Case:** White polyester or Antron yarn dyed light blue or light blue polyester yarn
- **Wing:** Clear Super Hair with pearl Krystal Flash
- **Eyes:** Light blue vernille

TYING THE FEATHER DAMSEL ADULT

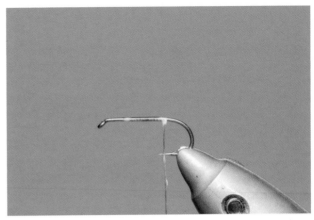

1. Attach the tying thread two eye widths back from the hook eye, taking a half-dozen wraps then trimming off the excess thread; the thread should be positioned even with the point of the hook.

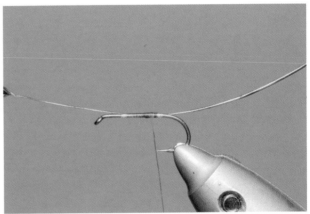

2. Select a large grizzly hackle from the neck of a Whiting Farms grizzly rooster cape; strip all the hackle fibers the entire length of the stem. Color the stripped stem with a light blue permanent marker. Attach the stem on top of the hook with the butt end of the feather facing toward the rear of the hook. Position the stem to the desired length or one and one-half the length of the hook shank. Tie in the stem securely with tying thread to form the abdomen of the damsel.

3. Attach a 3-inch length of light blue polyester yarn that has been divided in half lengthwise at the tie-in point of the abdomen. Take one of the strands of yarn and trim off the tag end if needed and wrap thread over the yarn to force it toward the rear of the hook; the yarn will be folded back over to create a wing covering and head.

4. Center and tie in four to six 2-inch strands of clear Super Hair directly in front of the yarn using a figure eight wrap to form the sparse wing of the damsel. Position the wing material so that it is perpendicular to the hook shank and tie in securely.

5. Take one or two pieces of pearl Krystal Flash, align it with the wing fibers, and trim to the same length. Fold the wing so it lies back toward the rear of the abdomen at

a 45-degree angle. Wrap tying thread over the base of the wing to gently cause it to stay in the swept-back position.

6. Fold the yarn forward over and in between the wing and tie in directly in front of the wing to form the wing covering. Tie in a grizzly dry-fly hackle.

7. Pull the yarn and hackle back slightly and dub a small amount of light blue dubbing onto the thread. Wrap the thorax so it is within two eye widths back from the hook eye; this will form the thorax and legs.

8. Wrap the hackle forward in evenly spaced wraps and tie off one eye width back from the hook eye.

9. Trim excess hackle. Fold polyester yarn over the thorax and legs and tie in as shown. Wrap tying thread forward over the yarn to the hook eye.

10. Tie in a small length of blue vernille in spent-wing style with figure eye wraps to form the eyes of the damsel, and then wrap the tying thread to the back side of the eye.

11. Fold over the polyester yarn and tie off behind the eye of the damsel; whip-finish and trim thread.

12. Trim the yarn behind the eyes as shown, then trim the tag ends off the vernille to form the eyes.

13. The Feather Damsel Adult has great imprint on the water's surface. Sometimes I move the fly ever so slightly at a slow retrieval rate; sometimes I let it rest, then move it in jerky short strips of line to mimic the struggling damsel trapped in the surface film. Hold on to your fly rod.

Water Boatmen

Another insect that is sometimes overlooked by stillwater fishermen is the water boatman. Often found in stillwaters and slow-moving streams, this insect is eagerly consumed by trout. These beautifully marked little insects are most recognizable by their oar-like hind legs and can be observed darting around in the shallows. On a few occasions in the spring, I have seen water boatmen (also called backswimmers) darting around with their erratic swimming motion near shore. On those occasions, I often tie on a boatman pattern and have been surprised to have trout take them; in fact, friends of mine who keep an occasional trout have reported trout stomachs filled with water boatmen.

As per my usual tying style, I wanted to create a pattern that was somewhat easy and quick to tie. The first problem I had to overcome was creating a wing covering that replicated what I saw on the actual insect. I tried several types of material until I found Thin Skin Gator and Mottled Oak sheeting. These products give me the needed rigidity to hold the shape of the wing covering and have a shiny look, and I color these materials with a permanent marker if needed.

For the underbelly of the insect, I use Ice Dub or Kevin Compton's Performance Sybai Pearl Dubbing. You can order any of the European materials that Kevin distributes by looking up Performance Flies on the internet. These types of dubbing create the appearance of trapped air bubbles. I use a thread body for the thorax portion of the pattern, preferring to build up a tapered effect. I then cover the thread area with UV resin in the final step of the fly to give the appearance of a trapped air bubble on the underside of the wing.

For the legs, I've found that the fiber from a pheasant tail, when stripped from the stem, will leave a little piece of the stem fiber on the butt, which to my mind's eye looks like a paddle that mimics the legs of the boatmen. The little piece that peels off when you strip the herl from the stem looks reasonable for a paddle. I also use a trimmed hackle stem with the fibers left on the tip of the feather, then trimmed to form the paddle shape. Spanflex, stretch floss, and round rubber legs can be used for the legs if needed.

To create the transparent appearance of the shellback covering of the boatman, I like to put a coating of Solarez Thin UV resin on the entire length of the shellback. I used to coat the shellback with clear fingernail polish, but I've stopped using fingernail polish because I suspect it may emit a scent that the fish can detect. I have no proof, but some of my guide friends from North Park Anglers, Joey Solano and Tim Drummond, have mentioned to me that they suspect this might be happening, and I want to err on the side of caution. So I will stick to using UV resin as a coating. I need every advantage I can get to catch fish.

I tie my boatman patterns to have different sink rates, from neutral buoyancy to various sink rates. I use lead or lead-free wire to weight my flies to get them to sink below the surface of the water. I use a small-diameter wire, then flatten it out after I've covered it with thread. You could also use metal beads to provide weight. Use a darting type of movement when fishing the water boatman, with frequent pauses and short bursts of movement. Sometimes I won't weight the pattern and instead will let the stripping-in action of the fly retrieval take the fly under the surface.

GATOR BOATMAN

- **Hook:** #14-16 Daiichi 1260, Tiemco 2302, or Dai-Riki 280
- **Thread:** Tan 70-denier UTC
- **Underbody:** Pearl or yellow Ice Dub
- **Weight:** Brass bead sized to match hook size
- **Legs:** One herl from a pheasant tail with the stem piece of the base of the herl left on
- **Wing Covering/Shellback:** Black/tan Thin Skin Gator covered with UV resin
- **Thorax Underside:** Tying thread coved with UV resin

TYING THE GATOR BOATMAN

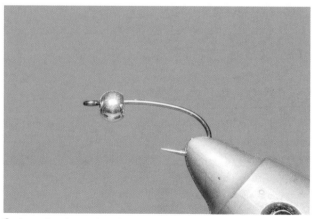

1. Attach a brass bead to the hook and slide to the hook eye.

Water boatmen are not one of the patterns that I consistently fish in stillwaters; however, I never want to be on the water without a couple of these patterns in my box.

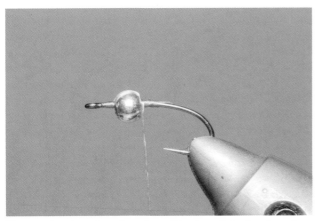

2. Attach tying thread to the midpoint of the hook and wrap back toward and slightly down the hook bend.

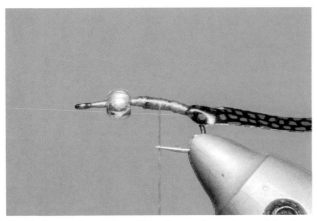

3. Tie in a strip of Thin Skin Gator about the width of half the gape of the hook; wrap thread to the midpoint of the hook over the Thin Skin.

4. Dub a small amount of dubbing, then wrap the dubbing forward to the midpoint of the hook.

5. Strip two fibers off the stem of a pheasant tail feather; the butt end of the fiber that is attached to the stem will be the foot of the paddle, like the legs of the water boatman. Tie in each fiber directly in front of the dubbed abdomen; each should extend slightly longer than the body, then trim excess. If desired, you can make these paddle legs any length you like. Dub on a small amount of dubbing and wrap in front of the legs as shown.

6. Slide the brass bead back until it is snug against the dubbing.

7. Fold the Thin Skin over the abdomen and bead as shown and tie off, then trim excess Thin Skin.

8. Tie in a neat tapered head and apply head cement.

9. The Gator Boatman is a pattern that all stillwater anglers should have in their fly box. You can put a small amount of Solarez Thin UV resin on the wing covering or shellback if desired.

Callibaetis

The Callibaetis nymph, dun, and spinner are must-have patterns to fish during the summer months on stillwaters.

The *Callibaetis*, or speckled-winged mayfly, is one of the major hatches I look forward to fishing on stillwater each year. The *Callibaetis* mayfly is a multi-brood, resulting in more than one generation per year; anglers can count on several generations of this insect throughout the summer months.

Callibaetis adults have mottled wings with bodies tending to be in the tan to light gray range. The hatch usually starts at around 8:30 or 9 a.m. and can last until midmorning or sometimes into the early afternoon. I've had spectacular days fishing the adult *Callibaetis*, and I keep a good supply of various patterns to mimic the adult as well as the nymph stage.

These mottled-wing beauties often bring on a trout eating frenzy in the lakes that I fish. I appreciate that the *Callibaetis* adult keeps reasonable hours to start the hatch on the lakes in our region, often starting around nine o'clock

in the morning. I have been fortunate to fish this hatch on many occasions, with some of the best dry-fly fishing in the spring. As with other lake-dwelling insects that have multi-brood characteristics, such as the chironomid, the first broods are larger in size in the spring and grow smaller with each succeeding hatch. I generally start with a size 12 and continue to go a size smaller as the season progresses.

Back in the late 1970s and early into the 1980s, still early in my stillwater fishing journey, I first encountered good hatches of *Callibaetis* on North Delaney Butte Lake west of Walden, Colorado, in the North Park area. Back in those days we primarily fished North Delaney Butte for the large population of brown trout; Colorado Parks and Wildlife harvests all their brown trout eggs from the fish in North Delaney Butte.

My friend Larry Moth and I would always start fishing the lake on July 6; we tried to be on the water by 8 a.m. After getting out our belly boats and putting on all of our gear, we'd take a breather and watch what was going on in the lake. We'd look to see if any insects were hatching on the surface of the water or if there were fish close to the shoreline.

Around nine o'clock in the morning we'd start to see rise forms close in to shore and out in the middle of the lake. Upon close inspection I'd see *Callibaetis* mayflies drifting on the surface of the water; often the duns would remain on the surface for a lengthy period of time. We'd target a *Callibaetis* mayfly floating along on the surface of the water, waiting to see how long it took before a big brown would suck it in. Many times I was amazed to see hundreds of rise forms all over the lake.

When out on the water, I noticed damsel adults trapped on the surface of the water, struggling to escape only to be consumed by a trout picking up an easy meal. I concluded that I only needed two fly patterns to fish: a Callibaetis dun and an adult damsel. For several years those were the only two flies I fished at North Delaney Butte Lake; I spent many hours designing dry patterns to replicate those two insects.

Often we would get confused trying to figure out what fish we should cast to, because they were rising all around us. When the hatch was on, one of my favorite tactics was to look for a cruising trout and try to anticipate which direction it was swimming, then cast the fly into the feeding lane and wait for the trout to get near. A slight twitch was

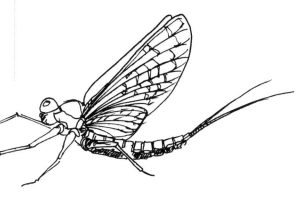

all that was needed for them to notice the movement and intercept the dun.

Fishing the nymphs (tied with varying weights) on a floating intermediate line along the shallower shoreline is also a good tactic. Often an unweighted or lightly weighted fly that sinks slowly is the ticket. I've had success catching fish by positioning myself 10 to 20 feet from shore and casting to the bank, allowing the flies to sink slowly as I make slow strips and pauses with my retrieves. Most of the time I fish on stillwaters using intermediate sinking fly lines, which sink slowly, some at 1 to 1½ inches per second. I feel that this gives the best presentation of many of the insects that hatch in the lakes.

QUILL BODY CALLIBAETIS DRY

- **Hook:** #14-18 Daiichi 1220 or 1222 or Tiemco 100
- **Thread:** Cahill 8/0 UNI
- **Tail:** Dun tapered paintbrush fibers
- **Underbody:** Tying thread
- **Body:** Stripped Nature's Spirit or Spirit River dyed Callibaetis peacock herl
- **Wing:** White polyester yarn mottled with black Sharpie
- **Hackle:** Dun Whiting Farms saddle

TYING THE QUILL BODY CALLIBAETIS DRY

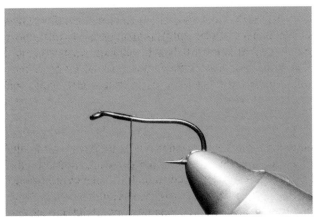

1. Attach tying thread one-third the distance back from the hook eye.

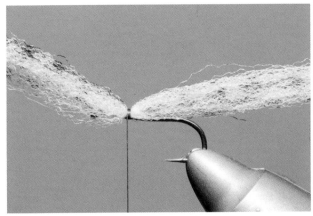

2. Tie the polyester yarn in the middle of the yarn, then fold the yarn pieces together and pull perpendicular to the hook shank. If desired, you can color in the wing material or create a mottled effect with a black permanent marker. This helps to replicate the mottled wing of the *Callibaetis* dun.

3. Wrap the tying thread in front of wing to create a dam of thread to hold the wing upright and behind the wing post to secure into position. Wrap tying thread back to the hook bend opposite the barb.

4. Tie in two strands of tapered paintbrush fibers, then wrap thread over the tail material to behind the wing; trim off excess tail material.

5. Strip the fibers off the stem of the peacock herl by rubbing with an eraser or using your thumbnail to scrape off the fuzz (place stripped quill on a damp folded paper towel if the quill appears to be brittle; this will soften the quill). Place the tip end of the stripped quill at the bend equal to the tail and tie in, then wrap the tying thread back to the hook bend opposite the barb.

6. Wrap the quill forward in touching wraps to the base of the hook; tie off and trim excess quill. Place a sparse coating of thinned-out head cement over the quill to protect it. Thinned-out head cement is less likely to crack under pressure from hemostats.

7. Tie in one dun Whiting Farms saddle hackle behind the wing with the shiny side facing forward. Wrap the tying thread in front of the wing behind the eye. Wrap hackle forward to one eye width back from the hook eye. Tie off and trim thread.

8. The Quill Body Callibaetis Dry.

Crawfish (aka Crayfish)

As a youngster I'd go to a local pond and spend hours collecting crawfish to bring home to my grandma to cook in traditional Japanese style—I don't recall how she cooked them, but I remember how good they tasted. I had no knowledge of the Cajun tradition of preparing a boil until my adult years, and today relish a good ole crawfish boil. Crawfish are also a delicacy for trout, both in streams and stillwaters. Trout can often be seen cruising the shoreline in the early morning, picking them off in the shallows.

I have designed a couple of crawfish/crayfish patterns that I fish when stillwater fishing for trout or when I'm chasing bass. There are so many wonderfully conceived patterns on the market today that I don't feel the need to tie my own necessarily, but as a fly designer I have a few thoughts on design. I center on tying smaller versions than the larger, more adult types; I figure the trout are less intimidated by a smaller crawfish than a larger one with bigger pincers. At least, I am less frightened by a small crawfish, and I project that to the thoughts of a trout.

One of the best crawfish patterns I have ever seen is the pattern tied by the famous deer hair fly tier Tim England; his was one of the patterns I hated to fish for fear of losing it or breaking it off. I would rather frame the pattern as a work of art than fish it. In designing my Crawdaddy Crawfish, I wanted to incorporate Swiss Straw, one of the materials that made Tim's pattern so effective, and also weight it so that it rode hook up to make this pattern almost weedless, as well as to possibly mimic the defensive position of a crawfish.

I have developed a number of patterns, which I have provided recipes for, for different conditions and species:

- **Big Craw:** a pattern with a lot of moving parts to represent a fleeing crawfish.
- **Mini Craw:** inspired by my friend Steve Thrapp's design. His pattern was designed as a small crayfish pattern to target trout cruising the shallows for smaller crawfish and bass in warmwater lakes.

Crawfish, or crayfish or crawdaddy depending on what part of the country you are in, are among trout's favorite foods; trout take them with relish when available. Try casting the fly near the shoreline, allow the fly to rest on the bottom, and then make a series of short pulls to "puff" the fly off the bottom or slowly troll one from a belly boat.

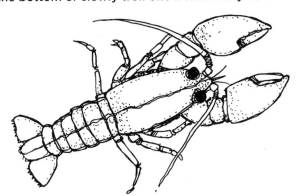

- **Baby Craw:** a variation on the Mini Craw using Swiss Straw, which I first saw on Tim England's crawfish pattern.
- **Candy Crawdaddy:** a tastier variation on a theme.

DAMSEL NYMPHS

BIG-EYED DAMSEL NYMPH (OLIVE)

- **Hook:** #10-16 Daiichi 1770 or TMC 400T
- **Thread:** Olive 70-denier UTC
- **Tail:** Olive grizzly marabou
- **Underbody:** Tying thread
- **Rib:** Fine gold wire
- **Wing Case:** Mottled Medallion Sheeting
- **Thorax:** Olive nymph dubbing
- **Legs:** Olive hare's ear in dubbing loop
- **Eyes:** Black bead chain

BIG-EYED DAMSEL NYMPH (TAN)

- **Hook:** #10-16 Daiichi 1770 or TMC 400T
- **Thread:** Tan 70-denier UTC
- **Tail:** Tan grizzly marabou
- **Underbody:** Tying thread
- **Rib:** Fine gold wire
- **Wing Case:** Tan Swiss Straw
- **Thorax:** Tan nymph dubbing
- **Legs:** Hare's ear in dubbing loop
- **Eyes:** Black bead chain

BIG-EYED DAMSEL NYMPH (OLIVE BROWN)

- **Hook:** #12-16 Daiichi 1770 or TMC 400T
- **Thread:** Olive brown 70-denier UTC
- **Tail:** Olive marabou
- **Underbody:** Tying thread
- **Shellback:** Marabou pulled straight over hook
- **Rib:** Fine gold wire
- **Wing Case:** Mottled Medallion Sheeting
- **Thorax:** Olive nymph dubbing
- **Legs:** Dark olive hare's ear in dubbing loop
- **Eyes:** Black bead chain

CDC DAMSEL NYMPH (OLIVE)

- **Hook:** #10-16 Daiichi 1770
- **Thread:** Olive 70-denier UTC
- **Tail:** Olive CDC feather fibers
- **Underbody:** Tying thread
- **Rib:** Silver wire
- **Thorax:** Olive Ice Dub
- **Wing Case/Head:** Olive Swiss Straw
- **Legs:** Olive CDC
- **Eyes:** Dark olive glass bead using monofilament line burnt ends

CDC DAMSEL NYMPH (LIGHT OLIVE)

- **Hook:** #10-16 Daiichi 1770
- **Thread:** Light olive 70-denier UTC
- **Tail:** Light olive CDC feather fibers
- **Underbody:** Tying thread
- **Rib:** Silver wire
- **Thorax:** Light olive rabbit dubbing
- **Wing Case/Head:** Light olive Swiss Straw
- **Legs:** Light olive CDC
- **Eyes:** Light olive glass bead using monofilament line burnt ends

CDC DAMSEL NYMPH (TAN)

- **Hook:** #10-16 Daiichi 1770
- **Thread:** Tan 70-denier UTC
- **Tail:** Tan CDC feather fibers
- **Underbody:** Tying thread
- **Rib:** Gold wire
- **Thorax:** Tan Ice Dub
- **Wing Case/Head:** Tan Swiss Straw
- **Legs:** Tan CDC
- **Eyes:** Brown glass bead using monofilament line burnt ends

GLASS-EYED DAMSEL NYMPH (LIGHT OLIVE)

- **Hook:** #10-16 Daiichi 1260 or TMC 2302
- **Thread:** Light olive 70-denier UTC
- **Tail:** Light olive marabou
- **Underbody:** Marabou wrapped the length of the abdomen
- **Rib:** Gold wire
- **Thorax:** Light olive nymph dubbing
- **Wing Case/Head:** Olive Swiss Straw
- **Legs:** Olive mottled hen fibers
- **Eyes:** Light olive glass bead

GLASS-EYED DAMSEL NYMPH (TAN)

- **Hook:** #10-16 Daiichi 1260 or TMC 2302
- **Thread:** Tan 70-denier UTC
- **Tail:** Tan marabou
- **Underbody:** Marabou wrapped the length of the abdomen
- **Rib:** Gold wire
- **Thorax:** Tan nymph dubbing
- **Wing Case/Head:** Tan Swiss Straw
- **Legs:** Mottled hen fibers
- **Eyes:** Brown glass bead

GLASS-EYED DAMSEL NYMPH (DARK OLIVE)

- **Hook:** #10-16 Daiichi 1260 or TMC 2302
- **Thread:** Olive 70-denier UTC
- **Tail:** Olive marabou
- **Underbody:** Marabou wrapped the length of the abdomen
- **Rib:** Light olive wire
- **Thorax:** Olive nymph dubbing
- **Wing Case/Head:** Olive Swiss Straw
- **Legs:** Olive brown mottled hen fibers
- **Eyes:** Olive glass bead

SWISS DAMSEL NYMPH (OLIVE)

- **Hook:** #10-16 Daiichi 1260
- **Thread:** Olive 70-denier UTC
- **Tail:** Medium olive marabou
- **Underbody:** Marabou wrapped along the hook shank
- **Rib:** Monofilament
- **Thorax:** Olive Superfine Dubbing
- **Wing Case/Head:** Olive Swiss Straw
- **Legs:** Whiting Farms olive Coq de Leon
- **Eyes:** Olive glass bead

SWISS DAMSEL NYMPH (TAN)

- **Hook:** #10-16 Daiichi 1260
- **Thread:** Tan 6/0 UNI
- **Tail:** Tan marabou
- **Underbody:** Marabou wrapped along the hook shank
- **Rib:** Monofilament
- **Thorax:** Tan Superfine Dubbing
- **Wing Case/Head:** Tan Swiss Straw
- **Legs:** Whiting Farms olive Coq de Leon
- **Eyes:** Tan glass bead

KISS ASS DAMSEL NYMPH (DARK OLIVE)

- **Hook:** #10-16 Daiichi 1260 or TMC 280
- **Thread:** Dark olive 6/0 Danville
- **Tail:** Dark olive select marabou
- **Body:** Dark olive select marabou wrapped around hook
- **Rib:** Small silver or gold wire
- **Thorax:** Dark olive hare's ear dubbing
- **Legs:** Rabbit dubbing using dubbing brush
- **Eyes:** Black bead chain eyes

SWISS DAMSEL NYMPH (LIGHT OLIVE)

- **Hook:** #10-16 Daiichi 1260
- **Thread:** Light olive 6/0 UNI
- **Tail:** Light olive marabou
- **Underbody:** Marabou wrapped along the hook shank
- **Rib:** Monofilament
- **Thorax:** Light olive Superfine Dubbing
- **Wing Case/Head:** Light olive Swiss Straw
- **Legs:** Whiting Farms olive Coq de Leon
- **Eyes:** Light olive glass bead

KISS ASS DAMSEL NYMPH (LIGHT OLIVE)

- **Hook:** #10-16 Daiichi 1260 or TMC 280
- **Thread:** Olive 6/0 Danville
- **Tail:** Light olive select marabou
- **Body:** Light olive select marabou wrapped around hook
- **Rib:** Small silver or gold wire
- **Thorax:** Dark olive hare's ear dubbing
- **Legs:** Rabbit dubbing using dubbing brush
- **Eyes:** Black bead chain eyes

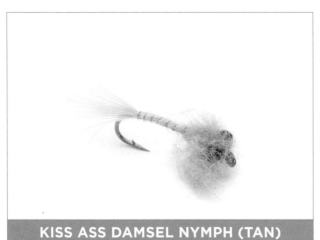

KISS ASS DAMSEL NYMPH (TAN)

- **Hook:** #10-16 Daiichi 1260 or TMC 280
- **Thread:** Tan 6/0 Danville
- **Tail:** Tan select marabou
- **Body:** Tan select marabou wrapped around hook
- **Rib:** Small silver or gold wire
- **Thorax:** Tan nymph dubbing
- **Legs:** Tan rabbit dubbing using dubbing brush
- **Eyes:** Black bead chain eyes

STATIC DAMSEL NYMPH (TAN)

- **Hook:** #10-16 Daiichi 1230 or TMC 400T
- **Thread:** Tan 6/0 Danville
- **Tail:** Three tan ostrich herls
- **Underbody:** Cream Coats & Clark sewing thread
- **Shellback:** Pheasant tail fibers pulled straight over hook shank
- **Rib:** Cream Coats & Clark sewing thread
- **Wing Case:** Tan Swiss Straw
- **Thorax:** Nymph dubbing to match color scheme
- **Legs:** Brown partridge fibers
- **Eyes:** Dark amber glass beads

STATIC DAMSEL NYMPH (LIGHT OLIVE)

- **Hook:** #10-16 Daiichi 1230 or TMC 400T
- **Thread:** Light olive 6/0 Danville
- **Tail:** Three light olive ostrich herls
- **Underbody:** Chartreuse Coats & Clark sewing thread
- **Shellback:** Light olive Swiss Straw pulled straight over hook shank
- **Rib:** Cream Coats & Clark sewing thread
- **Wing Case:** Light olive Swiss Straw
- **Thorax:** Olive Ice Dub
- **Legs:** Olive partridge fibers
- **Eyes:** Light olive glass beads

STATIC DAMSEL NYMPH (OLIVE)

- **Hook:** #10-16 Daiichi 1230 or TMC 400T
- **Thread:** Olive 6/0 Danville
- **Tail:** Three olive ostrich herls
- **Underbody:** Olive Coats & Clark sewing thread
- **Shellback:** Light olive Swiss Straw
- **Rib:** Olive Coats & Clark sewing thread
- **Wing Case:** Light olive Swiss Straw
- **Thorax:** Olive brown Ice Dub
- **Legs:** Olive partridge fibers
- **Eyes:** Olive glass beads

MARABOU DAMSEL NYMPH (OLIVE) (VARIATION OF RANDELL KAUFMANN'S DAMSEL)

- **Hook:** #10-16 Daiichi 1230 or TMC 400T
- **Thread:** Light olive 70-denier UTC
- **Tail:** Light olive marabou
- **Underbody:** Olive marabou
- **Rib:** Olive fine UTC wire
- **Thorax:** Peacock herl
- **Legs:** Olive brown marabou

DAMSEL ADULTS

TWISTED POLY DAMSEL ADULT (TAN)

- **Hook:** #10-16 TMC 5210
- **Thread:** White 16/0 Veevus colored with marker
- **Abdomen/Thorax/Head:** Tan polyester yarn
- **Underbody:** Tying thread
- **Wing:** Pearl Micro Flash and white Near Hair
- **Hackle:** Whiting Farms grizzly saddle
- **Eyes:** Tan vernille

TWISTED POLY DAMSEL ADULT (LIGHT BLUE)

- **Hook:** #10-16 TMC 5210
- **Thread:** White 16/0 Veevus colored with marker
- **Abdomen/Thorax/Head:** Light blue polyester yarn
- **Underbody:** Tying thread
- **Wing:** Pearl Micro Flash and white Near Hair
- **Hackle:** Whiting Farms grizzly saddle
- **Eyes:** Light blue vernille

FEATHER DAMSEL ADULT (RUST)

- **Hook:** #10-16 TMC 5210
- **Thread:** White 16/0 Veevus colored with marker
- **Abdomen:** Stripped Whiting Farms grizzly neck stem, colored rust
- **Thorax/Head:** Rust polyester yarn
- **Underbody:** Tying thread
- **Wing:** Pearl Micro Flash and white Near Hair
- **Hackle:** Whiting Farms brown saddle
- **Eyes:** Tan vernille

FEATHER DAMSEL ADULT (TAN)

- **Hook:** #10-16 TMC 5210
- **Thread:** White 16/0 Veevus colored with marker
- **Abdomen:** Stripped Whiting Farms grizzly neck stem, colored tan
- **Thorax/Head:** Tan polyester yarn
- **Underbody:** Tying thread
- **Wing:** Pearl Micro Flash and white Near Hair
- **Hackle:** Whiting Farms grizzly saddle
- **Eyes:** Tan vernille

BRAIDED DAMSEL ADULT (RUST)

- **Hook:** #10-16 TMC 5210
- **Thread:** White 16/0 Veevus colored with marker
- **Abdomen:** Monofilament braid core backing, colored rust
- **Thorax/Head:** Tan polyester yarn
- **Underbody:** Tying thread
- **Wing:** Pearl Micro Flash and white Near Hair
- **Hackle:** Whiting Farms light brown saddle
- **Eyes:** Dark tan vernille

FEATHER DAMSEL ADULT (LIGHT BLUE)

- **Hook:** #10-16 TMC 5210
- **Thread:** White 16/0 Veevus colored with marker
- **Abdomen:** Stripped Whiting Farms grizzly neck stem, colored light blue
- **Thorax/Head:** Light blue polyester yarn
- **Underbody:** Tying thread
- **Wing:** Pearl Micro Flash and white Near Hair
- **Hackle:** Whiting Farms grizzly saddle
- **Eyes:** Blue vernille

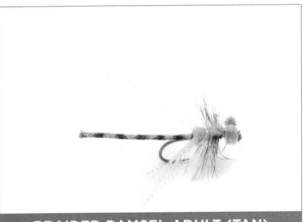

BRAIDED DAMSEL ADULT (TAN)

- **Hook:** #10-16 TMC 5210
- **Thread:** White 16/0 Veevus colored with marker
- **Abdomen:** Monofilament braid core backing, colored sand
- **Thorax/Head:** Tan polyester yarn
- **Underbody:** Tying thread
- **Wing:** Pearl Micro Flash and white Near Hair
- **Hackle:** Whiting Farms dyed orange grizzly saddle
- **Eyes:** Tan vernille

BRAIDED DAMSEL ADULT (LIGHT BLUE)

- **Hook:** #10-16 TMC 5210
- **Thread:** White 16/0 Veevus colored with marker
- **Abdomen:** Monofilament braid core backing, colored light blue
- **Thorax/Head:** Light blue polyester yarn
- **Underbody:** Tying thread
- **Wing:** Pearl Micro Flash and white Near Hair
- **Hackle:** Whiting Farms grizzly saddle
- **Eyes:** Blue vernille

Water Boatmen

EZ H20 BOATMAN

- **Hook:** #14-16 Daiichi 1260 or TMC 2302
- **Thread:** Tan 70-denier UTC
- **Underbody:** Pearl or yellow Ice Dub
- **Weight:** Lead (.020)
- **Legs:** Pheasant tail fiber tied in with butt of fiber out
- **Wing:** Pellon 808 cut in an oval shape, colored with permanent marker
- **Thorax Underside:** Tying thread covered with UV resin
- **Note:** Coat wing with UV resin.

GATOR BOATMAN

- **Hook:** #14-16 Daiichi 1260 or TMC 2302
- **Thread:** Brown 8/0 70-denier UTC
- **Underbody:** Pearl or yellow Ice Dub
- **Weight:** Lead (.020)
- **Legs:** Trimmed hackle stem
- **Wing Covering:** Brown/clear Thin Skin Gator
- **Thorax Underside:** Tying thread covered with UV resin
- **Note:** Coat wing with UV resin.

THIN SKIN BOATMAN

- **Hook:** #14-16 Daiichi 1260 or TMC 2302
- **Thread:** Tan 70-denier UTC
- **Underbody:** Pearl or yellow Ice Dub
- **Weight:** Lead (.020)
- **Legs:** Trimmed hackle stem
- **Wing Covering:** Tan/black Thin Skin Gator
- **Thorax Underside:** Tying thread covered with UV resin
- **Note:** Coat wing with UV resin.

Callibaetis Duns

QUILL CALLIBAETIS DUN

- **Hook:** #12-16 Daiichi 1220 or 1222 or TMC 100
- **Thread:** Tan 8/0 UNI
- **Tail:** Whiting Farms Coq de Leon fibers
- **Underbody:** Tying thread
- **Body:** Nature's Spirit stripped peacock herl
- **Wing:** Dun poly yarn with natural mallard
- **Hackle:** Whiting Farms grizzly saddle hackle

THREAD-BODIED CALLIBAETIS DUN

- **Hook:** #12-16 Daiichi 1220 or 1222 or TMC 100
- **Thread:** Tan 8/0 UNI
- **Tail:** Tapered polyester fibers
- **Underbody:** Tying thread
- **Rib:** Tying thread colored with sand permanent marker
- **Wing:** Dun poly yarn with natural mallard
- **Hackle:** Whiting Farms grizzly saddle hackle

MALLARD WING CALLIBAETIS DUN

- **Hook:** #12-16 Daiichi 1220 or 1222 or TMC 100
- **Thread:** Tan 8/0 UNI
- **Tail:** Dun tapered paintbrush fibers
- **Body:** Cahill Superfine Dubbing
- **Wing:** Mallard flank feather
- **Hackle:** Whiting Farms badger saddle hackle

LOPPED WING CALLIBAETIS DUN

- **Hook:** #12-16 Daiichi 1220 or 1222 or TMC 100
- **Thread:** Tan 12/0 Veevus
- **Body:** Tying thread
- **Rib:** Tying thread colored with dark brown permanent marker
- **Wing:** White polyester yarn
- **Hackle:** Whiting Farms badger saddle hackle

CALLIBAETIS CRIPPLE
(VARIATION ON QUIGLEY CRIPPLE)

- **Hook:** #12-16 Daiichi 1220 or 1222 or TMC 100
- **Thread:** Tan 12/0 Veevus
- **Shuck:** Amber Antron
- **Tail Topping:** Mallard dyed wood duck fibers
- **Body:** Light dun ostrich herl
- **Rib:** Fine gold wire
- **Wing/Back Strap:** White polyester yarn
- **Hackle:** Whiting Farms grizzly saddle hackle

CALLIBAETIS PARACHUTE

- **Hook:** #12-16 Daiichi 1220 or 1222 or TMC 100
- **Thread:** Tan 8/0 UNI
- **Tail:** Dun tapered paintbrush fibers
- **Body:** Gray Superfine Dubbing
- **Wing:** Dun poly yarn with teal feather fibers
- **Thorax/Head:** Light dun Superfine Dubbing
- **Hackle:** Whiting Farms badger saddle hackle clipped top and bottom

CALLIBAETIS POLY WING EMERGER

- **Hook:** #12-16 Daiichi 1260 or TMC 2302
- **Thread:** Tan 8/0 UNI
- **Tail:** Amber/light olive Antron
- **Body:** Rust pheasant tail fibers
- **Rib:** Fine gold wire
- **Wing:** Dun poly yarn
- **Thorax:** Rust Ice Dub
- **Legs:** Whiting Farms badger saddle hackle clipped top and bottom

Callibaetis Nymphs

BH CALLIBATIS NYMPH

- **Hook:** #12-16 Daiichi 1260 or TMC 2312
- **Thread:** Tan 12/0 Veevus
- **Bead:** Gold brass
- **Tail:** Mallard dyed wood duck fibers
- **Underbody:** Tan nymph dubbing
- **Rib:** Fine gold wire
- **Wing Case:** Medium brown Swiss Straw
- **Thorax:** Olive brown Nature's Spirit peacock herl
- **Legs:** Light hare's ear dubbing loop

BH CALLI NYMPH

- **Hook:** #12-16 Daiichi 1260 or TMC 2312
- **Thread:** Tan 12/0 Veevus
- **Bead:** Gold brass
- **Tail:** Tan ostrich herl
- **Underbody:** Tan nymph dubbing
- **Rib:** Fine gold wire
- **Wing Case:** Medium brown Swiss Straw
- **Thorax:** Olive brown Nature's Spirit peacock herl
- **Legs:** Brown mallard flank feather fibers

BH CALLIBAETIS NYMPH (BROWN)

- **Hook:** #12-16 Daiichi 1260 or TMC 2312
- **Thread:** Brown 12/0 Veevus
- **Bead:** Brown Togen bead
- **Tail:** Hare's ear guard hairs
- **Underbody:** Light hare's ear dubbing
- **Rib:** Fine gold wire
- **Wing Case:** Medium brown Swiss Straw
- **Thorax:** Hare's ear dubbing
- **Legs:** Partridge feather
- **Collar:** Dark hare's ear dubbing

PT CALLIBAETIS NYMPH

- **Hook:** #12-16 Daiichi 1260 or TMC 2312
- **Thread:** Wood duck 70-denier UTC
- **Bead:** Gold brass
- **Tail:** Brown pheasant tail fibers
- **Underbody:** Tan nymph dubbing
- **Rib:** Fine gold wire
- **Wing Case:** Medium brown pheasant tail fibers
- **Thorax:** Olive brown nymph dubbing
- **Legs:** Light hare's ear dubbing

CALLI NYMPH

- **Hook:** #12-16 Daiichi 1260 or TMC 2312
- **Thread:** Rust 12/0 Veevus
- **Tail/Legs:** Dark tan CDC fibers
- **Underbody:** Tan nymph dubbing
- **Rib:** Fine gold wire
- **Rib 2:** Dark tan ostrich herl
- **Wing Case:** Hareline Synthetic Quill, colored brown
- **Thorax:** Dark tan ostrich herl
- **Wing Case:** Light gray Larva Lace foam

HARE LEG CALLI NYMPH

- **Hook:** #12-16 Daiichi 1260 or TMC 2312
- **Thread:** Tan 12/0 Veevus
- **Bead:** Copper
- **Tail/Dorsal Stripe/Wing Case:** Rust brown pheasant tail fibers
- **Underbody:** Tying thread
- **Rib:** Fine gold wire
- **Wing Case:** Hareline Synthetic Quill, colored brown
- **Thorax:** Rust Life Cycle Dubbing
- **Legs:** Dark hare's ear dubbing

Crawfish

CRAWDADDY (OLIVE)

- **Hook:** #10 Daiichi 2720 or Saber 7060
- **Thread:** Olive 140-denier UTC
- **Weight:** Spirit River Real Eyes Plus
- **Mouthparts:** Pheasant tail fibers
- **Eyes:** Burnt mono
- **Pincers:** Olive micro pine squirrel Zonker strip
- **Shellback/Tail:** Olive Swiss Straw
- **Thorax:** Olive rabbit dubbing
- **Legs:** Whiting Farms dyed olive/yellow saddle hackle
- **Underbody:** Peacock micro Estaz
- **Rib:** Brown D-Rib

BIG CRAW (OLIVE)

- **Hook:** #10 Daiichi 2720 or Saber 7060
- **Thread:** Olive 140-denier UTC
- **Weight:** Spirit River Real Eyes Plus
- **Mouthparts:** Pheasant tail fibers
- **Pincers:** Olive micro pine squirrel Zonker strip
- **Back/Tail:** Olive bucktail
- **Thorax:** Olive micro pine squirrel Zonker strip
- **Legs:** Harelines olive/black barred Crazy Legs

BABY CRAW (VARIATION OF STEVE THRAPPS'S CRAZYDADDY)

- **Hook:** #10 Daiichi 2720 or Saber 7060
- **Thread:** Olive 8/0 UNI
- **Weight:** Spirit River Dazl-Eyes
- **Mouthparts:** Natural pheasant tail fibers
- **Feelers:** Brown/black Sili Legs
- **Pincers:** Olive or orange, natural Micro pine squirrel Zonker strip
- **Tail:** Olive brown bucktail
- **Body:** Rust Ice Dub
- **Legs:** Whiting Farms olive dyed grizzly saddle

MINI CRAW (NATURAL)

- **Hook:** #10 Daiichi 2720 or Saber 7060
- **Thread:** Olive 8/0 UNI
- **Mouthparts:** Natural pheasant tail fibers
- **Feelers:** Brown/black Sili Legs
- **Pincers:** Olive or orange, natural Micro pine squirrel Zonker strip
- **Shellback/Tail:** Olive Swiss Straw
- **Underbody:** Olive Arizona Dubbing
- **Hackle:** Whiting Farms yellow grizzly Euro hackle
- **Weight:** Spirit River Dazl-Eyes
- **Tail:** Olive brown marabou
- **Body:** Rusty copper UV Polar Chenille
- **Legs:** Whiting Farms olive dyed grizzly saddle
- **Note:** Coat shellback with UV resin.

CANDY CRAWDAD (OLIVE)

- **Hook:** #6-10 Dai-Riki 950
- **Thread:** Black 140-denier Danville Flymaster Plus
- **Head:** Olive brown Ice Dub
- **Feelers:** Yellow/black Sili Legs
- **Pincers:** Dark olive micro pine squirrel Zonker strip
- **Shellback/Tail:** Dark part of chartreuse bucktail
- **Body:** Olive brown Ice Dub in dubbing loop then brushed out
- **Weight:** Spirit River gold barbell eyes
- **Back Legs:** Yellow/black Sili Legs
- **Note:** Coat thread tail with UV resin.

-12-

TERRESTRIAL SERIES

Land-borne insects such as beetles, grasshoppers, bees, ants, moths, and mice often end up in the water due to any number of circumstances. Any insect or rodent born on land can be classified as a terrestrial. I've fished beetles of all sizes and shapes and have been surprised at how often I've had fish take a beetle all day long. I fish beetles on long leaders and usually cast them out, let them sit for a few moments, then give a slight movement to the fly. As soon as I moved the pattern, the trout struck. I like to incorporate a highly visible indicator so that I can more easily spot the fly in the surface film. Try adding some Krystal Flash to the underside of the beetle to mimic the beetle trying to take flight but trapped in the surface film.

Bopper Hopper

Grasshoppers

One of the blessings of living in Colorado are the mountains. In those pine-covered hills flow some of the most beautiful rivers and in those rivers live some of the most beautiful trout: cutthroat, rainbows, brookies, and browns. As a young kid growing up and venturing into the mountains near the town of Deckers, Colorado, I often found myself along the banks of the famed South Platte River. On occasion I'd sit on the bank with a handful of freshly caught grasshoppers; I loved to toss those "hoppers" in the water and watch them float downstream in anticipation of a trout intercepting the struggling insect.

That youthful activity would someday play an important role in my development as a fly fisher and fly tier. Truth be known, I really didn't like handling those grasshoppers (or any bugs) much, but watching trout eagerly take this big mouthful of protein was well worth the discomfort. As I evolved into an angler, I understood the importance of terrestrial insects as a food source for trout and soon developed

a desire to replicate these insects at the fly-tying bench.

A fortunate occurrence happened the day a friend of mine gave me my first "hopper"-type pattern—Ed Shenk's Letort Hopper, a pattern I continue to tie a variation of and have supreme confidence in its fish-catching qualities. As time progressed, I learned of other grasshopper patterns like Dave's Hopper and found that many tiers had developed their own designs for this insect. I am always seeking ways to improve on a hopper pattern and see how far I can push the design using different types of materials. I developed a drowned hopper version to simulate a hopper that has been in the water a long time and pulled under the surface.

I incorporate foam into many of my terrestrial patterns to provide flotation. I like to use 2 mm craft foam because of its easy availability and range of colors. I also use Evazote foam for many of my patterns; I like this foam because of its ability to compress easily (which makes it easier to tie onto the hook), its shiny appearance, and its floatability. For the bodies of other types of terrestrials such as ants, beetles, and cicadas, I like to use the 2mm thick craft foam, which

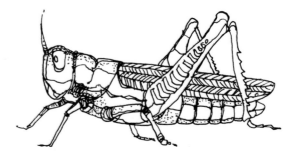

Grasshoppers are often blown into the water and should not be overlooked by the stillwater angler.

comes in a wide palette of colors; I can create as many color combinations as I can imagine or use a solitary color to meet my tying needs.

Several materials can be used for wings on many terrestrials. I use Pellon 808 (sewing material used for interfacing) because it accepts permanent markers well for coloration, holds up fairly well, and will not pull apart as easily as some wing materials. River Road Creations produces one of my favorite wing materials, called River Wing, which comes in eighteen different colors; their mottled wing materials work especially well for hoppers. Montana Fly Company also has a great variety of wing materials; I like to tie with their mottled brown wing material.

The variety of rubber leg materials ranging in types and colors, from round rubber legs to Sili Legs to molded legs and beyond, gives the fly tier a wealth of materials to choose from. I like to use Montana Fly Company's rubber leg assortments for many of my patterns.

Many more materials can be incorporated into tying terrestrials; I have only begun to explore all the possibilities on the fly-tying materials market and this process should keep me busy for years to come.

VARIATIONS

Most hoppers that I have designed in the last few years have centered on the use of foam. I am just amazed at the versatility of the foam and how many different tying techniques I can apply to create a whole host of body shapes,

like a Chernobyl Ant–type body or cut thin and wrapped around a hook to give a segmented look. You are limited only by your imagination. Many of my fly-tying friends have developed some interesting patterns with foam as one of the main ingredients. The development of all these different patterns prompted me to write my second book, *Modern Terrestrials: Tying & Fishing the World's Most Effective Patterns*, which features a variety of land-borne insects, not just hoppers. I favor tying patterns much like Allan Woolley's Chernobyl Ant, Juan Ramirez's Hopper Juan, and Charlie Craven's BC Hopper.

I also get tremendous satisfaction tying deer hair hoppers in the style of Ed Shenk, Dave Whitlock, and Tim England. I'll often sit down at my vise and get lost in the amount of concentration it takes to tie these types of flies

Many of my patterns utilize techniques I have borrowed as well as a few of my own. I always look at any type of material as fair game for tying new patterns, items such as artificial flower petals or Pellon 808 colored with a marker or spray paint for hopper wings.

Pellon 808 is an effective substitute for wing materials that I use on some of my terrestrial patterns. I still favor using River Road Creations' wing materials and Montana Fly Company mottled wing materials for some of my tying; however, when I'm out of those materials, I can always use the Pellon 808. Pellon 808 is strong and less resistant to tearing. I color it with permanent markers or spray-paint the fabric.

It doesn't get much better than this at the end of the day, fishing a favorite stretch of the Poudre River in Colorado. ISRAEL PATTERSON PHOTO

When spray-painting, I set the Pellon 808 on the floor of my garage on top of newspaper to catch any overspray. I lightly press the spray nozzle until it barely starts to spray; it sounds like someone sticking their tongue out, pressing their lips together, and blowing out air. This causes the spray paint to sputter out of the nozzle, which is ideal for creating a splattered look on the fabric. The downside is that it takes a lot of time to paint the fabric, but the result is worth it. Be sure to move the spray pattern around, and at times press the nozzle down fully and make long, sweeping spray patterns to cover the exposed areas.

I like to use River Road Creations wing cutters in various hopper wing sizes; they make well-defined wing shapes.

In this chapter, instead of explaining the design process behind each pattern, I am just presenting the patterns to give you an idea of the design process.

TAN BOPPER HOPPER

- **Hook:** #10-16 Daiichi 1260, Tiemco 2302, or Dai-Riki 280
- **Thread:** Tan 140-denier UTC or color to match the overall color scheme
- **Abdomen/Body/Head:** Tan River Road Creations foam (2 mm) or color to match the overall color scheme
- **Body Hackle:** Brown Whiting Farms midge saddle
- **Underwing 1:** Precut brown River Road Creations mottled wing material
- **Underwing 2:** White MFC Widow's Web
- **Top Wing:** Elk hair
- **Hackle:** Brown Whiting Farms saddle hackle
- **Legs:** Black/brown MFC Sexi Floss or color to match the overall color scheme

TYING THE TAN BOPPER HOPPER

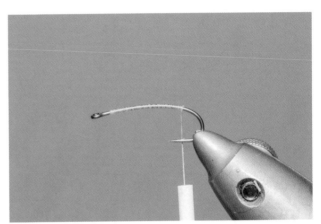

1. Attach tying thread one-third the distance from the hook eye and wrap thread back to the hook bend opposite the barb.

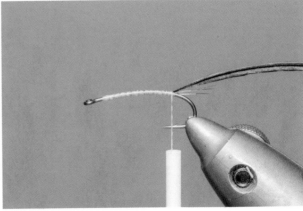

2. Tie in one brown Whiting Farms saddle hackle with the shiny side facing forward.

3. Wrap the saddle hackle forward in evenly spaced wraps to two eye widths back from the hook eye. Wrap thread back to the hook bend opposite the barb through the saddle hackle.

4. Place the precut foam body with the round end of the foam extended beyond the hook bend; tie in securely. Wrap thread forward through the hackle to the end of the hackle in front about two eye widths back from the eye of the hook. Fold the foam body over the hook shank and tie in as shown.

5. Tie in the precut mottled wing as shown.

6. Tie in the MFC Widow's Web as shown.

7. Trim the rear section of the Widow's Web even with the hook bend, and trim the front end of the yarn even with the hook eye.

8. Stack a small bunch of light elk hair about a quarter of the diameter of a pencil and tie in at the same position the front foam piece was tied in on top of the yarn underwing. Measure the stacked elk hair so that the tips of the hair are even with the hook bend, then grasp the elk hair in your left hand and trim the butt ends even with the hook eye. Position the butt ends of the elk hair even with the hook eye. Make several loose wraps of tying thread as shown, then tighten each successive wrap to flare the hair out.

9. Tie in one piece of MFC Sexi Floss on each side of the body and secure with several tight wraps. Whip-finish, trim thread, and apply head cement onto the tie-in point of the elk hair and legs. Trim legs to desired length.

10. Top view.

11. The Tan Bopper Hopper. Try tying this pattern with as many colors as you'd like, even colors such as pink, purple, or blue. Umpqua Feather Merchants has selected this pattern for their catalog.

Beetles

Beetles are one of my favorite stillwaters patterns; I've had great success using beetles as one of my main dry flies to fish from midmorning until dusk on lakes. In the midmorning to when the *Callibaetis* stop hatching, I have used a two-fly setup with about 18 inches between each pattern. There have been a few times when fish took both patterns at the same time, and it was fun to try landing both fish. My approach to tying beetles is similar to other flies: I've found that different types of foam lend themselves well to creating the shape of a beetle without too much manipulation on the part of the tier. I've used the River Roads Creation beetle foam cutter as well as a Chernobyl Ant foam cutter to cut the shape of the beetles I wanted out of the foam. My friend John Harder introduced me to Evazote foam—it is easy to work with, looks realistic, and floats high. Rainy's Flies produces a wide variety of colors of Evazote foam, as does Wapsi Fly. At times I will also use other types of foam, including 2 mm craft foam and Rainy's Flat Foam material, which I cut in half lengthwise as instructed by Rainy.

On a beetle, the shape of the pattern when viewed from the underside of the fly (the trout's view) is important. Therefore, I play closer attention to the underside of the beetle than I do to the top side. I had an interesting conversation with A. K. Best at a Denver fly-fishing show. We were discussing fishing beetles on stillwaters and he stated that one element fly tiers often leave off when tying beetle patterns is the underwing of the beetle. He suggested that tiers should tie the flashy appearance of the wing as the beetle struggles to become airborne. The flash is added to fan out on the sides of the beetle's underbody. I took that bit of information and added this underwing to some of my beetle patterns.

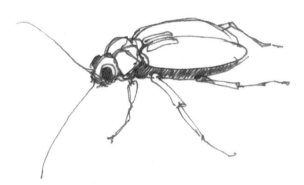

Beetles are a common insect found in stillwaters, rivers, and streams. When fishing a dry/dropper in stillwaters, I usually use the large black foam beetle from size 10 to 14 as my dry fly.

VW BEETLE
(VARIATION OF A. K. BEST BEETLE)

- **Hook:** #10-16 Daiichi 1260, Tiemco 2302, or Dai-Riki 280
- **Thread:** Black 70-denier UTC
- **Underbody:** Black/red Arizona Simi-Seal Dubbing
- **Body:** Black Evazote foam
- **Legs:** Brown or black round rubber legs
- **Underwing:** Orange Krystal Flash
- **Indicator:** Pink foam (2 mm) strip

TYING THE VW BEETLE

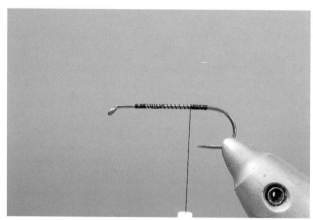

1. Attach tying thread behind the hook eye and wrap thread to the hook bend opposite the barb.

2. Cut a piece of black Evazote foam a little wider than the gape of the hook and cut a point at one end of the foam.

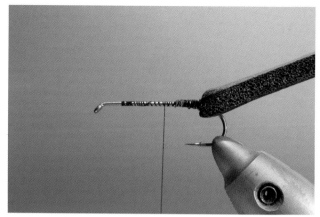

3. Tie in the foam by the pointed end a short distance from the hook bend opposite the barb, then wrap thread over foam to the hook bend opposite the barb. Cover up the excess foam with tying thread; you'll find that the Evazote foam compresses down tightly.

4. Dub the black/red Arizona Simi-Seal Dubbing onto the thread.

5. Wrap the dubbing forward to the one-third to one-quarter position on the hook shank.

6. Tie in about six or seven stands of orange Krystal Flash spent-wing style, then wrap thread over the flash to force the flash to bend back toward the rear of the hook.

7. Fold the black Evazote foam over the hook and between the Krystal Flash and tie in; this will form the head of the beetle.

8. Tie in the round rubber legs on each side of the head as shown.

9. Tie in the pink foam for the indicator as shown

10. Trim the Evazote and the pink foam for the indicator even, with both foam pieces slightly over the hook eye.

11. Whip-finish the fly as shown

12. Trim the flash even with the rear of the beetle.

13. The VW Beetle has been a proven fish catcher for me over the years.

Cicadas

My experience with adult cicada fly patterns was very limited until three years ago. I had heard of the annual cicada hatch on the Green River out of Flaming Gorge Dam, but had never had the opportunity to witness the hatch nor fish when the cicadas were present. I'd hear stories from my friends about fish coming from great distances to intercept cicadas that had fallen into the water, and about the large bulky flies tied to represent these terrestrial insects.

Ethan Emery, a former student, Green River guide, and now an educational administrator in Denver, invited me to fish the Green River once during his time as a guide; we'd talk about the beauty of the river, the high canyon walls, and the legendary hatches he'd been witness to. Often our conversation turned to fishing the cicada hatch—the great opportunities for his clients to catch perhaps a fish of a lifetime or how the trout would throw caution to the wind to take these giant mouthfuls of protein. I'd always hoped that I could someday be on the river at the right time to "catch" the cicada hatch; to this day that time has not presented itself.

Four years ago a good friend of mine, Mark Mills, told me about a cicada hatch on a river close to where I live. The Big Thompson River originates out of the mountains of Rocky Mountain National Park and travels downstream through the Big Thompson Canyon along Highway 34 to the town of Loveland, Colorado, then out to the plains to join the South Platte River drainage. The Big T, as it is called by those who access the river for recreational use, has many stretches of river that are easily accessible from the main highway. I fish this river as often during the spring, summer, and fall as time allows with great success; sadly, the Big T was devastated by a major flood in 2013 and is now in a rebuilding stage along its entire length from Estes Park to Loveland.

My dear friends Lyle and Diane Honstein own a piece of property along the river near Cedar Cove and invited me to fish. I decided to try to time my visit during a cicada hatch on the river. In all the years I've fished that river, I had never heard nor witnessed a cicada hatch, but my luck was about to change.

I came to the river equipped with cameras for taking photographs of these magnificent insects, hoping to get photos of fishing the hatch for my book *Modern Terrestrials: Tying & Fishing the World's Most Effective Patterns.*

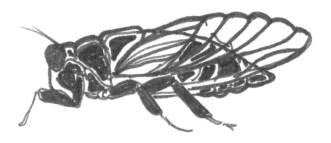

What I found was a concerto of the song of the cicada, a wonderful joyful noise that spoke to the beauty of nature. Along the banks, on the limbs of the trees, were thousands of these large, bulbous insects, which I was able to photograph and inspect closely. I spent several days fishing the Big Thompson using the patterns that I had quickly gone home to tie after each day's outing. I enjoyed seeing the trout traveling great distances to take the struggling Cicada just like the stories I had heard about the Green River.

TAK'S CICADA

- **Hook:** #14-16 Daiichi 1260 or 1760, Tiemco 2302, or Dai-Riki 285
- **Thread:** Black 140-denier UTC
- **Body:** Black craft foam (cut out foam using River Road Creations Chernobyl Ant body cutter)
- **Underbody:** Fluorescent orange fly line backing
- **Bottom wing:** Pellon 808 (cut using River Roads Chernobyl body foam cutter)
- **Wing:** Nature's Spirit bleached deer hair
- **Indicator:** Orange 2 mm foam strip
- **Legs:** Orange and black round rubber legs
- **Eyes:** 1-inch piece of orange round rubber legs

TYING TAK'S CICADA

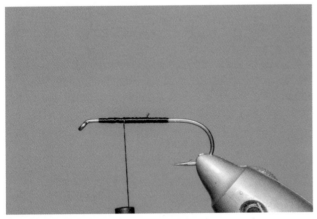

1. Attach tying thread behind the hook eye and wrap to the rear of the hook to opposite the barb; trim excess thread. Wrap thread back to one-third or just past the midpoint of the hook toward the eye.

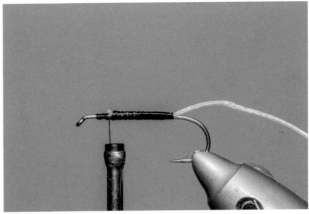

2. Tie in orange fly line backing by the tag end and wrap thread over the fly line backing to the rear of the hook, then wrap thread back to one-third the distance from the hook eye.

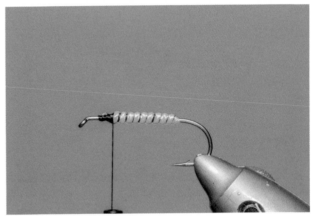

3. Wrap fly line backing in touching wraps forward to the one-third position; tie off and trim.

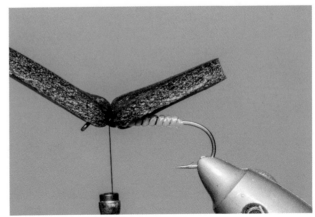

4. Tie in the foam body so that the rear end extends just slightly longer than the hook bend and secure tightly.

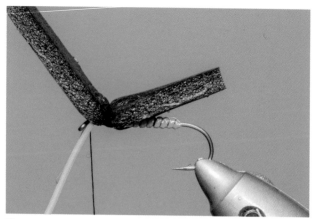

5. Tie in a short piece of orange rubber leg material; this will be cut shorter to form the eyes.

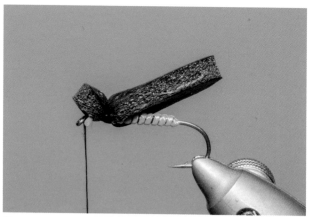

6. Trim the rubber leg material to form the eyes. Trim the foam body even with the outer edge of the hook eye. Cut the eyes the same width as the foam body.

7. Tie in the bottom wing material cut from Pellon 808 using River Road Creations hopper wing cutters in the size to match the fly being tied.

8. Stack a small bunch of Nature's Spirit bleached deer hair, about two-thirds the length of the body, and then trim deer hair even before tying onto the fly. Wrap the thread around the deer hair without any pressure; tighten the thread to cause the deer hair to flare out.

9. Tie in the legs on each side of the foam body. Whip-finish and trim excess thread. Turn the fly over and add head cement to the tie-in points on the legs and wings to secure.

10. Trim legs to desired length. Tie in the 2mm orange foam strip as the indicator and trim to size as shown.

San Juan Ants

Fishing the South Platte River with my friend Donn Johnson, a passionate dry-fly angler and my fly-fishing mentor, would often find us fishing the soft edges of the river with small ant patterns when the water was too high to safely wade or during runoff. Armed with this knowledge, I started to build an arsenal of terrestrial patterns I always carried when fishing during the summer months. The legendary "ant fall" on the San Juan River also illustrated the fact that trout do like to eat ants when they are available. The ant fall brings up lots of large fish that had been feeding on size 24-26 midge pupae to feast on these large insects.

My favorite times of year to fish the San Juan River, located in the northwest corner of New Mexico, are the summer months, when the occasional rain shower stimulates the carpenter ant into its mating rituals. I have been fortunate enough to witness this phenomenon several times in my fishing lifetime and have watched with awe when larger rainbow trout rise to the surface of the water to take advantage of this cornucopia of high-protein fare.

When the ants are on the water, the trout seem to throw caution to the wind and switch their diets from diminutive midge pupae to the much larger ants; I've seen large rainbows travel great distances to consume carpenter ants, reminiscent of the cicada hatches on the Green River. My initial experience with the ants had me searching my fly boxes for anything that was large to match the size of the ants falling on the water's surface. I found the Stimulator in black was an acceptable imitation as well a large Royal Coachman; these patterns, while effective, left me with the desire to come up with a pattern of my own.

Ray Johnston, owner of Float-n-Fish located in the small burg of Navajo Dam in New Mexico, gave me a sample of ants he had collected, preserved in a small insect collection bottle used by entomologists. Inspecting the ants more closely, I found the flying carpenter ant resembles a smaller version of a wasp. The rear gaster of the ant has the classic wasp shape, and the wings are clear with an amber cast to them; the remaining portions of the ant have a much more enlarged structure than the common ant. With these images in mind, I set out to design my impression of the flying carpenter ant.

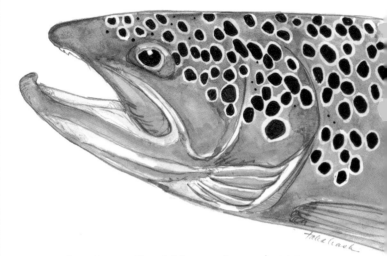

Poudre River Brown Trout. More and more brown trout are replacing the rainbow trout population that was decimated by whirling disease.

TAK'S SAN JUAN FOAM ANT

- **Hook:** #10-16 Daiichi 1270
- **Thread:** Black 12/0 Veevus
- **Rear/Thorax/Head:** Black Rainy's Float Foam
- **Hackle:** Brown Whiting Farms saddle hackle
- **Wing:** Clear Swiss Straw
- **Legs:** Brown speckled MFC Sexi Floss

TYING TAK'S SAN JUAN FOAM ANT

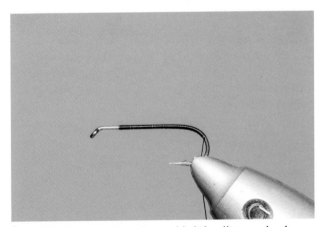

1. Attach the tying thread one-third the distance back from the hook eye, then wrap thread to the bend and just slightly down the hook bend; trim excess thread.

2. Cut a 1-inch section of Rainy's Float Foam and cut in half lengthwise. Turn the foam piece and cut a small section of the foam at one end of the half-shaped foam tube. This will allow the foam to collapse when tied onto the hook. Tie on the foam piece with the shiny rounded side facing down at the hook bend opposite the barb. The foam should extend toward the rear from the hook bend. Wrap the tying thread forward to the one-third position of the hook shank as shown.

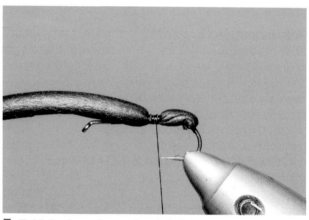

3. Fold the foam forward and tie in with several wraps to form the gaster, or rear portion of the ant. Wrap the thread forward in touching wraps to form the waist portion of the ant.

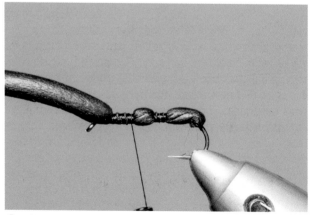

4. Lift the foam perpendicular to the hook and wrap the thread forward to form another short separation from the

gaster to form the thorax of the ant. Fold the foam over to create the thorax. Wrap the thread over the foam to form another separation, then wrap thread to just behind the hook eye to form the head. Take wraps back between the thorax and head; this is where the wings, hackle, and legs will be tied in.

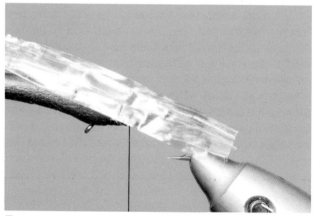

5. Prepare the wing material by taking a strip of clear Swiss Straw or Medallion Sheeting about the width of the gape of the hook and color with a permanent amber marker.

6. Twist the wing material in the middle. This is a technique used by the late Shane Stalcup that will help when tying in the wing.

7. Tie in the wing material as shown between the thorax and head using figure eight wraps. Fold the wings back, and take several wraps over the base of the wings to force them to slant back. Cut the wings a little longer than the bend of the hook, then cut a slant to form a point on each wing tip.

8. Tie in one round rubber leg on each side of the hook in front of the wing.

9. Tie in the brown Whiting Farms saddle hackle.

10. Wrap the saddle hackle with several wraps; tie off and trim excess hackle. Whip-finish and trim excess thread. Trim the ends of the legs as desired.

11. The San Juan Foam Ant has been a successful ant pattern on rivers and lakes. I also created a version of this fly tied out of Evazote, a closed-cell foam. I recommend that you tie this pattern in various sizes to match the naturals on your favorite water.

Terrestrials

TAKAHOPPER (VARIATION OF ED SHENK'S LETORT HOPPER)

- **Hook:** #14-16 TMC 5210 or Daiichi 1220
- **Thread:** Yellow 3/0 monocord
- **Body:** #9 Golden yellow Fly rite dubbing
- **Underwing:** River Roads River Wing Speckled Medium Tan
- **Overwing:** Natural deer hair
- **Head:** Clipped deer hair

TAK'S FOAM HOPPER

- **Hook:** #4-12 Daiichi 1260 or TMC 2302
- **Thread:** Hopper yellow 140-denier UTC
- **Abdomen:** Tan River Road Creations foam (2 mm)
- **Rib:** Tying thread
- **Underwing:** River Roads River Wing Speckled Medium Tan
- **Rear legs:** Metz Hopper Legs, femur colored with orange marker
- **Over Wing:** Natural Nature's Spirit mule deer

TAK'S HOT HEAD FOAM HOPPER

- **Hook:** #8-12 Daiichi 1260 or TMC 2302
- **Thread:** Yellow 140-denier UTC
- **Underbody:** Tying thread
- **Abdomen:** River Road Creations tan, yellow, or olive foam (2 mm)
- **Underwing:** Rootbeer Krystal Flash
- **Wing:** White MFC Widow's Web
- **Legs:** Red/black/yellow Centipede Legs
- **Indicator:** Hot McFlylon

MONSTER HOPPER

- **Hook:** #6-10 Daiichi 1260 or TMC 2302
- **Thread:** Hopper yellow 140-denier UTC
- **Underbody:** Tying thread
- **Abdomen:** River Road Creations tan, yellow, or olive foam (2 mm)
- **Underwing:** Pearl Krystal Flash
- **Wing:** Pellon 808 colored with permanent brown marker
- **Thorax:** Tan Superfine Dubbing
- **Rear Kicker:** Metz Hopper Legs
- **Legs:** Black/yellow Centipede Legs
- **Head:** River Road Creations tan, yellow, or olive foam (2 mm)

LIGHT HOPPER

- **Hook:** #6-10 Daiichi 1260 or TMC 2302
- **Thread:** Hopper yellow 140-denier UTC
- **Abdomen:** River Road Creations tan, yellow, or olive foam (2 mm)
- **Underwing:** Pellon 808 colored with sand permanent marker
- **Wing:** White Spirit River Near Hair
- **Legs:** Red/black/yellow Centipede Legs
- **Indicator:** Red foam (2 mm)

SILVER LINING HOPPER

- **Hook:** #4-10 Daiichi 1260 or TMC 2302
- **Thread:** Olive 140-denier UTC
- **Abdomen:** Tan River Road Creations foam (2 mm)
- **Wing:** Pellon 808 colored with olive permanent marker
- **Overwing/Head:** Olive Nature's Spirit deer hair
- **Rear Kicker:** Metz Hopper Legs, femur colored with orange permanent marker
- **Head:** Brown River Road Creations foam (2 mm)

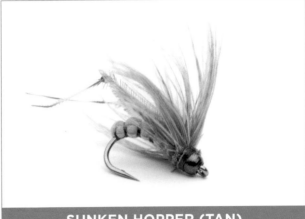

SUNKEN HOPPER (TAN)

- **Hook:** #4-10 TMC 8089
- **Thread:** Olive 140-denier UTC
- **Bead:** Black brass
- **Abdomen:** Tan River Road Creations foam (2 mm)
- **Wing:** Mottled brown MFC wing material
- **Overwing:** Olive Whiting Farms chickabou
- **Wing:** Pellon 808 colored with olive permanent marker
- **Collar:** Olive Whiting Farms chickabou
- **Legs:** Metz Hopper Legs

TAK'S DROWNED HOPPER

- **Hook:** #4-10 TMC 2499SP-BL
- **Thread:** Olive brown 140-denier UTC
- **Bead:** Black brass
- **Tail:** Red Whiting Farms neck spade hackle
- **Abdomen:** Natural latex colored with sand Chartpak marker
- **Wing:** Mottled brown MFC wing material
- **Overwing:** Olive Whiting Farms chickabou
- **Wing:** Pellon 808 colored with olive permanent marker
- **Hackle:** Olive Whiting Farms chickabou
- **Collar:** Olive brown Ice Dub
- **Legs:** Metz Hopper Legs

NINJA HOPPER (TAN)

- **Hook:** #8-10 Daiichi 1260 or TMC 2302
- **Thread:** Tobacco brown 3/0 monocord
- **Abdomen:** Tan River Road Creations foam (2 mm)
- **Wing:** Artificial flower petal dyed yellow
- **Overwing:** Natural Nature's Spirit deer hair
- **Legs:** Brown medium Wapsi round rubber legs

MINI SKIRT HOPPER (TAN)

- **Hook:** #8-10 Daiichi 1260 or TMC 2302
- **Thread:** Wood duck 140-denier UTC
- **Underbody:** Golden yellow Fly Rite #9 dubbing
- **Abdomen:** Yellow River Road Creations foam (2 mm)
- **Wing:** Artificial flower petal dyed yellow
- **Overwing:** Natural Nature's Spirit deer hair
- **Legs:** Black/yellow Centipede Legs

BOPPER HOPPER (TAN)

- **Hook:** #10-16 Daiichi 1260 or TMC 2302
- **Thread:** Chartreuse 140-denier UTC
- **Abdomen/Body/Head:** Tan River Road Creations foam (2 mm)
- **Body Hackle:** Brown Whiting Farms midge saddle
- **Underwing:** White MFC Widow's Web
- **Wing:** Elk hair
- **Hackle:** Olive Whiting Farms saddle hackle
- **Legs:** Black/brown MFC Sexi Floss

BOPPER HOPPER (YELLOW)

- **Hook:** #10-16 Daiichi 1260 or TMC 2302
- **Thread:** Chartreuse 140-denier UTC
- **Abdomen/Body/Head:** Yellow River Road Creations foam (2 mm)
- **Body Hackle:** Brown Whiting Farms midge saddle
- **Underwing:** White MFC Widow's Web
- **Wing:** Elk hair
- **Hackle:** Olive Whiting Farms saddle hackle
- **Legs:** Yellow round rubber

BULLET HEAD FOAM HOPPER

- **Hook:** #8-12 Daiichi 1260 or TMC 2302
- **Thread:** Olive brown 140-denier UTC
- **Abdomen/Body/Head:** Tan River Road Creations foam (2 mm)
- **Rib:** Tying thread
- **Wing:** Pellon 808 colored with brown permanent marker
- **Over wing:** Natural Nature's Spirit mule deer hair
- **Kicker Legs:** Knotted Pheasant Tail fibers
- **Legs:** Black/olive MFC Centipede Legs

Cicadas

BLACK FOAM CICADA

- **Hook:** #8-10 Daiichi 1260 or TMC 2302
- **Thread:** Black 6/0 Danville
- **Body:** Black craft foam
- **Underbody:** Black foam (2 mm)
- **Underbody Rib:** Fluorescent orange 140-denier UTC
- **Back:** Black foam (2 mm)
- **Wing:** White Spirit River Near Hair
- **Eyes:** Hot orange Ultra chenille
- **Legs:** Orange round rubber

ORANGE EYED CICADA

- **Hook:** #8-10 Daiichi 1260 or TMC 2302
- **Thread:** Black 6/0 Danville
- **Body:** Black craft foam
- **Underbody:** Orange foam (2 mm)
- **Underbody Rib:** Tying thread
- **Back:** Black foam (2 mm)
- **Wing:** White Spirit River Near Hair
- **Indicator:** Orange McFlylon
- **Rear Legs:** Orange goose biot
- **Legs:** Orange round rubber

EZ CICADA

- **Hook:** #8-10 Daiichi 1260 or TMC 2302
- **Thread:** Black 6/0 Danville
- **Body:** Black craft foam (2 mm) cut out with River Road Creations caddis wing cutter
- **Underbody:** Tying thread
- **Underwing:** Pearl Krystal Flash
- **Wing:** White Spirit River Near Hair
- **Indicator:** Orange foam (1 mm)
- **Hackle:** Whiting Farms dyed orange saddle hackle
- **Legs:** Orange Dacron backing line

GREEN RIVER CICADA

- **Hook:** #8-10 Daiichi 1260 or TMC 2302
- **Thread:** Black 140-denier UTC
- **Body:** Black foam (2 mm)
- **Underbody:** Orange foam (2 mm)
- **Underbody Rib:** Tying thread
- **Back:** Black foam (2 mm)
- **Wing:** White organdy
- **Over wing:** Black Nature's Spirit deer hair
- **Indicator:** Orange McFlylon
- **Legs:** Orange round rubber

Ants

S.J. FLYING ANT

- **Hook:** #12-18 Daiichi 1180 or TMC 100
- **Thread:** Black 16/0 Veevus
- **Rear Gaster:** Brown Rainy's ant body
- **Waist:** RIO bendable wire
- **Thorax:** Black foam (2 mm)
- **Underbody Rib:** Tying thread
- **Legs:** Black brush bristle
- **Wings:** Clear Medallion Sheeting
- **Antennae:** Dun
- **Note:** Coat underside with UV resin.

CINNAMON ANT

- **Hook:** #12-18 Daiichi 1180 or TMC 100
- **Thread:** Black 16/0 Veevus
- **Rear Gaster:** Brown Rainy's ant body
- **Waist:** RIO bendable wire
- **Thorax:** Black foam (2 mm)
- **Underbody Rib:** Tying thread
- **Legs:** Black brush bristle
- **Antennae:** Polyester tapered paintbrush fibers
- **Note:** Coat underside with UV resin.

EVAZOTE ANT

- **Hook:** #12-18 Daiichi 1180 or TMC 100
- **Thread:** Black 8/0 UNI
- **Body/Thorax/Head:** Black Evazote foam
- **Underbody Rib:** Tying thread
- **Legs:** Black round rubber
- **Indicator:** Red foam (2 mm)

ANT LION ADULT

- **Hook:** #12-18 Daiichi 1260 or TMC 2302
- **Thread:** Tan 8/0 UNI
- **Body:** Muskrat dubbing
- **Wing:** Cow elk
- **Hackle:** Brown Whiting Farms saddle hackle

CHERNOBYL ANT

- **Hook:** #12-18 Daiichi 1260 or TMC 2302
- **Thread:** Black 8/0 UNI
- **Body/Thorax/Head:** Black Evazote foam
- **Underbody Rib:** Tying thread
- **Legs:** Black/brown MFC Sexi Floss
- **Indicator:** Red foam (2 mm)

SAN JUAN FLYING ANT

- **Hook:** #12-18 Daiichi 1260 or TMC 2302
- **Thread:** Black 16/0 Veevus
- **Body/Thorax/Head:** Black Evazote foam
- **Underbody Rib:** Tying thread
- **Legs:** Black/brown MFC Sexi Floss
- **Hackle:** Brown Whiting Farms saddle
- **Wing:** Clear Swiss Straw

Beetles

BLACK FOAM BEETLE

- **Hook:** #12-18 Daiichi 1180 or TMC 100
- **Thread:** Black 8/0 UNI
- **Body/Thorax/Head:** Black Evazote foam
- **Underbody Rib:** Brown Whiting Farms midge saddle
- **Legs:** Black round rubber
- **Indicator:** Red McFlylon

EZ FOAM BEETLE

- **Hook:** #12-18 Daiichi 1180 or TMC 100
- **Thread:** Black 8/0 UNI
- **Body/Thorax/Head:** Black Evazote foam
- **Underbody Rib:** Brown Whiting Farms midge saddle
- **Legs:** Black/brown Sexi Floss
- **Indicator:** Hot orange foam (2 mm)

EZ PRE-FLIGHT BEETLE

- **Hook:** #12-18 Daiichi 1180, TMC 100, or Dai-Riki 305
- **Thread:** Black 8/0 UNI
- **Body/Thorax/Head:** Black Evazote foam
- **Underbody:** Olive Ice Dub
- **Side Wings:** Pearl Krystal Flash
- **Hackle:** Brown Whiting Farms saddle
- **Legs:** Black round rubber
- **Indicator:** Light orange foam (2 mm)

EZ CRYSTAL LEGGED BEETLE

- **Hook:** #12-18 Daiichi 1180 or TMC 100
- **Thread:** Black 8/0 UNI
- **Body/Thorax/Head:** Black Evazote foam
- **Underbody Rib:** Brown Whiting Farms midge saddle
- **Legs:** Black Krystal Flash
- **Indicator:** Red foam (2 mm)

SIMPLE BEETLE

- **Hook:** #12-18 Daiichi 1180 or TMC 100
- **Thread:** Black 8/0 UNI
- **Body/Thorax/Head:** Black Evazote foam
- **Underbody Rib:** Peacock herl
- **Legs:** Black/brown Sexi Floss
- **Indicator:** Orange foam (2 mm)

-13-
RIVER TECHNIQUES

Tackle

Tackle for rivers and streams is not only highly subjective but also a thoroughly covered subject; I will reserve most of the space here for focusing on techniques. However, because people frequently ask, I'll go into a few details regarding my favorite setup for fishing in moving water.

I like to fish a 3- or 4-weight 7½-foot to 9-foot fly rod for small streams, a 5- or 6-weight 9-foot fly rod for larger rivers and bigger fish, and a 6- or 7-weight fly rod for lakes and bass ponds. One of my favorite nymphing fly rods is the Beulah 10-foot 4-weight in the Platinum Series Single Hand. This fly rod is an ideal rod for me to fish all the nymphing styles being used today; everything from high sticking to European-style nymphing can be done with this fly rod. The 10-foot length gives me added line control and makes it easier for me to do the European-style nymphing, with the flies just off your rod tip.

I do use rods of various flex to match the water and conditions I'll be fishing. Wind always seems to be a factor in the region of the country I fish. Fly rods with medium-fast to fast action will generate the right amount of line speed needed to help overcome wind. In selecting a fly rod for lake fishing in my area, I use a 5-weight medium-fast action

Kevin Browning drifting through the morning fog on the Arkansas River. JIM BROWNING PHOTO

Fly lines are manufactured to match the weight and type of line needed by fly fishers. Fly lines have been developed to meet all the needs of the angler for every type of fishing condition and water condition, from fresh water to salt water, from floating to sinking lines that can sink at a very slow rate or can sink quickly.

for most of my dry-fly fishing, then go to a 6- or 7-weight for any flies that are fished subsurface.

There is controversy as to which line is better for dry-fly fishing, with individuals supporting one camp or the other. Personally, I prefer the weight forward line over the double taper because of the shorter casting distances I generally fish. Having said that, I can fish both lines equally well. My favorite fly lines for the majority of my dry-fly fishing are RIO's Gold and LT series. I find that if I use a longer leader and tippet and stop the cast above the horizon line, the line will turn over more delicately.

I use floating fly lines for the majority of my dry-fly fishing, which stands to reason; you don't want to use a sinking line that has the potential of dragging your fly under the surface. I use floating fly lines to fish nymphs when using longer leaders and maybe some added weight. I also use a floating fly line when fishing chironomid patterns in a vertical or inclined presentation. I favor using a fly line with a welded loop on the front and rear ends of the line. The welded loop keeps water from migrating into the core of the fly line, which often causes the front end of the line to sink. The rear loop makes for a smooth connection of backing to the fly line. Floating lines also come in weight sizes, from 1- to 15-weight lines and from double tapers all the way to weight forward.

There are several types of sinking lines that will descend to various depths dependent on the type of fly line used.

Sink-tip fly lines are designed to allow the front portion of the fly line to sink while the remaining fly line is floating. There are many types of sink tips with various weight configurations that allow the sinking portion to sink at different depths and at different rates of speed, which is usually designated as ips, or inches per second.

Intermediate lines are fly lines that sink gradually to the desired depth. For much of my stillwater fishing, I like to use an intermediate line that has a very slow sink rate when I'm fishing many of the patterns of insects found in stillwaters. I feel that an intermediate line allows my flies to stay in the "zone" for a longer period of time than does a full sinking line.

Full sinking lines are designed to sink at various rates from ultraslow to fast. I use a full sinking line when I want to get my flies to the bottom quickly.

For most of my fishing in rivers and streams, I select a tapered leader from 9 to 12 feet long with the tip end tapered to 5X; I will go to a larger leader diameter when conditions require a stronger leader. For the majority of my stream fishing, I usually attach a 6X tippet material to the leader when fishing dry flies in sizes 12-22 and when fishing midges. If conditions warrant the use of larger flies, I prefer to go to a larger-diameter tippet such as a 4X or 5X tippet, depending on the condition and size of the flies. Sometimes I will use a 2X and 3X tippet when fishing stillwaters. I will trim back the leader material if

JIM POOR'S METHOD OF CONNECTING FLY LINES AND LEADERS

Jim Poor, original owner of Angler's All in Englewood, Colorado, used this technique to make all of the butt sections on fly lines for his customers. Dave Whitlock has a kit that will do nearly the same type of connection. This method of attaching a butt section onto a fly line is an "old school" technique that I've always thought was very cool and different from any other method I've seen. The stiffer butt section facilitates in the "turnover" of the leader system and helps lay out the fly line more efficiently.

1. Select an 18-inch length of stiff monofilament line. I prefer Mason Tippet material and like to use .019 to .021 diameter for most of my needs. Orvis, Maxima, Amnesia, and Umpqua Tough Nylon Butt Material are also available.

2. Trim the butt material with a sharp razor to create a long tapered point, resulting in a fine point that will be put through the eye of a beading needle (which I'll explain).

3. Take a long beading needle, such as a number 10, and push the needle up the center core of the fly line. Many of the new fly lines use a welded loop to attach the leader. If I decide to use this type of butt section I'm describing, I will cut off the welded loop on the end of the fly line. However, the welded loop will prevent the water from migrating up the core of the fly line. The new butt connection will be covered in the final step with Pliobond or a flexible UV resin, thus mitigating the water entering the end of the fly line.

4. Insert the sharpened pointed end of the butt material into the eye of the beading needle and fold over the end to help secure the butt material to the hook. It may take several tries to accomplish this step.

5. Pull the needle as far as you can through the core of the fly line; take your time and be safe. Once you can no

longer push the needle up the core, bend the fly line as shown and push the needle until the needle point exits out the side of the fly line. Pull a short length of the butt material through the opening of the fly line to expose a short length of the butt material. Needle-nose pliers will help with this process.

6. Pull a short length of the butt material from the end of the fly line back; it's important to leave a tag end of the butt out of the line so you'll be able to apply some superglue to the tag end. Pull the butt material forward, exposing enough of the butt material—i.e., as long as what was inserted into the fly line. Take a piece of sandpaper and roughen up the surface of the butt material, then apply superglue. Grasp the tag end of the butt material sticking out of the fly line and pull backward; this will cause the glued end to slide back into the fly line. Pull enough of the butt material back into the fly line so that the none of the butt is exposed and allow to dry.

7. Wrap the fly line with 6/0 fly-tying thread in touching wraps the entire length of the butt section concealed under the fly line. Cover with a thin coating of Pliobond, then put a weight on the end of the butt material and allow to hang vertically. Be sure to secure the fly line so it won't slide off the shelf or whatever you are allowing the fly line to hang from. Allow the Pliobond to dry, then tie in a perfection loop or a blood knot to the butt end of a tapered leader; I prefer a small blood knot. Cover the connection with a UV resin such as Loon Knot Sense and set with a UV light or exposure to sunlight. This type of setup will allow a smoother slippage of leader and fly line through the tip of the fly rod.

Right: This display features a variety of leader materials in various line weights and lengths, as well as the tippet material for attaching to the leaders.

Reading Water

There are areas in the trout stream where anglers should concentrate their presentation of flies, whether dry flies, nymphs, or streamers. These feeding lanes often carry the most concentration of food and are places where trout focus on feeding.

One fact I've learned about trout's feeding behavior is their need to feel safe from predation in their environment, from above as well as in the stream itself. A number of animals will feed on trout when the opportunities present themselves. Birds such as herons, ospreys, eagles, kingfishers, cormorants, and ducks all feed upon all types of fish in the stream including trout. Mammals such as bears, weasels, otters, and others also rely on trout as part of their diet. So while it seems that trout are leery of shallow areas when feeding, they will take advantage of the opportunities to feed in the shallows for short periods of time.

Depth, cover, and speed of the water appear to be factors where trout feel relatively safe from predation from above. When I speak of depth, I am speaking of the depth of the water where the fish feed; the deeper the water, the less likely it is that predation from above will occur. In my experience, fish feeding in shallow waters can be more easily spotted from predation from above. Fish feeding in the shallows are there for one reason, and that is to feed; otherwise they will return to deep water for safety. Areas in the stream where this occurs can be worthwhile places to investigate to see if a hungry trout is waiting for food to pass by.

Cover such as undercut banks, overhead foliage, and trees that have fallen into the water can provide safe havens for fish to hang out because they are more difficult to see from above. This gets them out of direct sunlight and gives them the opportunity to dart out into the open water to snatch or inspect food, then dart back into relative safety.

Speed of water can also obscure the presence of fish because the breakup of the surface makes seeing what is beneath the surface a little more difficult (breaking up the outline of the fish obscures the vision from above). This gives the feeding fish a more comfortable environment in which to feed.

Trout will not expend energy to capture their food if that energy is greater in calories than the caloric value of the food; otherwise the trout would not be able to grow and survive.

The ability to read water is important to locate possible feeding areas for trout. For the most part, trout are opportunistic and will not pass up an easy meal; I've caught fish whose throat was crammed full of bugs and yet they were still feeding.

Streams are usually composed of pools, riffles, and runs. A pool is a section of stream with deeper water and a slower current. Riffles are sections of the stream where the depth of the water is much shallower and the speed of the current is much faster. A run is usually characterized by a greater depth of water with long stretches of much slower current speeds than a riffle.

needed to accommodate the larger diameter of the tippet I'm adding to the leader. I try to follow the rule of connecting leaders or tippets that are the next size up or down; linking materials that are more than one size apart can cause a hinging effect that has the potential to weaken your setup.

I use fluorocarbon tippet material when nymph fishing almost exclusively. The reasoning behind this choice is based on the visible fact that fluorocarbon almost disappears underwater. Increasing the chance that the trout will not be able to see it is of great advantage to the nymph angler. When fishing dries I use regular monofilament because the mono will float better, while the fluorocarbon has a tendency to sink. I can get a longer drift if I use mono.

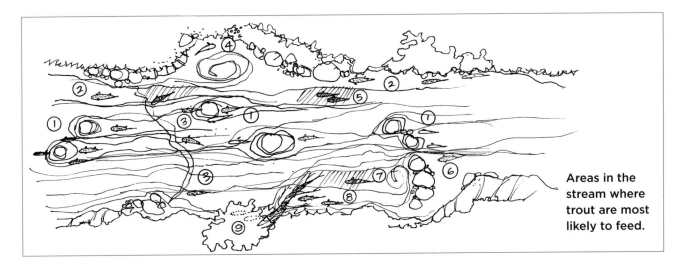

Areas in the stream where trout are most likely to feed.

BOULDERS AND ROCKS (1)

Boulders and rocks provide a diversion of the pressure of the stream's flow or current both at the surface and underwater. Trout can often be found in front of a boulder or rock; because of the nature of the hydraulics of water, a cushion is formed where the trout will not have to expend as much energy as when swimming in the current. If a tasty morsel should pass by, the trout can leave its lie and grab the food then return.

The underside of the boulders or rocks often provides a slower current speed where a trout can hold its position without expending too much energy, again a function of the hydraulics of the water.

The backside of the rock often forms a "pocket" of calm water where the current flow is reduced greatly and food is funneled into these pockets of water. Fishing these areas is often referred to as "pocketwater" fishing—one of my favorite places to present my flies.

These areas can provide a greater sense of security to the trout and are often dictated by the depth of the water. The breakup surface flow can also disguise the trout from being seen from above.

SLOW WATER (1-6)

Slow, calm water downstream of a major obstruction of the water's flow can also harbor fish resting or feeding casually. I look for these stretches of calm or "soft" water next to a seam as excellent places to try out a dry fly.

RIVERBANKS (2)

Riverbanks are often excellent places to fish your flies. I have found fish near the banks feeding regardless of water depth. The banks are outstanding areas for trout to intercept food that has fallen into the water from overhanging bushes or tree branches; often these insects are in the form of terrestrials such as grasshoppers, ants, and crickets. Look for undercut banks and curves in the bank where trout can hide out.

DROP-OFFS (3)

Drop-offs from rock shelves or from formations in the stream bottom structure creating deeper water are also productive places to present flies. Drop-offs provide security, oxygenate the water, and concentrate the drift of food.

BACK EDDIES (4)

Back eddies also provide excellent feeding lanes for trout; sometimes you will see a change in direction of the current and the trout facing into the stream flow waiting for food to drift by.

FAST WATER (5)

Fast water can also be excellent holding water for trout. The hydraulics of the water provide a cushion of slower water at the stream bottom where a trout can swim easily, while just a few inches above the bottom the current is much faster. The trick is to get your flies down to the bottom if nymph fishing.

SEAMS (6)

Seams are places in the current where slower water butts against a faster current. The slower current is generally in shallower water, whereas the faster water generally is a result of deeper water. Trout often will sit in the faster water and dart out to grab a bite to eat.

DEPRESSIONS (7)

Depressions in the stream bottom often create deep troughs that can result in deep pockets of water where the fish can stay in relative security while feeding. The food is often concentrated in these troughs.

OBSTRUCTIONS (8)

Calm water behind fallen trees or branches can be excellent holding and feeding areas for trout, where food is filtered down to them and the obstructions often hide the trout from sight from above.

OVERHANGING FOLIAGE (9)

Overhanging branches and bushes offer trout a great hiding spot, a greater sense of security, and shade from the sun.

Israel Patterson hooks one of the legendary trout in the South Platte River of Cheesman Canyon.
ISRAEL PATTERSON PHOTO

There is nothing more exhilarating than seeing a trout come to the surface and pluck a morsel off the surface of the water. I remember as a youngster throwing a grasshopper into the current of the South Platte River and watching it float downstream, its progress interrupted by a rainbow intercepting it, sometimes with a showy take, other times like a hole opening up on the surface of the water and the grasshopper disappearing into it.

One of my most memorable catches was a 24-inch brown trout taking my Takahopper in a back current of a small stream. I cast the fly into the slack water and watched as it just disappeared off the surface of the water, leaving just a telltale bubble, nothing more, not a big swirl or splashy show, just a bubble. I had to be very careful to play the fish in such a manner as to keep it out of the willow branches on the opposite bank and to land it quickly. I believe that was the first time I kissed a fish as I released it. I relish the times I can dry-fly fish.

Dry-fly fishing isn't simply throwing the fly on the water hoping to catch fish; I know because that is precisely what I did for several years. I'd spend days on the water flailing around like I knew what I was doing. I had the same flies as all the other anglers—a nice fly rod, vest, hat, sunglasses, waders, and a plaid shirt. The only difference was that those anglers where catching fish and I was not. I could cast as far as they did, I was using the same flies, and everything

I did mimicked what I thought they were doing. I was determined to not give up, but I should have asked for some help or taken a basic fly-fishing lesson—but heck, I'm a guy and should know how to do this stuff. Wrong! If you can afford to take a fly-fishing lesson, it will help you acquire the skills necessary to improve your understanding of what it takes to catch a fish. In my case I asked a good friend of mine, Dr. Donn Johnson, who in my opinion is the best dry-fly angler I know, to teach me the skills of becoming an angler.

One of the premier rivers to fish in Colorado is the famed Cheesman Canyon section of the South Platte River. Donn had invited me to spend a couple of days fishing the river; a Trico spinner fall was anticipated and I had never fished that type of mayfly before. I had always felt the trout in that section of river all had their PhDs; they were very selective and some of the most difficult trout to catch, in my opinion. Cast after cast yielded no fish for me; in fact, I didn't have one fish look at my fly. I looked upstream to see Donn catch a fish on what seemed to be every cast.

I ventured up to where Donn was fishing, put my fly rod up against a tree, and sat down to watch him catch over thirty fish. I realized I was witnessing a master fly fisher and asked him if he could show me how to catch fish. What followed was my education in the true art of fly fishing, fly tying, entomology, fly-fishing literature, and the aesthetics

TAKING CARE OF DRY FLIES

All the techniques and skills will be for naught if the flies being fished are not able to float for an extended period of time. There is any number of floatants available to fly fishers; most of these have silicon as part of their makeup. Silicon helps to repel water for an extended period but will need to be regenerated as the floating ability lessens. As a fly designer for Umpqua Feather Merchants, I rely on Umpqua Dry Magic. It comes in a tube and you squeeze out the contents onto your fingers, liquefying the floatant, then rub it on the surface of the fly. I also use C and F's dry-fly floatant.

When the need arises for a reapplication of the floatant, I will use one of two materials to wick away the moisture from the fly: Amadou or C and F's Rubycell foam pad. I first rinse the fly off in the water, then sandwich the fly between the Amadou or Rubycell foam pads. The majority of the moisture is removed from the fly and it's ready for another coating of fly floatant.

However, I re-dress my dry flies using Shimizaki's Dry Shake, which is a powered desiccant that coats the surface of the fly. The residual moisture on the dry fly allows the desiccant to adhere to the surface of the fly. I then blow off the excess desiccant or false cast the fly to remove any overcoating of the desiccant; the result is a high-floating dry fly ready for service. When fishing with dry flies that incorporate CDC feathers in their design, I use Shimizaki's Dry Shake instead of another floatant. Care must be taken when applying floatant to a CDC-type dry fly; most floatants will mat down the individual fibers of the CDC feather, thus eliminating the CDC's ability to float. Use a dry desiccant that will not mat down the individual fibers of the CDC: Shimazaki Dry Shake for most dry-fly patterns and Frog's Fanny (which has a brush applicator) for larger flies.

Preparing to fish the banks of the river with a large terrestrial pattern.

of fly-fishing equipment. Donn has one of the largest collections of fly-fishing literature I've ever seen; I would not be surprised to learn that he has over 1,000 books. In addition, he has a huge collection of original fishing art from some of the most respected artists in the genre.

Prior to successfully learning the skills to catch fish on a consistent basis with a dry fly or any fly, you'll need to acquire a number of skill sets that will ultimately result in fish caught. Learning to determine where to find fish, fly selection, casting techniques, proper presentation techniques, and line control are all parts of the formula. Missing any part of the formula will result in a longer learning curve. Don't be put off by any of this; these challenges are what make the act of fly fishing fun and rewarding. I will explain how I go about using these processes to help you learn to catch trout.

The most important aspect of fly fishing is developing the ability to achieve a drag-free drift with the fly. Drag refers to the movement of the fly on the surface of the water that is not moving at the same speed as the current; drag can often be seen as a small wake created by the mass of the fly moving the water to the side. At times you may feel the fly is not dragging at all and at other times it seems the fly is being dragged at almost a microscopic pace. Trout often will not take a dry fly that appears to be dragging, even if the drag is minimal.

Once you've mastered the techniques of presenting the fly in a dead-drift manner, your catch rate will increase and your enjoyment of fly fishing will be enhanced. I often look at items floating on the surface of the water, like small air bubbles, a leaf, or other insects, and try to have my flies travel at the same rate of speed as those items. As you learn how to control your drift, it will almost become second nature to do so *if* you are concentrating on fishing. I'm often not paying attention to what is going on with my flies but rather looking at the landscape and the beauty of nature. It is a challenge for me to concentrate on fishing at times.

Dry-Fly Techniques

Let's reduce the complexity of dry-fly fishing methods to five presentations: upstream, across and upstream, across stream, across and downstream, and directly downstream.

Fishing directly upstream is a favorite presentation technique of Rick Takahashi, high up in the Poudre Canyon of Colorado. STEVE SOLANO PHOTO

These techniques cover most fishing situations when fishing streams or rivers.

UPSTREAM PRESENTATION

Useful casts when fishing the upstream approach are curve casts and reach casts. Curve casts allow the fly to land on the water ahead of the tippet and leader and not allow the leader and tippet to "line" the trout. Having said that, the upstream presentation does "line" the fish, but I feel the use of the longer leaders and tippets reduces the alarm factor for the trout.

The upstream approach is a technique that I often use for fishing shallow streams that are not obstructed by overgrown brush or a canopy of trees. I look for water that can be easily waded, with shallow runs that result in adjacent deeper runs (seams) parallel to the shallow water. I position myself facing directly upstream. This upstream approach is not considered the most effective method of fly fishing, but it works for me

I generally make casts that are between 15 and 30 feet long directly upstream, casting as close to the bank as possible on my first cast. Trout often are found close to the bank when feeding to take advantage of insects falling into the water or close to the bank. Trout found close to the bank are there for one reason: to feed. Otherwise, trout would rather have the safety of deeper water, safe from the predators from above.

I employ a leader and tippet section that is long with as fine a tippet as I can use yet still be strong enough to overcome the fighting movements of a trout. Leaders in the range of 12 to 15 feet long are a general rule of thumb, and I'll lengthen the leader and tippet according to the conditions.

I use a serpentine-type cast, which consists of a series of curves in the line that absorb the pressure of the current if the water speed is fast; this type of cast is made by casting in a straight line, then wiggling the fly rod tip side to side in a rapid motion as the line is cast forward. Another cast I make is a straight-line cast, generally upstream. I then allow the fly to drift about 5 feet toward me, keeping my rod tip positioned just a few feet above the water. If the fly is taken, I gently lift the rod tip to set the hook.

If the fly is not intercepted, I lift the rod tip slowly and make an upstream roll cast. As the line is being rolled out, I time the forward progress of the line and make a back cast. I then make a forward cast the same distance as the previous cast, but 5 to 10 inches to the side of the previous cast, and work my way across the stream until I reach deeper water or the seam of the current. If no fish has taken the dry fly, I take one step forward and repeat the sequence.

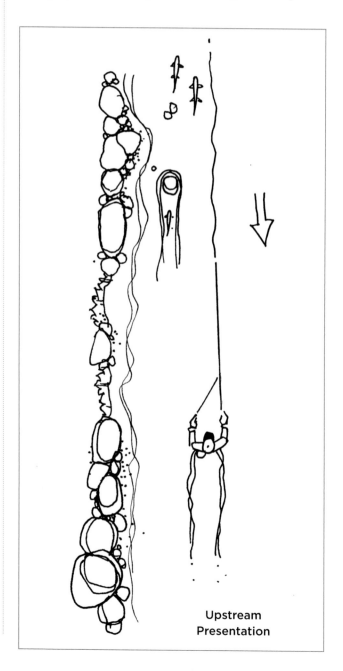

Upstream Presentation

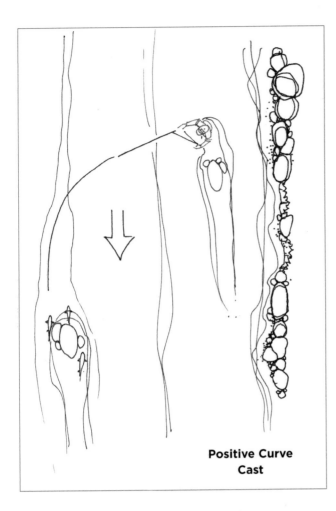

Positive Curve Cast

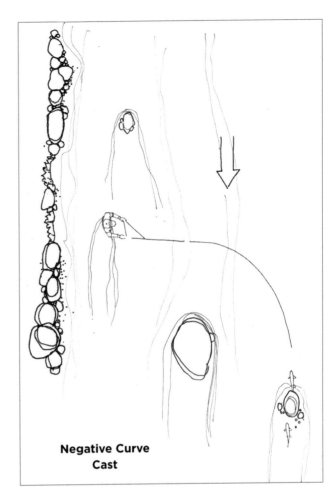

Negative Curve Cast

The seam is a section in the stream where one current meets parallel to a different current speed. Often I am looking for the shallower water with a slower current to butt up against a faster and deeper depth.

I continue my casts to the side of the previous cast until I reach the seam, then make one or more casts on the faster side of the seam. If the water is relatively deeper than the shallow section, trout will not expend the energy to swim up to the surface to take a dry fly—too much energy expended than taken in.

I only repeat a cast in the same lane as the previous cast if I sense there are more fish in the feeding lane. I look for visual clues such as movement under the surface of the water, a flash, or spotting a portion of a fish, or if I have a feeling a fish is there. I do not have to see rising trout to use a dry fly. I've learned over the years that trout are opportunistic and are looking up in shallow water and will take a fly presented to them. I figure fish are in shallow water to do only one thing: eat.

Positive Curve Cast. The function of the positive curve cast is to allow the fly to land downstream of the tippet, leader, and fly line with a drag-free drift. I make this type of cast when the flow of the river is moving from right to left. To produce a positive curve cast, I change my casting plane to a 45-degree angle to the right of the casting stroke, then slightly overpower the forward cast and stop the rod tip above the horizon. This allows the power of the

forward cast to continue and abruptly stop, causing the line to turn over to the left. I then lower the rod tip, completing the cast. The positive curve cast can also be accomplished using a twist of the hand in the forward stroke of the cast, much like throwing a curve ball—more difficult but doable with practice.

Negative Curve Cast. The function of the negative curve cast is to allow the fly to land downstream of the tippet, leader, and fly line. I make this type of cast when the flow of the river is moving from left to right. The negative curve cast is created by making your casting stroke on the left side of your body by crossing the rod tip over your left shoulder at a 45-degree plane, to the left if you are right-handed, opposite if you are left-handed. The forward cast is overpowered and stopped above the horizon as in the positive curve cast. The line is forced to curve to the right, and the rod tip is lowered after the completion of the cast. You can also affect a negative curve cast by underpowering your forward casting stroke, not allowing the line to extend fully. With this type of cast, you are casting in the normal forward casting stroke.

ACROSS AND UPSTREAM PRESENTATION

The cast can be short or you can make a longer cast if needed for a good presentation. You will need to mend your fly line upstream of the current to help affect a drag-free drift and get the leader, tippet, and fly line above the fly as

Across and Upstream Presentation. The objective of the across and upstream cast is to position the fly upstream and across the current.

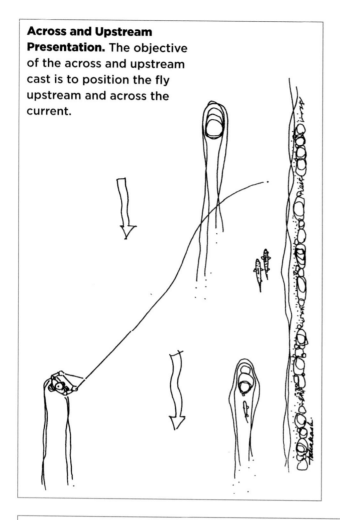

Across Stream Presentation. Across stream presentation often requires casting across several different current speeds, so introducing slack into your line is generally necessary. Using the serpentine cast will help reduce the change of different current speeds and give your flies a bit more time to dead-drift.

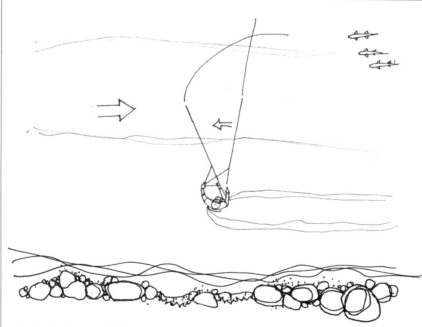

Reach Cast. Reach casts are easy to master, and they help with line management during the drag-free drift. Essentially you are trying to place the tippet, leader, and line upstream of the fly, so that the fly reaches the fish first. To create a reach cast, move the fly line upstream after your forward cast by moving the rod tip to the left or right side of the cast, depending on the direction of the current. You may need to mend the fly line upstream several times to maintain a drag-free drift.

it travels downstream. You can also use an upstream reach mend at the end of your cast to position your fly line and tippet above the fly. In any case, the objective again is to maintain a drag-free drift.

ACROSS STREAM PRESENTATION

Sometimes you need to cast directly across the stream to reach the target area where you suspect fish may be positioned. Often this requires you to cast perpendicular to

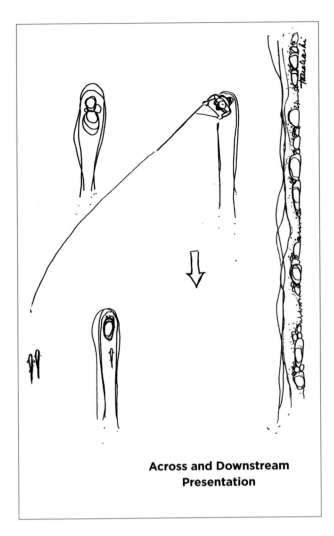

Across and Downstream Presentation

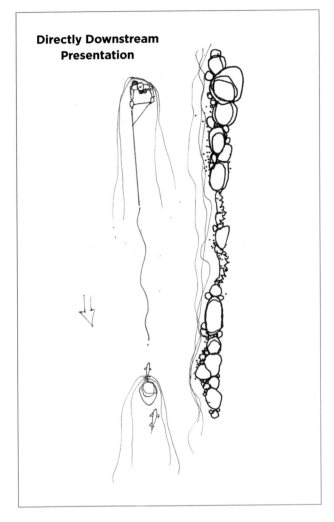

Directly Downstream Presentation

several current speeds. Casting a straight line across the currents may result in the fly being immediately dragged across the surface of the water, which often ends in the fish refusing to take your offering. I like to use a serpentine or S shape across the currents. This type of cast requires that on your forward cast you wiggle your rod tip horizontally in rapid, short, side-to-side movements, causing the line to make a series of serpentine curves across the surface of the water. This S-shaped curve allows for a short, drag-free drift of the fly and may be just enough for the trout to take the fly. Remember to mend your line upstream to position your fly line above your fly and reduce drag.

ACROSS AND DOWNSTREAM PRESENTATION

If you are upstream of the trout, you may need to cast across and downstream. A reach cast upstream may be the best way to position the fly in a drag-free drift; mending the fly line upstream will help create a longer drag-free drift of your fly. I've often used the serpentine cast in this situation with great success to allow the flies to drift drag-free.

This presentation positions the fly ahead of the leader and tippet, allowing the fly to be seen by the fish first. I mend the line upstream as soon as the fly lands on the

surface of the water, but there are times you'll need to mend the fly line upstream several times to allow the fly to reach the desired water depth. At the end of the drift I slowly raise the rod tip in preparation to re-cast but have found in many situations the trout follows the fly downstream and as soon as the fly rises to the surface the trout takes it as if it was emerging.

DIRECTLY DOWNSTREAM PRESENTATION

I do not normally fish downstream, but sometimes while drifting in a drift boat or when fishing streamers I use this type of cast; it really is a matter of what conditions you are facing. In some areas fishing directly downstream in line with your position is not allowed, especially when casting a short distance. I'm referring to what is called the San Juan shuffle, where an angler disturbs the bottom structure of the streambed in order to dislodge immature insects so they float downstream, effectively chumming the trout. This is considered unsportsmanlike conduct. I try to keep my downstream drifts more at an angle from my position, but having said this, when fishing streamers I often allow them to drift directly downstream of me and then bring the streamer back up toward me as if it were swimming upstream in the current.

Fall fishing on the main branch of the Poudre River, outside of Fort Collins, Colorado. ISRAEL PATTERSON PHOTO

Nymph Techniques

I have been evolving as a nymph fisherman over the last 40-plus years. I love to catch fish, and I realized that most of the feeding activity of trout is below the surface. I love to see a trout pluck a morsel off the surface of the water, and nothing gets me stumbling over myself more than seeing rising trout, but I've come to understand that the immature stage of an insect's life cycle is at the heart of a trout's diet.

PRESENTATION

The key to catching fish when fly fishing is the ability to control the drift of your fly to travel at the same speed of the current to mimic the drift of natural insects. The term most widely used is "dead drift," which simply implies that the fly is progressing downstream in the same manner as all the other objects in the water, including the insects both surface and subsurface. I often try to keep pace with other objects such as bubbles or leaves traveling near or in the same lane that I'm fishing. Once you have learned to control your fly, your ability to attract and catch fish will increase dramatically.

Dead drifting is not always the answer, however. Fish can also be caught when skating the fly along the surface, pulling it across the current, pulling it faster than the speed of a dead drift, swinging it across the current, and the list goes on.

Nymph fishing generally means the flies you'll be fishing are just below the surface of the water, continuing through the entire water column to bounce off the bottom of the stream. It is important to be observant of what is going on subsurface. Take the time to survey what is happening in the stretch of river you are fishing. Try to observe any movement of fish by seeing either the entire fish or portions of the fish, flashes from the side of the fish, or any sort of movement. Observe if insects can be seen moving about, and if fish are taking nymphs just under or close to the surface of the water. Polarized sunglasses and a wide-brimmed cap will facilitate your ability to see into the water and reduce glare from the sun.

If I see none of the above, I often opt to put enough weight on my tippet to ensure the fly will get down to the bottom of the run. This may require some guesswork on your part, but you can determine the bottom if you add weights in an amount that will get the nymph starting to pick up any bottom-type materials or becoming hung up once in a while. It's said that if you don't get hung up every once in a while, you are not fishing deep enough. I constantly adjust my weight, check on my rigging, check the fly, and adjust the strike indicator if using one as I progress up or down the stream.

RIGGING

My basic setup for fishing nymphs incorporates a 7½-foot 4X leader attached to a fairly stiff butt section if possible. I like to use Mason's Monofilament in .019 to .021 diameter, no longer than 8 inches in length, with a perfection loop at the tag end used to connect the butt section to the leader. If I use a fly line such as RIO's Gold with a weld loop connection, I will forgo the Mason butt section.

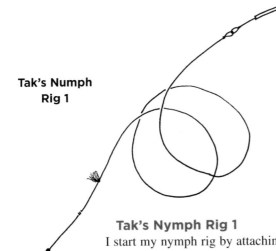

Tak's Numph Rig 1

Tak's Nymph Rig 1

I start my nymph rig by attaching a 7½-foot knotless tapered leader to the butt section of my fly line, or if the fly line has a welded loop, I'll tie on the leader. I tie on a 16- to 18-inch section of 5X tippet to the tapered leader. I know it would be easier to use a 9-foot tapered, but I've been so used to doing it this way that I continue to do so. I then take a 10- to 12-inch section of 6X tippet and attach it to the 5X tippet. I tie on my first fly, which I call the "point" fly, using a clinch or improved clinch, then slide the knot to the side of the hook eye. I attach another 10- to 12-inch section of 6X tippet through the eye of the point fly, using a clinch or improved clinch knot, and then slide the knot to the opposite side of the eye of the hook. This forms what I call a "T" connection, where the fly is positioned in a perpendicular angle to the leader. I attach the "dropper" at the end of the tippet.

When adding weight to the leader, if needed, place the split shot above the knot of the 5X and 6X junction; the weight will not travel any farther down the leader using the knot to stop the weight from sliding down to the point fly. If using a strike indicator, I will attach the indicator at a position on the leader that is equal to one to one and a half the depth of the water. My measurement is based on the weight and not the dropper fly. I reason that the weight will get the flies to the desired depth, and the more reasonable assumption is from the weight to the strike indicator. This nymph rig is used for more technical types of fishing such as in slow to moderate speeds of the current. If the speed of the water is swifter, I'll lengthen the distance to the strike indicator to accommodate the speed of the water

I add weight above the connection of the 5X and 6X if needed. If the water is deeper or faster in speed, I'll add more weight as conditions dictate to get the flies to the depth the fish are feeding. I add some tungsten putty to the weight if I need added weight instead of adding another split shot, which was a tip from Pat Dorsey.

This setup allows for the two-fly rig to be at the lowest level required, with the point fly and the dropper pushed up into the water column a bit higher by the hydrodynamics of the stream flow.

One of the reasons I set up a nymph rig in this fashion was relayed to me by Jude Duran, who guided on the San Juan River and who I consider to be one of the best guides on the river because he not only helps the anglers he's

guiding catch fish but also teaches them *how* to catch them. His reasoning was that having the flies 10 or so inches from each other will allow the trout to see both flies in the window of vision, which is cone-shaped from their head up toward the surface of the water, which gives anglers a better chance at fish taking one or the other fly. The distance stated about the placement of the strike indicator is based on being able to detect a strike sooner than when using a strike indicator placed in a more traditional location of two to three times the depth of the water.

One technique I use is a system for creating a connection of fly line to leader, which was taught to me 30 years ago by Terry and Lori Nicholson of Anglers All. This system, developed by Jim Poor, the original owner of Anglers All, creates a connection of butt material positioned through the core of the fly line with the use of a needle and superglue to hold the fly line in place; there is minimal increased material in the connection point, thus creating a very smooth transition. (I've explained this technique earlier in the book.)

I have started to use fluorocarbon tippet material when fishing nymphs because of the visual qualities of the material, as mentioned in Pat Dorsey's *Nymph Fishing* DVDs. When I encounter the possibilities of catching larger fish, I'll adjust the diameter size of the tippet material accordingly.

Drop Shot Rig

The second setup I use is borrowed from my experience steelhead fishing. The prime difference with this setup over the previous method is in the knot used for attaching the flies and the placement of the weight. This setup is commonly referred to as drop shot.

I use a 9-foot leader tapered to 3X and attach a 36-inch piece of 4X tippet material. Approximately 12 inches from the connection of the 3X leader to the 4X tippet, tie in a small dropper loop and then another small dropper loop 12 to 18 inches from the previous knot. This will leave a tag end of tippet remaining.

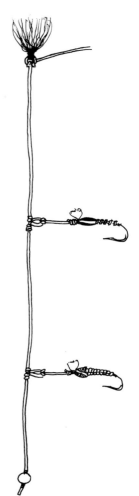

Drop Shot Rig

The dropper loop was shown to me by Brian Yamauchi; this setup was used to fish vertically in the water column and can be used in stillwaters as well as rivers and streams.

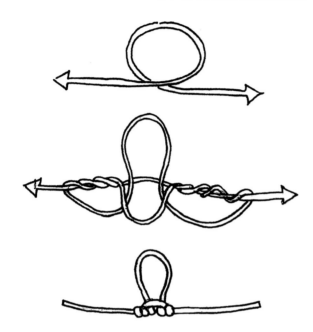

Dropper loop knot

Form a loop in the line as shown in the illustration, then twist the line around several times, open the loop where the twisted lines comes together, grasp the bottom of the line opposite the twist, and insert through the opening created. Form the size of loop you want, then pull the ends of the lines in opposite directions, cause the opening to close. You should have now formed a small loop in which to attach the tippet material.

To make the knot I use for tying the fly to the dropper loop, take a 3- to 5-inch length of whatever-size tippet you want to use and make an overhand knot in one end of the tippet, making sure there is a small section of tippet at the tag end. Thread the knotted end of the tippet through the dropper loop and complete another overhand knot; tighten the overhand knot so that the knotted end with the overhand knot snugs up to the knot. For the point fly I tie on the nymph so that it is no longer than 1 to 2 inches away from the dropper loop; this helps prevent the tippet from wrapping around the leader. I repeat the same process for the dropper fly.

I mentioned earlier that I leave a small tag end on the tippet material that I attach to the dropper loop. When the time comes for me to change out the tippet because it has become too short, I grasp the short tag end with hemostats; pulling the tag end allows the remaining tippet to become undone without having to cut the tippet material. I can then add a fresh length of tippet to the dropper loop without damaging the dropper loop.

The remaining leader section can hold a split shot on the end of the tippet. I generally do not put a knot on the end of the leader, which allows the weight to slip off the tippet

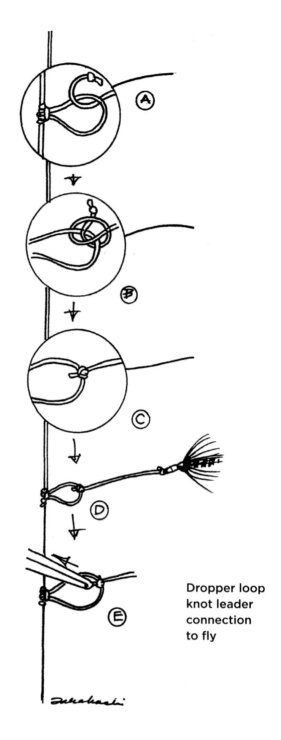

Dropper loop knot leader connection to fly

should it become lodged on the bottom of the stream. I can also clip the end tippet material if the flies happen to have enough weight to sink them to the desired depth.

A fishing friend of mine, Phil Iwane, makes a dropper loop knot using a larger loop. He cuts one end of the dropper loop to create a long piece of leader that he uses to attach his flies. He ties an additional overhand knot above the knot, using the longer section of tippet created for added insurance that the knot will not come undone. Make sure that the dropper knot is snugged up tight before cutting the leader.

I fish this rig with or without a strike indicator, depending on the situation. Jude Duran taught me to use this

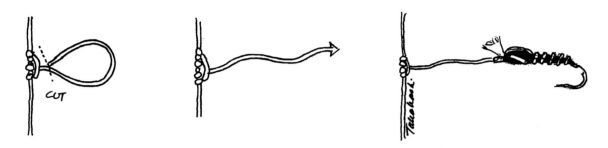

Iwane's dropper loop knot extension

technique when fishing the deep main channel of the San Juan River. He would place a strike indicator high up on the leader, then place the flies as you would a dropper loop type of setup. In this instance the flies were between 10 and 12 inches apart with a tag end about 12 to 14 inches below with the appropriate amount of weight to get the flies down quickly. Jude did not form a knot below the weight to keep the split shot from slipping off, but rather, it was opened ended. If the split shot should get caught up on the bottom, a pull on the line would dislodge the split shot without breaking off the entire rig. The indicator was held above the water in the same fashion as "high sticking" and not used until the rig was well downstream.

I lower the indicator to the water to finish out the drift of the flies and then lift the rig slowly to the surface at the end of the drift as in the Leisenring Lift–type method to entice the trout to eat the ascending nymphs.

TECHNIQUES

Direct Upstream, Straight Line

I prefer to use rigging setup 1 when using this technique. I cast the line directly upstream, starting from the bank out. I generally look for water that is shallow and no deeper than 5 to 6 feet, adding sufficient weight to get the fly down but not sink too rapidly. I immediately lower the rod tip to the surface of the water while constantly stripping in the line with enough speed to not allow the rigging to get caught up in the rocks. I can often feel the flies as they are drawn toward me, and can often feel the take. I watch the water for any signs of movement, flash, or indication that the fish has intercepted the fly.

If I have difficulty feeling the take, I put a 2- or 3-inch bend in the tip of my fly line and wait for a take when the bend straightens out. I let the flies drift past me and downstream at an angle before I make my next cast; the dragging fly line often helps me load up the rod for the next cast. If the cast is coming directly at me, I'll use a roll cast pickup and re-cast the fly. I position the next cast a few inches from the previous one and work my way across the stream.

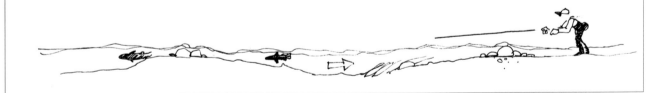

Direct Upstream Indicator

I often nymph fish with a strike indicator using an upstream cast of no more than 30 feet, much like when fishing streams using a dry fly. I also only allow the rig to drift drag-free for a short distance, then use a roll cast pickup followed by a forward overhand cast to cast the same distance as the previous one, except I place this cast within a few inches of the previous one. I mostly cast across the piece of the water where I feel trout will be, and since I'm fishing a nymph I can fish across the stream if needed.

If no fish take the nymph, I'll take one step forward upstream and start the whole process over, continuing to fish upstream until conditions won't allow forward progress.

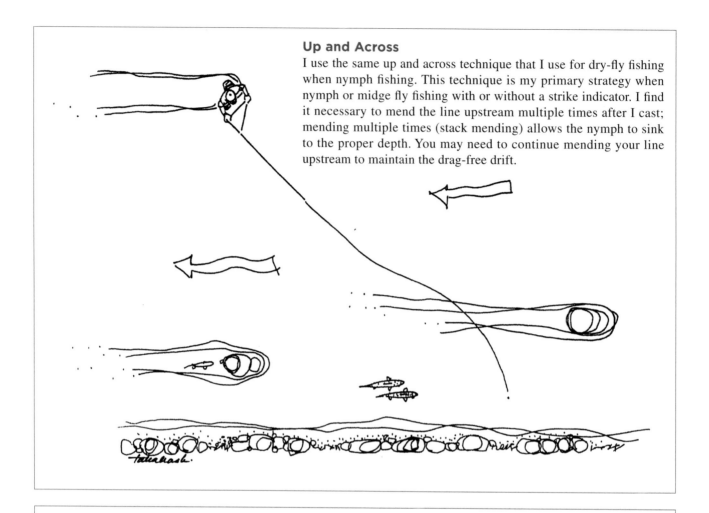

Up and Across

I use the same up and across technique that I use for dry-fly fishing when nymph fishing. This technique is my primary strategy when nymph or midge fly fishing with or without a strike indicator. I find it necessary to mend the line upstream multiple times after I cast; mending multiple times (stack mending) allows the nymph to sink to the proper depth. You may need to continue mending your line upstream to maintain the drag-free drift.

High Sticking

High sticking is an effective technique for nymph fishing close to your position in the stream; it offers excellent line control, allows you to feel the take of the fly, and requires you to pay attention to your fishing. High sticking refers to staying in contact with the entire drift of the fly by holding your fly line and some of the leader off the surface of the water as you follow the fly drift downstream.

You can fish this technique with an indicator if desired. You need to have the appropriate amount of split shot on to get the flies down quickly, and you can place the weight above or below the flies as in the drop shot technique. It's important to adjust the tippet material size to the water you are fishing, and the use of fluorocarbon tippet will result in less visibility of the tippet material.

To high stick, cast your flies upstream of your position and throw an upstream mend or several mends to allow the nymphs to get to the bottom. Bring in the slack line, then hold your rod tip high above the water and follow the fly's progress downstream by following the fly with your rod tip. Be sure to put the fly line under your index finger of your rod hand but not tightly; with your off hand, keep control of the fly line. I do not pull all the line in but keep an adequate amount of line available in case the fish should take off, in which case you can feed line out and take line back in as you gain control over the fish.

Morning frost on the Arkansas River tailwater below Pueblo Reservoir. JIM BROWNING PHOTO

Induced Take

I use this technique when I see fish in the upper column of water rising close to the surface to take emerging nymphs, then sliding down deeper into the water column, then rising again. I cast up and across upstream of the position of the fish, stack mend the fly line to allow the flies to sink deeper, then put a downstream mend in the fly line. When I feel I've reached the area where I saw the rise, I start to retrieve the line to cause the nymphs to ascend to the surface.

With this technique I induce the trout to take the nymph as it rises to the surface, imitating an emerging nymph. If no trout has intercepted the flies, I often allow the nymphs to extend down to the end of the drift, then slowly tighten up the drift, causing the nymphs to again rise to the surface, which will often trigger a take.

Down and Across Stream

Here I cast the flies across the stream and then make a series of upstream mends to allow the flies to sink. I drift the flies downstream, following the flies with my rod tip, which is held up slightly, until the line begins to drift below my position but at an angle. I then lower the rod tip, allow the flies to drift, and slowly lift the rod tip slightly (Leisenring Lift) before making another cast; this often elicits a take at the end of the drift. Re-cast to a new position when you have ended your downstream drift; the cast can be a few inches to the side of the previous cast.

INDICATOR TECHNIQUES

When fishing in a river and you are required to suspend the nymphs at a given level in the water column, the use of a strike indicator is the most efficient method of presentation. There are times when I just don't have that intuitive instinct to know when a fish has taken my fly, nor the skill level to do so.

When sight fishing, I often use a strike indicator as an aid to help me judge the proper distance I need to drift the flies into the feeding zone. I know the distance from the strike indicator to the flies, and so I can cast above the lie of the fish and adjust for the distance and direction the flies are traveling. I make my adjustments and do not look at the indicator for the take. Rather, I look at what the fish is doing; if I detect any movement up, down, or sideways

or an opening of the mouth, I will lift my rod tip to set the hook in case the fish has taken my flies.

If blind indicator fishing, I try to imagine that there is nothing under the surface of the water that would impede the strike indicator's smooth float down the river. If the strike indicator pauses or its float is disrupted, I lift the rod and hope for a solid hookup. Of course, we know there are all sorts of structures under the water that can cause the strike indicator to alter its course, but if you can lift the rod at any movement, this will increase your catch rate.

There are many types of indicators available on the market today; the following describes a few of the more common indicators available.

1. Pinch-On Indicators are usually made out of foam with highly visible sides. The pinch-on types are made up of two identical halves that have a sticky surface. To attach the indicator to the fly line, you simply fold the two halves together to form a bond.

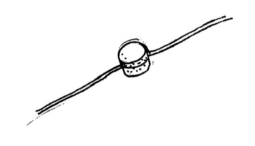

2. Twist-On Indicators are a long, rounded cylinder with a slit wide enough to insert a leader and a rubber band type of attachment that is twisted around the leader to hold it in place.

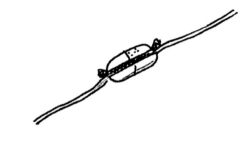

3. Yarn Indicators are an excellent way to nymph fish and are very sensitive; you can make your own or buy yarn indicator kits. I like to make my own on-stream indicator using Rainy's Float Foam in the small diameter. I cut a short section of the foam, then force a pointed end of a hemostat up through the center. I open the hemostat so that I can grasp the leader material, which I pull through the foam to create a large enough loop in which I can place the polyester yarn. I pull the leader tight, thus trapping the yarn, then clip the yarn even and apply floatant; this indicator slides up and down the leader with ease. See my book *Modern Midges* for an illustration of this indicator.

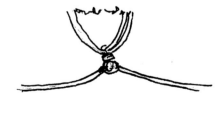

4. Hot Head Indicators, which I fish most of the time, are produced by Spirit River and come in two sizes. You can attach the indicator to your line by using the O ring. I loop my leader and pull it through the ring and then slide over the body of the indicator. I then pull both ends of the leader in opposite directions rather than pull the loop tight, which doesn't allow movement. Pulling the leader in opposite directions until the O ring flattens out allows the indicator to move freely up and down the leader.

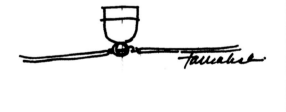

5. Loon BioStrike Indicator material has a dough-like consistency, which I form into a small ball then mold that small ball onto the leader; submerging in water hardens the ball. I use this indicator when fishing dries or patterns just under the surface where I can't see the fly. I can spot the BioStrike and can react to any surface activity near it.

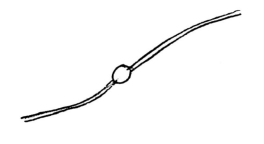

6. Foam Ball and Peg Indicators are small foam balls with a hole through the center of the ball. The leader is inserted through the hole and pegged into place with a toothpick.

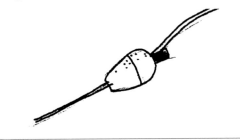

7. Slip Strike Indicators are foam balls with tapered hollow pegs. The leader is placed through the hollow center section of the peg, which is positioned with the larger end facing toward the flies. A loop is formed and the peg is placed back into the hole in the foam ball, trapping the loop; the peg should be tight enough to hold the loop but not so tight that the loop can't be pulled out with a little force. The objective is that when a fish strikes the loop, it will be pulled free and the strike indicator will slide freely down the leader. This allows the angler to fish at greater depth without the indicator stopping the retrieval of the line. It's a great way to present the fly at a greater depth, yet allow it to successfully land a fish without the line stopping at a statically placed indicator.

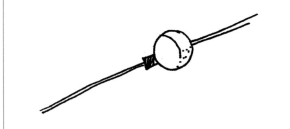

Dry Dropper Combination

Using a larger dry fly as an indicator and dropping a weighted nymph off the bend of the hook is an effective method of presenting flies and is not as likely to scare off a fish while presenting a second option to a fish feeding subsurface. A larger, high-floating dry fly like a grasshopper, Madam X, or Stimulator style of fly can serve as an indicator with the added advantage of possibly also catching a fish. I generally drop off a weighted fly about 1 to 3 feet below the surface or as conditions warrant from the hook bend. I have also tied my dropper tippet in front of the dry fly with a clinch knot. I do this when I think I may want to switch out the dry pattern; I simply slip the dropper tippet up the leader and change the dry fly.

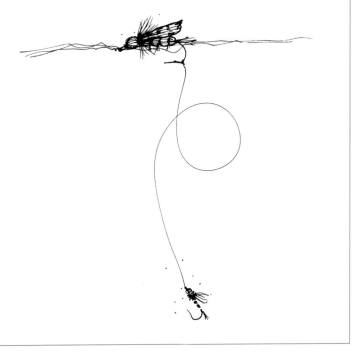

A Cable Hole section rainbow from the upper
San Juan River below Navajo Dam, New Mexico.
JUDE DURAN PHOTO

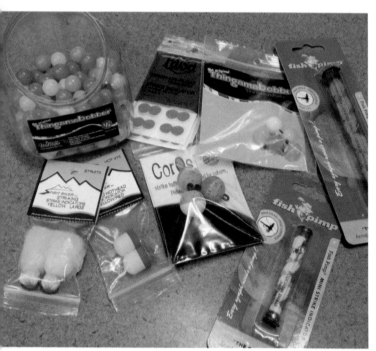

Strike indicators come in a variety of shapes and
sizes to meet most anglers' needs.

Balloon Indicators

A small balloon can make a highly effective indicator. Take a small, party-type balloon and fill it with a small puff of air to the size desired. Guide Gary Okizaki likes to tie two overhand knots next to each other. He then takes a small dental brace rubber band and wraps it several times around a closed pair of hemostat tips. He opens up the hemostats and grasps the leader, then pulls the leader through the knotted rubber band until an opening in the trapped line will accommodate the knotted end of the balloon. He pulls the knotted balloon through the opening until the leader is between the two knots. He then pulls the opposite end of the leader taut until the open loop is secured between the two knots of the balloon. This type of indicator is very sensitive to any take of the flies attached to the tippet, and the angler will find that these indicators cast easily.

When fishing depths less than 10 feet, I opt for one of the static or nonslip types of indicators. There are several brands available that work on the same principle of using a peg or a rubber band–type stopper to hold the indicator in place. To ensure that the line is attached to the indicator securely, twist the rubber band–like material, causing the leader to wrap around the rubber band to hold it in place.

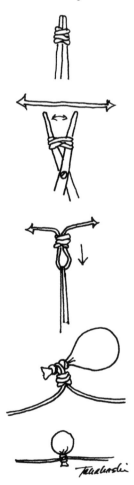

-14-
STILLWATER TECHNIQUES

Fly-fishing lakes opens up a whole new arena for the angler who has spent the majority of their time fishing rivers and streams. One of the main factors that prompts many anglers to consider fishing stillwaters is runoff or adverse water conditions that will not allow them to fish in flowing waters. During the runoff phase, many streams and rivers will experience an increased water flow caused by snowmelt that results in high, swift water. Fishing is marginal at best, and the high water levels are often difficult and dangerous to wade and to fish. During the runoff many lakes are just starting to "turn on." Lakes are not necessarily affected by runoff, but fishing stillwaters for the first time presents some interesting dynamics to those not accustomed to fishing these types of waters.

Thunder Lake in the high alpine region of Rocky Mountain National Park above Estes Park, Colorado.
ISRAEL PATTERSON PHOTO

Fishing from a belly boat or some other type of floating device will give you the opportunity to reach more favorable areas to fish and allow better access than you would have from shore. SCOTT STISSER PHOTO

Rods, Line, and Other Tackle

Ultimately, the selection of a fly rod's action will be a personal choice. However, experience has shown a fly rod of medium-fast to fast action may be beneficial to the lake angler. Windy conditions often occur when lake fishing. A fly rod of this action is stiffer and aids in casting into the wind or when pulling a sunken fly line out of the water. Fly rods in the 9- to 10-foot lengths, in weights 5 to 7, will meet the needs of most anglers fishing lakes. The longer length of rods in the 10- or 11-foot range allows for better control of the fly line, especially when fishing from a belly boat, pontoon boat, or other boat.

I am not necessarily an advocate of fishing lightweight fly rods in lakes unless circumstances allow. My reasoning is based on my experience fishing lakes—that is, lakes typically hold much larger and stronger fish than are found in most streams and rivers. That is not to say there aren't bigger western rivers that produce large fish to rival those found in lakes. My reason for selecting a 5- to 7-weight fly rod is to not overplay the fish. Using a lighter fly rod weight may require a longer time to land the fish, thus increasing the possibility of the fish dying even after successfully returning it to the water. Lactic acid buildup in a struggling trout may cause its death after the release.

A 5-weight fly rod can be ideal when fishing dries. When the wind becomes a factor, you might think of using a 6- or 7-weight rod; the heavier line weight will aid in casting during windy conditions. Consider using a 7-weight setup

Fly rods already rigged wait on the windshield of the car as anglers put on their gear as they prepare to fish.

for fishing any sinking types of lines. I prefer a fast-action fly rod for fishing with sinking lines; a faster-action fly rod with enough backbone to lift sink tip and full sinking lines out of the water is an added advantage. A fly rod with a stiffer butt section and a softer tip may be a rod to consider; the softer tip can help protect the tippets. Five- to 7-weight fly rods are ideal when conditions warrant their use; a 6-weight is a nice compromise. Fly rods with a fighting butt will also aid in fighting the larger fish you might encounter in stillwater conditions. I would highly suggest you bring a brace of fly rods in the 5- to 7-line weights with a variety of line types such as floating, intermediate, sink tip, and full sinking with varying sink rates, if you are able.

I have recently been using a switch fly rod in the 11-foot, 5-weight range for fishing from shore. I selected this style of fly rod because the lakes and reservoirs I fish are often windy. A switch fly rod can facilitate overcoming wind when you are forced to fish from shore. I fish a Reddington or Elkhorn switch fly rod in a 5-weight class that allows me to use the overhand and Spey styles of presentation. I also fish a 4-weight switch (for both lakes and streams), which helped me overcome slight wind while allowing me to fish from shore. Using a switch rod and learning how to cast properly will result in less effort when casting into the wind. Casting a switch rod takes less effort for me than casting a conventional fly rod.

One of the factors that may be encountered when fishing a switch rod is setting the hook when the fly line is at a greater distance than normally found. The softer tip of the switch rod may inhibit a proper hook set when the rod tip is in an up position. I find that keeping tension on the line and holding the rod to the side using a slip strike helps eliminate this problem of setting the hook.

FLOATING, INTERMEDIATE, SINK TIP, AND FULL SINKING LINES

There is a whole range of fly lines used for fishing lakes. Many manufacturers have developed lines for very specific uses. I favor RIO fly lines because the company has developed lines for specific as well as general fishing conditions. The types of lines run the gamut of floating, intermediate, sink tip, full sinking lines, and so on. I use a floating line for 30 percent of my lake fishing, coupling it with long leaders of 12 to 15 feet, which allows me to fish dries and subsurface patterns without drawing attention to the leader and fly line.

I use intermediated fly lines for the majority of fishing I do in lakes using subsurface patterns. Intermediate lines sink at a slower rate of descent, keeping your flies in the zone for a longer period of time but still allowing the fly line to sink to a deeper depth if required. I feel confident fishing emerging chironomids just under the surface of the water as well as fishing streamers in all different depths of the water column. I have used an intermediate line to fish with a strike indicator when fishing vertical; the indicator was of sufficient size to hold in the surface of the lake even though the intermediate line was slowly sinking from my rod tip to the indicator. This scenario allowed me to use a vertical presentation when warranted and not have to switch out line while out in the water. It worked long enough to allow me to fish and not have to re-rig with a floating line.

Because depth is key, I recommend that you buy three lines. First, choose a floating fly line in a weight-forward type for fishing flies on the surface. The addition of a longer tippet works well with a floating line when you want to fish subsurface. I like using a floating line for fishing dries and for presentation of the subsurface flies at various angles on long leaders. I often present the flies in a vertical plane

Nearing dusk on Yellowstone Lake. TOM FLANAGAN PHOTO

Brian Yamauchi with a beautiful rainbow trout taken from North Delaney Butte Lake with his chironomid pupa.

under a strike indicator. If only one line is in your budget, then I would suggest a floating line.

The second type of line is an intermediate sinking line. The intermediate line has a slower sink rate than a full sinking line and allows you to stay in the "zone" for a longer period of time. I find that using an intermediate type of fly line catches more fish just under the surface or in slightly deeper water because it sinks slowly instead of quickly passing through the upper water column like a full sinking line. Some line manufacturers are producing lines with a clear tip or where the entire line is clear throughout its length. The theory behind using clear lines is to reduce the visibility of the line to the fish. The intermediate fly line that I use has camouflage coloration.

The third type of line is a full sinker when you need to get the flies down quickly. I use a full sinking line when I'm fishing from a float tube or a boat. I'll often cast as far as I can, then move away while stripping out additional line until I get the line as far out as I feel comfortable in handling. I'll then strip in the fly line as fast as I can, sometimes putting the handle of the rod and reel under my arm and retrieving hand over hand in rapid succession. I don't use this technique very often, but it has proven to be a fish catcher at times.

Long leaders are essential when fishing a floating line, to allow the presentation of the subsurface fly to reach the desired depth. As stated previously, the use of a fluorocarbon leader or tippet material can be helpful when fishing subsurface flies due to the leader being nearly invisible. Monofilament is my choice for dry flies. You will have to determine what size and length of leader you will need to use when fly fishing stillwaters. The fish in most lakes are generally good fighters and can be larger than the typical stream trout (at least in my area), and the use of a larger-diameter tippet will help land fish. I generally start with a 9-foot 2X leader. I attach a 24-inch section of 3X tippet and then the flies I'll be using. If conditions warrant I will shorten the tippet to meet the requirement of getting the flies down to the level of the fish in a timely manner.

When fishing an intermediate or sinking fly line, the leader and tippet can be much shorter in length. I generally fish a leader that is in the 9- to 12-foot range, or about the length of my fly rod, and 2X or 3X in size. As with most fly fishing, you have to experiment when it comes to selecting what length, size, and X factor to use for your terminal gear. In some lakes the trout will tolerate a larger leader and tippet as large as 1X. Using a leader of this size diameter helps land fish quicker than using a lighter tippet. Using lighter tippets requires you to fight the fish more cautiously, which often means playing the fish longer. Try to land the fish as quickly as possible; remember that fighting a fish for an extended period of time is detrimental to the fish.

The length of the leader and tippet may require constant adjustment until you start catching fish. Shorten or lengthen the tippet as needed. It's not uncommon to fish a leader of 15 feet or more in length. When using any type of full sinking fly line, use a shorter leader setup as opposed to longer, as this will help keep the fly at the same level as the fly line.

Stillwater Rigs

DROPPER LOOP SETUP RIG

The dropper loop setup is used with a floating fly line incorporating a static type of indicator that is set to not slide on the leader or a slip-type indicator that will release when you set the hook and slide down the leader while fishing in a vertical plane. I use a very small dropper loop, then attach a short piece of tippet to the loop to tie the fly on. In Colorado you are allowed to use a two-hook rig, which means that you can use two flies.

With this type of setup I often space the flies about 12 to 18 inches apart, I might extend a 12- to 18-inch length of leader below the dropper fly and add weight if needed. In other instances I allow the weight of the flies to sink them to the desired depth, or sometimes use a heavier-weighted fly as the dropper to sink the fly. Guide Gary Okazaki likes to use a swivel as his weight to get the flies to depth. I generally start by fishing the flies about 3 to five 5 below the surface of the water and will adjust this distance as the condition dictate.

When fishing stillwaters, I often use a 3X tippet for the majority of my fishing; by using a 3X tippet I feel I can dictate how I fight the fish and find I can land the fish quicker than when using lighter tippets.

HOOK BEND SETUP

When I am using a retrieval technique where I'm pulling the flies toward me, I tie the dropper fly off the hook bend of the point fly. In this instance I feel it is alright to tie the dropper fly off the bend of the point fly since you are retrieving the line toward you. I like to use a nonslip knot tied to the point fly and dropper fly.

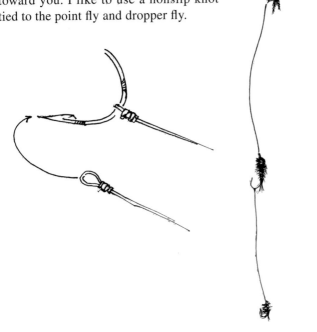

EYE TO EYE SETUP

When using a two-fly setup, I like to tie the point fly on with a clinch knot and position the knot on the side of the eye, then tie the tippet for the dropper onto the opposite side of the eye and tie on the dropper fly. I use this setup when fishing vertically, similar to the dropper loop setup using a slip strike indicator. The weight is positioned above the point fly. I feel that if the point fly is perpendicular to the leader, it won't impede the exposed hook point with tippet material, which might cause the fish to reject the fly because it can feel the tippet material. I generally use 2X leader and tie on an 18-inch piece of 3X, then tie my point fly on using a clinch knot. Then I slide the knot over to the side of the eye. I then attach 18 inches of 3X to the eye of the hook using a clinch knot and slide the knot opposite the first knot. I'll tie the dropper using a clinch knot. This is the same sort of setup I use for my regular nymph rig. If I need the flies to sink, I'll add weight to the junction of the 2X and 3X leaders. I'll often place a bead-head fly as my dropper and allow that weight to sink my flies instead of using weight on the line.

DROP SHOT RIG

The drop shot setup is an excellent method of presenting flies in a vertical plane with weight attached to the end of the line. The drop shot rig is similar to the dropper rig except the tippet is extended off the dropper fly about 10 to 18 inches from the fly. I use this setup when fishing vertically; I attach a weight on the tag end of the leader, and the weight at the end of this setup will suspend straight down. When using this rig in moving water, I sometimes will not put a knot at the tag end of the tippet, thus allowing the weight to be pulled off the tippet in cases where it might hang up on the bottom. I use this setup when I feel the need to get the flies down fast.

SLIP STRIKE INDICATOR

The use of indicators can help present the fly in a vertical plane and hold it at the desired depth. A variety of strike indicators are currently used for stillwater fly fishing. Many of the indicators are designed to allow some movement up and down the leader and still provide resistance to a freely sliding indicator. One of the drawbacks of using this type of indicator occurs when held in a position that does not allow movement. These types of indicators are useful when fishing depths that still allow you to land the fish without the indicator being stopped when it reaches your tip top.

When fishing depths one and a half times longer than your fly rod, I suggest using a slip strike indicator, one of my favorite indicators to use when fishing stillwaters. I use the slip indicator when fishing my flies vertically at depths greater than the length of my fly rod. I sometimes fish depths over 15 feet and have fished beyond 20 feet. The main characteristic of this indicator allows it to slip down the leader when you set the hook. Becoming unhitched from the leader and sliding down freely allows the angler to land the fish closer to hand, as opposed to using a static, nonslip type of indicator.

This indicator uses a hollow peg that the leader slides through and is held in place by looping up the leader and inserting one end of the leader next to the peg, which is then inserted into the opening of the strike indicator. This allows the indicator to stay in place. When the angler sets the hook, the weight of the fish and the action of pulling the line forces the loop inserted into the indicator to pull out, thus allowing it to slide down the leader. You can also use a static type of indicator when fishing water depths no deeper than the length of your fly rod; you determine what depth to set the slip strike indicator depending on where the fish are feeding.

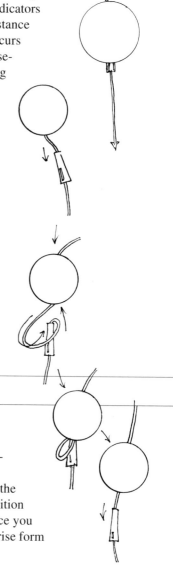

BIOSTRIKE INDICATOR MATERIAL

Take a small amount of Loon BioStrike material and form a ball, then press the ball onto the leader. Wet the material, which will harden up. You can see this type of indicator at a greater distance.

When fishing flies on or just under the surface, it is sometimes difficult to see where the fly is. Using a moldable type of strike indicator will help you locate the approximate position of the fly. By attaching a small amount of the Loon BioStrike to the leader at a distance you determine, you will have a better idea of where the fly is. Set the hook when you see a rise form in the general area of the BioStrike.

Todd Pipin holds up a beautiful rainbow caught in the shallows of Delaney Butte with chironomids.

Fishing Techniques

Two important factors to remember about lake fishing are to use long leaders when fishing floating lines and to use slow, very slow, retrieval rates. This does not mean that all retrieves must be slow; in fact, you should vary the retrieval rates but don't neglect the slow retrieve approach. Most insects do not typically move at break-neck speeds; rather, they move at a much slower rate and sometime pause in their movement. This does not

Dave Mosnik with one of many fish caught and landed at Red Feather Lakes.

After the thaw on Fern Lake in Rocky Mountain National Park. ISRAEL PATTERSON PHOTO

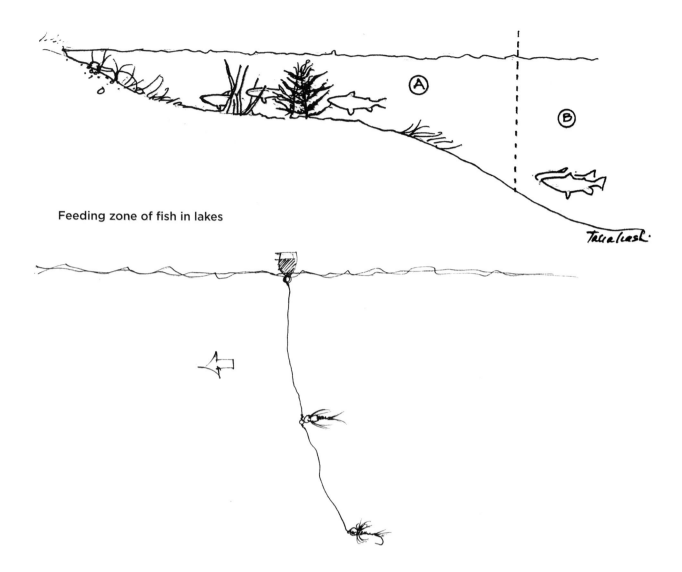

Feeding zone of fish in lakes

mean you should abandon a quicker retrieval rate, but do remember that immature insects move at slower speeds than you might expect. Insects such as chironomid pupae, damsel nymphs, scuds, and *Callibaetis* nymphs are just a few examples.

Some insects do dart around in the water; organisms such as scuds and water boatmen will flit around a bit, and you'll have to develop retrieval rates to mimic those creatures. But my point is, slow down when drawing the flies in.

Forage fish move faster, thus requiring a faster retrieve. Imagine how minnows and other forage fish might move in the water when being pursued by a predator; they generally move quicker to not be eaten. Crawfish often move quickly but usually pause after a short distance, so mimic that type of movement when fishing crawfish patterns. Scuds often exhibit these same types of movement characteristics.

When fishing vertically, retrieval rates vary depending on what insect you are trying to imitate. Generally I fish the majority of insects with very slow retrieval rates with pauses in between the retrieves. Most of the insects that I have observed move short distances, pause to (seemingly) rest, then continue on their way. Some creatures, such as

scuds, dart around with rapid movements, then pause, then move slowly, pause, and so on.

Generally speaking, you should concentrate some time fishing the shallower parts of the lake where the water is, say, 15 to 25 feet in depth. The reasoning is that the majority of insects and other aquatic invertebrates such as scuds and crawfish thrive where the sunlight reaches the plants, causing photosynthesis, development of oxygen, plant growth, and so on. These shallower areas of the lake attract all sorts of aquatic invertebrates. Remember, fish congregate where the food source is abundant, so fish will come into the shallows to feed then retreat back to the pro-tection of deeper water. In the illustration, the A portion is known as the littoral zone and B is deeper water.

When the fish move back into deeper water, anglers should follow suit. Use the countdown method to locate where the fish are feeding; a fish finder can be handy in these circumstances to determine the depth of the water. When using a floating line, adding extra tippet material will help you get to the desired depth of the feeding fish. When using an indicator, the slip strike type is very helpful.

GOING VERTICAL

Vertical presentation refers to presenting your flies perpendicular to the surface of the water, which, if you are planning on casting out any distance, is usually accompanied by the use of a strike indicator. I seldom use a vertical presentation directly from my fly rod tip while sitting in my belly boat or float tube; having said that, I've used this technique with success when I've been able to see the fish below me in clear water. The use of a strike indicator is the key element of this technique.

The slip strike indicator allows the flies to hang down into the water at a vertical plane; using an indicator that is easily slid up and down the leader makes changing the depth of the flies a simple maneuver. A slip strike indicator is my first choice; I can change the depth of the flies easily without having to switch to any other type of indicator. I prefer to use the dropper loop, drop shot, or the eye to eye setups for my presentation technique.

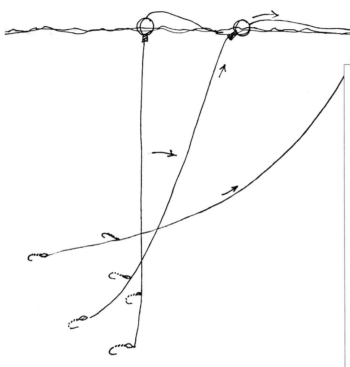

Bow Tie Boogie (Vertical)

I use this technique when I want to present the movement of the fly in a vertical plane. I use a long leader and tippet; length is determined by the depth of water that you are fishing or the depth at which the fish are suspended. Attach a slip-type indicator that will allow the patterns to sink to the desired depths without being pulled under the surface. Use a considerable amount of weight to get the flies to the level of the fish quickly. I usually attach the weight about 18 inches above the point fly. This is "chuck and duck" kind of fishing: cast the rig out, allow the flies to settle into position, and wait a short amount of time.

I next take two or three sharp and short strips of the fly line, let it settle down for a few seconds, then hand-twist retrieve very slowly. Be prepared for the take.

If you happen to be fishing a depth greater than the length of your fly rod, use of the slip strike indicator allows you to land the fish without the strike indicator impeding you. The slip indicator will become unsecured from the post that held it in place and will allow the indicator to slide down the length of your leader until it hits something that will stop its slide like a split shot or point fly. The use of the slip strike indicator allows the angler to fish greater depths of water, and when the fish takes and the angler strikes to set the hook, the indicator will be unhinged and slide down the line. This makes landing the fish so much easier.

Yamauchi Technique (Vertical)

This technique used by Brian Yamauchi has proven to be one of the better techniques I've seen. Basically, use a setup that includes a floating line, a strike indicator, a two-fly rig, and no weight. The length of the leader is set 3 to 5 feet from the indicator to the first fly; flies are spaced between 12 and 24 inches apart. No weight is used; allow the weight of the flies to reach the depth set. Allow the setup to sit still without imparting any movement, or use a very slow retrieval rate to add some movement to the flies. I've seen Brian outfish me 10:1 using this technique.

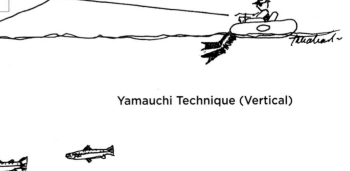

Yamauchi Technique (Vertical)

Inclined

Trolling

GOING INCLINED

Inclined simply refers to fishing at an angle to the surface of the water; I use this technique when the vertical approach is not working for me. I choose a floating fly line with long leaders of around 15 to over 20 feet and usually add some type of weight on the leader to help it sink at a more rapid rate. I often employ a countdown technique to allow adequate time for the flies to reach the desired depth, which is determined by how many seconds I counted down before the fish started taking my flies. I start off with a count of 10 seconds and fish this depth with a few casts; if nothing captures my flies, I add 5-second intervals until contact is made. Again, I generally use a slow/pause retrieve unless I'm fishing patterns that imitate forage fish. To retrieve forage fish–type patterns, I usually take in line at a faster speed. If it's a crawfish I'm fishing, I allow the pattern to settle on the bottom, rest, then make a short, rapid retrieve followed by a pause, or I "puff" the crawfish with very short retrieves, sometime accomplished with the raise of my rod tip.

I like to use an intermediate sinking line when fishing stillwaters because the slower sink rate allows the flies to be in the "zone" longer than with a full sinking line. I use weighted flies to get them to sink to the levels, but the use of the intermediate line helps sink the flies to the depth I want to fish. I will often troll with my fly line streaming a long distance behind my float tube.

I also use weighted lines such as a high-density sinking fly line when I'm fishing streamer-type patterns that I want to get deep quickly. Often I cast the lines out, then extend more line as I kick away from the cast, allowing time for the sinking line to reach deeper depths. I then put my fly rod under my arm and strip the fly line back as quickly as I can to imitate a forage fish trying to escape a predator. My friend Mike Seris showed me this technique many years ago, and it's one of the major retrieves I use when fishing sinking lines and forage fish–type patterns.

TROLLING

In this technique, a long leader of 12 to 15 feet or longer is used to get your flies down to the feeding zone; an intermediate or full sinking fly line is ideal for this technique. Constant movement in a belly boat, pontoon boat, or other boat is perfect for fishing any subsurface patterns.

Another effective method of fishing subsurface flies incorporates the use of an intermediate line and shorter-length leaders. The intermediate fly line sinks at a very slow rate of descent; this slow descent rate allows the fly to be in the "zone" for a longer period of time. The idea is to allow a long length of the fly line to be trolled behind your float tube or pontoon boat as you continually keep moving, thus slowing down the rate of descent; by stopping and allowing the line to sink, you will eventually get your flies deeper if desired.

When moving in your float tube or pontoon boat, do not retrieve the fly line but rather let it stream out, extend the line out as far as desired, and allow the line to become taut. You need to have a long length of fly line out to help create resistance, which will be felt like a pulling of the fly line and makes it easier to do the jigging motion. You can accomplish the jigging action by grasping the line and pulling on it in short jerks, sometimes varying the jigging motion to impart a variety of movement to the flies. My friend and fishing partner Dave Mosnik uses this technique while constantly moving in his float tube, and his success rate of hookups can't be ignored. I often refer to him as the "Energizer Rabbit" of float tubers. Simply put, he catches lots of fish no matter what type of fish it is.

Thunder Lake in the high alpine region of Rocky Mountain National Park. ISRAEL PATTERSON PHOTO

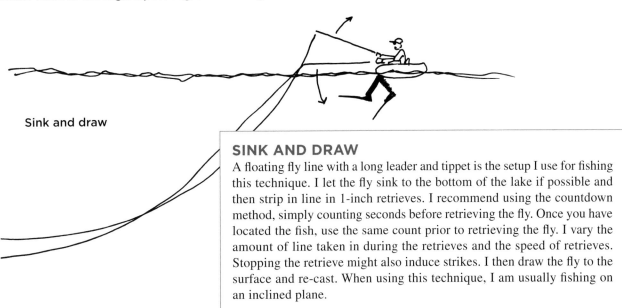

Sink and draw

SINK AND DRAW

A floating fly line with a long leader and tippet is the setup I use for fishing this technique. I let the fly sink to the bottom of the lake if possible and then strip in line in 1-inch retrieves. I recommend using the countdown method, simply counting seconds before retrieving the fly. Once you have located the fish, use the same count prior to retrieving the fly. I vary the amount of line taken in during the retrieves and the speed of retrieves. Stopping the retrieve might also induce strikes. I then draw the fly to the surface and re-cast. When using this technique, I am usually fishing on an inclined plane.

ANCHOR ACROSS WIND OR WIND DRIFTING

When fishing from a boat, putting out anchors at the bow and stern perpendicular to the wind is an effective method of fishing the downwind drift. This technique requires the use of two anchors, fore and aft, and is achieved more practically with the use of a drift boat or standard boat. The boat is positioned perpendicular to the direction of the wind; anchoring the fore and aft of the boat ensures that you're able to stay in that cross-section of wind and not move around. I fish the downwind side of the boat using a strike indicator and treat the water as if I were fishing in a stream to create a dead drift. It is important to remember to adjust the depth of your flies until you reach feeding fish, which is often just off the bottom of the lake. I then retrieve the fly at a slow rate in preparation to re-cast the flies.

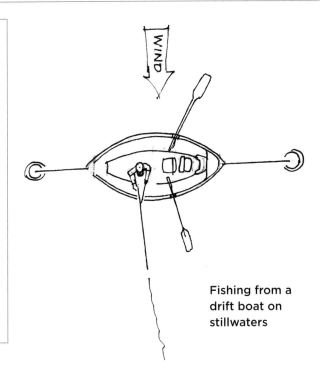

Fishing from a drift boat on stillwaters

INDEX